T0310474

Technocapitalism

Technocapitalism

A Critical Perspective on Technological Innovation and Corporatism

Luis Suarez-Villa

TEMPLE UNIVERSITY PRESS
Philadelphia

Temple University Press
1601 North Broad Street
Philadelphia, PA 19122
www.temple.edu/tempress

Copyright © 2009 by Temple University
All rights reserved
Published 2009
Printed in the United States of America

♾ The paper used in this publication meets the requirements of the
American National Standard for Information Sciences—Permanence
of Paper for Printed Library Materials, ANSI Z39.48-1992

Library of Congress Cataloging-in-Publication Data

Suarez-Villa, Luis.
Technocapitalism : a critical perspective on technological
innovation and corporatism / Luis Suarez-Villa.
        p. cm.
Includes bibliographical references and index.
ISBN 978-1-4399-0042-0 (cloth : alk. paper)
1. Capitalism. 2. Economics—Political aspects.
3. Corporations—Social aspects. 4. Technology—Social aspects. I. Title.
HB501.S93125 2000
338'.064–dc22

                                                    2009016384

2 4 6 8 9 7 5 3 1

Contents

Technocapitalism

Introduction

This book adopts a critical perspective to help us understand where we are and why we have become what we are. It is not apologetic of our current condition or the powers that dominate us. It is intended to be emancipative in word and spirit. In so doing, it attempts to break free from the overwhelming reductionism that characterizes most intellectual endeavors today.

Emancipation is the fundamental objective of a just society. Human emancipation involves not only freedom from oppressive and exploitive conditions but also participation in the governance of society and its creative activities at all levels. More than at any previous time, emancipative participation involves decisions that define the human condition and what it means to be human through the exercise of creativity in technology. Today, these decisions are overwhelmingly determined by corporatism and its authoritarian power over technology.

Corporatism is defined in this book as the power of business corporations over society. Such power now tends toward hegemony, but as we see later, it is not incontestable. This definition of corporatism varies from the traditional one that signifies collusion between corporate and government interests. Obviously, the traditional definition can be subsumed in the one used here, but the scope of the term is much broader. The term corporatism is therefore used to refer to the wide-ranging influence of corporate power on society, including its governance, and on nature. The corporate colonization of our social relations, of our identity as humans, and of life itself is an ongoing enterprise. This "enterprise" is crisis-prone, as it affects all aspects of our existence and of nature on a global scale. It creates crises at many levels that involve the entire context of our existence, including nature and the earth, along with human societies. The words of Richard Levins, a prominent scientist with a rare social sensibility, tell of this unfolding crisis: "It is more profound than previous crises, reaching higher into the atmosphere, deeper into the earth, more widespread in space, and more long lasting, penetrating more corners of our lives."[1]

As it colonizes human society, nature, and the planet, corporatism degrades us, turning our most precious human qualities into commodities. Our creativity, our knowledge, and our learning thus become not qualities that emancipate but commodities that bind us to our alienation from the human condition, from society, and from nature. This degradation of human values is not grounded in technology, in and of itself. *It is grounded in the character of a new kind of corporatism and its authoritarian control over technology.* It is a new kind of corporatism that is more clever, rapacious, and invasive than any previous form and that is imperial in its quest for power and profit as it tries to control any and all aspects of the public domain.

The creation of technology in our time is therefore a decision that has multiple consequences: social, political, economic, and natural, the composite of which may decide the human trajectory. The power of corporatism over these decisions should raise grave concerns about human society. Many of the social pathologies we encounter today are a product of that power, of its demeaning effects on human existence, on our social relations, and on the way we view our place in society. Only an emancipative trajectory that exposes the nature of the new corporatism and charts a new course can contain its pathological effects. And that course must necessarily involve greater accountability for corporatism and a democratization of social decisions on technology. Without them, technology cannot take up an emancipative role, nor can it help create a more just society.

This book exposes the character and pathologies of a new era. By awakening a sense of what the new era represents, its relations of power, and the challenges it poses, it hopes to raise our social consciousness. Such consciousness is the key to human emancipation in a society where the drive for profit and power overcomes most restraints. Through critical discourse, this book also seeks to promote an awareness of historical possibility without delving into messianic goals or utopian constructs.

This book breaks away from the pervasive reductionism and the narrow, microempiricist approaches that characterize most treatments of social phenomena nowadays. Its broad and often abstract perspectives follow a path taken by numerous authors in radical social criticism and radical political economy. The works of Marx, Braverman, Marcuse, Gramsci, Negri, Gorz, and many other authors enlightened readers by providing broad (and often abstract) vistas that created awareness, enlightened consciousness, and motivated readers to search for and work against the causes of injustice. By providing a broad panorama of an emerging social phenomenon, this book seeks to contribute to radical social criticism in our time and to kindle readers' awareness of injustice and the need for emancipative agendas. There is a place and a need for general perspectives and for broad conceptual constructs in our time to help us size up the ethos of technocapitalism, its contradictions, and its social consequences.

The critical perspective of this book is grounded on the premise that technology is neither completely "neutral" in a purely functional sense, nor is it wholly "cultural" as a sociocultural force unto itself. Technology is a result of human actions and decisions. These decisions have social, political, and economic dimensions, and are therefore not purely technical or indifferent to society. Technology is therefore subject to social intervention, which affects, and is affected by, both functional and cultural influences. It is through this difficult path between functionalism and culturalism that a consideration of the phenomenon of *technocapitalism* must traverse.

Technocapitalism is defined in this book as a new form of capitalism that is heavily grounded on corporate power and its exploitation of technological creativity. Creativity, an intangible human quality, is the most precious resource of this new incarnation of capitalism. Corporate power and profit inevitably depend on the commodification of creativity through research regimes that must generate new inventions and innovations. These regimes and the corporate apparatus in which they are embedded are to technocapitalism what the factory system and its production regimes were to industrial capitalism. The tangible resources of industrial capitalism, in the form of raw materials, production hardware, capital, and physical labor routines are thus replaced by intangibles, research hardware, experimental designs, and talented individuals with creative aptitudes. The generation of technology in this new era of capitalism is therefore a social phenomenon that relies as much on technical functionality as on the co-optation of cultural attributes.

The definition of technocapitalism used here therefore adopts neither a wholly functionalist nor a fully culturalist perspective.[2] The former, with its indifference to society and to the social character of technology, with its glorification of technical rationality above any human or social consideration, seems unsuited to any consideration of a socially emancipative role for technology. The dominant influence that corporatism exerts over technological agendas today, in its quest for power and profit, implicitly invalidates the purely functionalist view of technology. The culturalist view, which assumes that technology is a system unto itself from which there is no escape as society is molded and controlled by technological forces, also seems unsuited to any consideration of an emancipative role for technology.[3] From the culturalist perspective, attempting social interventions is pointless since there is no way to oppose technological forces, except to retreat to the primitive or the metaphysical.

The critical perspective of this book argues that the values of corporatism are embedded in the research agendas and design of technology.[4] Technological rationality is therefore not really "neutral" or "functional." Such rationality is also social, political, economic, and cultural, and it represents the power, the values, and interests of the dominant power: technocapitalist corporatism. The technological rationality of technocapitalism therefore combines technique (the rational character of technology) with social domination (the ideological character of corporatism). Such control is usually codified in the form of rules and conventions that govern how research is done and what it should look for. A critical perspective must therefore consider how these rules and conventions incorporate the values of corporatism, to systematize and justify its pursuit of power.

A critical approach must also analyze the forms of oppression associated with technocapitalism, and the challenges they pose. It must, perforce, consider the role of that new form of corporatism which is dominant in this phenomenon. Since the conquest of nature that technocapitalism and its corporatism represent occurs through social domination, the means to oppose their pathologies are to be found in a democratization of technological decisions. The democratization of these decisions must involve not only the adoption of technology but, most of all, the priorities and research agendas that generate the inventions and innovations in the first place.[5] Without such democratization, emancipation and justice remain futile notions, and a reconstruction of the sociotechnological platform of society, which is essential to offset the pathologies of technocapitalism, becomes no more than a dream.

The critical approach of this book also assumes that technocapitalism is not an outcome but a process that harbors contradictions and uncertainty. The latter are grounded in social values and in the struggle between corporatism and those who contest its power.[6] Their consideration distinguishes its approach from the merely "functional" view of technology, and thus recognizes that socially based contradictions and uncertainty are embedded in the research agendas and design of technology. The future trajectory of technocapitalism is therefore subject to change and is suspended between various possible paths. These paths can be created by the dominant, authoritarian power of corporatism *or* by democratic alternatives. Technocapitalism is therefore not necessarily a destiny but a platform of struggle, where the hegemony of corporatism is to be questioned, opposed, and overturned. On that platform of struggle rides the possibility of retracking technocapitalism toward an emancipative trajectory.[7]

All of these views and concerns were part of the motivation for writing this book. They reflect a personal trajectory toward critical thought and analysis, which has been marked by considerable difficulties. Overcoming these difficulties has given a social meaning to this project beyond the intellectual mission of grappling with a phenomenon that seems to have deep repercussions for humanity. Grasping the essence of technocapitalism in a critical way is an elusive enterprise that involves contradictory tendencies, opposition to established practices, and seeing through the walls erected by those who want to submit us to their influence.

In its scope and contents, this book may be considered controversial. Perhaps this should not surprise, in a time when most of the literature on technology is either supportive or apologetic of corporatism. How-to texts prescribing ways to improve corporate power and profit through technological innovation have little trouble gaining favor. Torrents of such books are published nowadays by university presses and commercial publishers, while critical works are all too often shunned. Critical works are often peremptorily dismissed as "unfit" for "publishing lists" that seem tailored to exclude radical critiques.[8]

The rejection of radical criticism by many publishers is part of a larger phenomenon, however. It would be remiss not to mention the inroads made by reductionism into every area of the social sciences, and its negative impact on critical dissent.[9] In the current climate, most any effort that is radically critical, broad, multidisciplinary, and that considers the "big picture" of social domination is vulnerable to pejorative comments. Such works are likely to be negatively tagged in favor of narrow or intensely microempiricist projects. Reductionism therefore commands the day and the publishing interest. Academics and publishers with vested interests in perpetuating and profiting from that mode of inquiry are not shy to disdain broadly based critical works, often brazenly and self-righteously.

It seems, therefore, that the review of critical scholarship nowadays all too often involves the opposite of Mertonian norms.[10] Vested interests, prejudice, topic-based biases, coupled with secrecy, are more common than most academics are willing to acknowledge. Subtle prejudice beyond the ideological sort is an additional obstacle faced by those who, being out of the mainstream ethnically or racially, attempt radical criticism. It seems as if some of the strategies and pathologies common to corporatism have made inroads into academia.

This book is the product of many years of research and reflection. The support and constructive feedback provided by many scholars over the years is deeply appreciated and acknowledged. They are too numerous to list here, but all who provided feedback on the topic of this book know about and share my gratitude for their efforts. To my spouse, I owe a special debt of gratitude, not only for her care and support but also for her progressive thoughts and philosophical acumen.

I must thank wholeheartedly the reviewers of the manuscript of this book, for their very critical (but nonetheless constructive) comments. They know, as I do, that no work of social criticism is ever truly complete, and no author can consider himself to be above criticism. I hope that this work contributes to the readers' understanding of our time and its social context. I also hope that they will find strength to oppose the injustices and pathologies that contemporary society imposes on us.

Experimentalism

Experimentalism is the driving force of technocapitalism. It underpins the ethos of this new era with its compulsions, exploitive schemes, and diverse pathologies. It contributes features that set the emerging paradigm apart from prior stages of capitalism. Experimentalism therefore transcends the context of the laboratory set by the experimental sciences in the nineteenth and twentieth centuries to encompass all of society. This chapter considers the characteristics that make experimentalism both a social phenomenon and a source of pathology in the nascent era of technocapitalism.

Experimentalism is defined here as technological and scientific inquiry whose overarching objective is commercial. It is therefore experimentation for the sake of profit and power above all ends, rather than experimentation for its own sake or for the sake of attaining new knowledge as an end in itself. Perhaps the most distinctive characteristic of experimentalism is that it sets a platform through which corporate profits and power are obtained from creativity and other intangibles. Obtaining profit and power from creativity involves research processes. Experimentalism and its research processes are to technocapitalism what the factory system and its labor processes were to industrial capitalism.

Experimentalism involves the subordination of research to corporate power and to its commercial ends to an extent never previously encountered. The harnessing of technology and science to corporatism exempts few experimental tasks or activities, as long as they bear the prospect of power and profit. Power and profit are usually the hope, measure, and judge of any experimental undertaking in the emerging context of technocapitalism.

Experimentalism is corporate, in spirit and praxis. Power and commercial ends thus tend to rule over the decision to experiment. For experimentation undertaken for its own sake and joy, for the simple pleasure of discovery or self-realization, has little scope in the context of technocapitalism. That context, which is corporate above everything, reaches into most every corner of society and respects few bounds. Its relations of power are therefore oriented toward domination, using technological creativity as the means to power and profit.

The definition of corporatism provided in the introduction—the power of business corporations over society—must therefore be revisited. Experimentalism provides the platform upon which corporatism extracts profit and power from creativity. The traditional definition of corporatism, which stipulates collusion between corporate and government interests, is subsumed in the broader definition of the term used here, as noted earlier. However, the advent of technocapitalism brings experimentalism into the definition of corporatism, given the symbiotic relationship between these phenomena. Experimentalism cannot exist without corporatism, and technocapitalist corporatism cannot exist without experimentalism. As we will see in this chapter, the accumulation modes that make it possible for experimentalism to emerge as a distinctive element of technocapitalism benefit corporatism most, above and beyond any other social entity.

As in previous stages of capitalism, new modes of organization, new technologies, and new accumulation regimes mark the emergence of technocapitalism. They are intimately related to experimentalism's emergence as a societal phenomenon and contribute to make experimentalism a social creation, one that transcends laboratory settings to encompass society in its power and pathologies.

Research dominates the new organizations spawned by experimentalism. Intangibles, and most of all creativity, are their most valuable resources. Several accumulation phenomena, built up over several decades, created platforms upon which critical masses of knowledge and experimental infrastructure could develop. The new technologies that are emerging are diverse and can be found in the fields that will become emblematic of the twenty-first century. Most every area of biotechnology, including proteomics, genomics, biopharmaceuticals, and biomedicine, the nascent field of nanotechnology and all its innumerable future medical and mechanical applications, molecular computing, bioinformatics, and the area of biorobotics are but a few examples of the fields that will represent this reincarnation of capitalism.

Society as Laboratory

At the core of experimentalism is the pervasive "socialization" of research. Socialization occurs at multiple levels, not only in the realm of social relations but also in the context of organizations, their networks, and in the broader sphere of governance. And this multifaceted process of socialization under technocapitalism is driven, first and foremost, by commercial objectives.

The socialization of experimentalism means that society as a whole becomes the laboratory of technocapitalism. This is a laboratory that is certainly quite different from the traditional labs of experimental science, not only physically but also in terms of scope, governance, and reach. And, it is a laboratory in which all of society is forcibly engaged, through the commercial compulsion of the new order. All of society, in essence, becomes the guinea pig of corporate experimentalism.

Many of the restraints that would allow society to resist this new order and its pathologies have collapsed. The emergence of technocapitalism is, in part, a result of the breakdown of these restraints, which are complex and involve myriad social, cultural, and institutional factors. And in some respects this breakdown repeats the collapse of restraints at previous stages in the advance of capitalism. In the earliest phase of industrial capitalism, for example, the factory system collapsed restraints that could have prevented its emergence.[1] Cultural conventions, mores, class structures, and governance arrangements that could not be co-opted were either discarded or radically reconfigured to serve the new order. Transcending preexisting conditions, the new mode typified by the factory system thus became more social than any of its predecessors as it took over or destroyed institutions, fostered new ones, generated new class arrangements, and otherwise changed the reality of the societies in which it was embedded.

And, as experimentalism transcends the laboratory context of the experimental sciences, it becomes more social than conventional experimentation could ever be. Experimentalism therefore becomes a *social creation* in its own right, especially since under technocapitalism, experimentalism is undertaken for the primary objective of extracting value. Such value is, moreover, generated through the exercise of *creativity*, a most precious and elusive quality. And, unlike the main resources of industrial capitalism, this most valuable resource of the technocapitalist era is *intangible* and therefore inherently social.

Although experimentalism's full dimensions and effects are still largely unknown, several features characterize its emergence as a social phenomenon. The *first* feature is that experimentalism involves *social mediation*, comprising both the exercise of technological creativity and its relations of power. Social mediation here refers to the intervention of society through, for example, the kind of relations that stimulate the generation of new knowledge and creativity. The term also refers to the governance of such relations, which affects the deployment of research creativity whenever it is applied as a resource of technocapitalism.

Social mediation, as we see later, occurs primarily through networks. But the networks that provide the mediation needed by experimentalism are rather different from those conventionally envisioned by social theorists. The networks of experimentalism are highly focused on research and on the communication of new knowledge obtained through research. Creativity is a fundamental resource for the latter. The social mediation of these networks is a major force in stimulating creativity to the extent that they regenerate imaginations, curiosity, and the motivation to search, tinker, or test.

Social mediation through networks also involves relations of power. Networks are not neutral insofar as the governance of social relations is concerned. Their extent, structure, and access are largely articulated by those who participate in them. Such participation can become a means to dominate other network participants *or* it can become a vehicle to collapse hierarchies, oligarchies, and exploitive control. The limits of either possibility must be understood in the context of techno-capitalism, however, and its overarching objective of extracting value. In this regard, it would be naïve to conclude that the kind of social mediation found through networks is necessarily emancipative.[2]

For example, research networks of the Open Source kind are often viewed as being contrarian to proprietary controls and corporate power.[3] Open Source research networks (such as the ones involving Linux software) are completely open to anyone's participation and collaboration. Their main requirement is that any results be shared with everyone, in or outside the network. Any individual or network-based property claims are therefore eliminated. Profit and property claims are banished in favor of sharing, collaborating, and making all results available to anyone who cares to use them, regardless of whether they participate in the network. In concept and practice, Open Source research networks have therefore come to symbolize free, socially driven experimentation.

However, the open character of these networks often leads to an unexpected outcome, as the freely available results (whether in the form of software code, biotech procedures, or a nanotech process) are taken and incorporated in proprietary corporate products or services. Corporations such as IBM are thus using Open Source (Linux) software—freely provided by networks involving thousands of volunteer programmers around the world—to reduce their costs and boost profits on the services and hardware they sell. Other corporate organizations, such as Sun Microsystems, develop hardware and applications based on the software kernels they obtain freely.[4] These applications are then sold to customers for a profit, usually with expensive service contracts that guarantee customers' dependence on the provider. The business models of many software service corporations have been built on free software provided by Open Source networks.

Therefore, social mediation cannot be divorced from the larger context of technocapitalism. The priority behind experimentalism is to extract value from research creativity through corporate power. Social mediation is subordinated to this overarching objective, and so are the relations of power that align interests with this priority. The days when cutting-edge experimentation might be undertaken for its own sake and joy (or for society's sake) without regard for commercial gain therefore seem to be coming to a close.

A *second* social feature of experimentalism is its emergence as a new form of *corporatism*. This new corporatism is defined here as a specific form of corporate organization that is primarily geared toward research (as opposed to a primary emphasis on, say, production or distribution). It is narrowly founded on the extraction of value from technological creativity through research, and can emphasize research to the exclusion of other traditional corporate functions. This means that for any extraction of value to occur, creativity must be turned into a commodity. On this basic premise rides the balance between success and failure for corporate experimentalism. The new corporatism is therefore part and parcel of the ethos technocapitalism and cannot be conceived as an entity divorced from the larger phenomenon.

Success in extracting value—rather than finding truth—becomes the prime objective of experimentalism. Extracting value from research creativity thus becomes the new "truth." Science at the service of corporate experimentalism does not involve the simple and unfettered search for truth for its own sake. If it occurs at all, the search for truth is subordinated to a higher priority: the attainment of commercial value, the higher the better, over all other possibilities.

This overarching priority poses serious challenges to corporate experimentalism. The main one is the imperative need to sustain creativity in order to turn it into a commodity. This is no simple endeavor, considering the intangible and fragile nature of creativity. Uncertainty and risk of the highest order are part of any effort to turn research creativity into cutting-edge results that might have any commercial value. Compounding the uncertainty is the fact that creativity defies efforts to standardize and measure it, unlike the raw materials or factory labor of industrial capitalism.

Examples of how corporate experimentalism turns the extraction of value into its overarching priority can be found throughout the contemporary corporate spectrum. In practically every sector, the foremost objective of research departments is to come up with innovations that can yield high profits in the shortest time. At Microsoft, this strategy has practically guaranteed that faulty software will be marketed, all the more so given the company's monopolistic power over the personal computer software market.[5] If achieving a trouble-free product is a form of "truth" (from a researcher's perspective), Microsoft has trumped it in the interest of high profits and short-termism. This occurs despite the fact that Microsoft's monopolistic hold over the software market has shielded it from the sort of do-or-die pressures that companies in competitive markets typically experience. Another factor affecting corporate experimentalism is the high cost of undertaking cutting-edge research. Expensive, complex, and highly sophisticated hardware is typically required in such fields as bioinformatics, nanotechnology, genetic decoding, and proteomics research, for example. The hardware utilized usually becomes obsolescent in a short time, needing high serial expenditures to update or replace it. Moreover, the complexity of the hardware requires teams of researchers with advanced university degrees to operate it, usually precluding the possibility of individual tinkering unrelated to commercial objectives or the research agenda set by corporate power.

Corporate experimentalism thus fosters organizations that are highly specialized in research. As we see later, traditional corporate functions, such as production, marketing, or distribution are often excluded or, if present, are subordinated to research. The experimentalist organization lives or dies by research. And research creativity is its main resource and commodity. The survival of corporate experimentalism, therefore, depends on how this most precious quality is exploited.

An example of this new kind of corporatism can be found in companies that are solely dedicated to decode genetic information to patent and retain the property claim. The early genetic decoding companies—such as Incyte and Celera Genomics—were built on this model and demonstrated a corporate path that other companies followed.[6] Utilizing supercomputers and very expensive laboratory hardware, and employing large numbers of highly talented researchers to do the decoding, along with dozens of lawyers to follow through on the patent filings, these companies are single-minded in purpose and scope. They have no production facilities and no distribution chains to speak of. Their only interest is in establishing intellectual (in this case technological) property claims, and their revenues are derived from licensing other companies who may put the patented genetic information to use in some product or service.

The social character of creativity makes corporate experimentalism more dependent on social mediation than any preceding corporate form. The experimentalist corporation cannot be considered to be separate

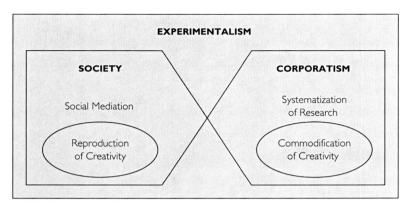

Figure 1   Context of Experimentalism

from society. A suggestive diagram of the relationship between experimentalist corporatism and society is shown in Figure 1. As we see in later chapters, the split between experimentalist corporatism *and* society is a major cause of pathology in the technocapitalist domain. Corporatism is primarily in charge of the commodification of creativity and cannot hope to reproduce it on its own because of the fundamentally social character of this resource. Only society can reproduce creativity effectively. This split between commodification (a corporate function) and reproduction (a social function) is a distinctive feature of the new era.

A major contradiction arises from the fact that experimentalist corporatism is part of society and is unavoidably embedded in it, mainly because its most valuable resource—creativity—cannot be sustained without the extensive mediation of society. This societal mediation limits the possibility of controlling creativity internally, by and through the sole intervention of corporate governance, making it necessary for the experimentalist corporation to be more "external" than any of its predecessors. As we see later, contradictions on this fundamental aspect of experimentalism introduce serious pathologies, not only in society but also internally in the corporate context.

A *third* social feature of experimentalism is its capacity to define *reality* to an extent never previously encountered. Until recently, the reality defined by experimental pursuits was confined to the impact of a certain technology or, more narrowly, to the laboratories where tinkering occurred. The reality of experimentalism under technocapitalism is defined, in turn, for *all* of society. Its scale is "mega," meant to be all-encompassing and deeply entwined with corporatism, to serve the latter. *Defining reality means that experimentalism increasingly sets the agenda for entire societies.* Its effects, therefore, go beyond issues directly related to technology and science, to encompass aspects that are seemingly far removed from their scope and range. It may be argued that the reach of this phenomenon goes far beyond that of previous epochs, such as the intrusion of the factory system on society and cultures during the nineteenth century or that of mass production in the twentieth. One of the means available for this intrusive reach is, for example, genetic engineering and its modification of life and nature, targeted to support the objectives of corporate experimentalism.

It does not seem too far-fetched to expect that new life forms, personalities, and behaviors may soon be "engineered" to suit the demands of corporate power. The time when human behavior is engineered to be "better adjusted" to corporate needs already seems to be upon us. Behavior modification drugs, for example, have turned into a growth sector for the pharmaceutical industry.[7] The incipient convergence between genetic engineering, biopharmacology, and biomedicine offers the frightening possibility of adjusting individual genetic makeups to suit corporate needs, not only in the manipulation of mass consumption habits but also in producing individuals who are pliant to corporate power and to its managerial priorities. "Medications" that engineer personalities and attitudes to suit corporate priorities are likely to become widespread with the expansion of the biopharmaceutical industry. By relying on genetics, the effects of such biopharma products are likely to be permanent.[8] The subordination of life, nature, and human values to the ethos of corporate experimentalism therefore seems more likely than ever, as social, cultural, and institutional restraints are collapsed by the new order.[9]

The relations of power are always, therefore, at or near the surface of the experimentalist order. A facade of democratic "process" (and governance) in society might provide an appearance of legitimacy, but the raw, compulsive nature of this phenomenon is not too difficult to detect. Moreover, its authoritarian impulse to conquer and colonize most every aspect of human existence (and nature itself) is enhanced by the incipient globalization of technocapitalism. Societies that might seem to be out of reach of technocapitalism are not likely to remain unaffected, especially since the capacity for intrusion of experimentalism is enhanced by market processes that are spreading to every corner of the globe. The prospect of experimentalism defining reality for entire societies is therefore a frightening one. As far as can be seen, this megaexercise in reality setting will be primarily oriented to benefit corporatism. Social elements and interests that diverge from those of corporate experimentalism are bound to become disadvantaged. Those that actively oppose the new order are likely to fare worse, as corporate power tries to conquer any and all institutions that can be of service to its interests. As we see in later chapters, new forms of governance and a radical democratization of technological decisions are needed to counteract the nefarious effects of this unfolding phenomenon.

Accumulation and Power

The emergence of experimentalism as a societal phenomenon is supported by processes of accumulation. Accelerating during the last part of the twentieth century, these processes made up the historical "platform" from which experimentalism's societal reach has been projected. Their influence in the emergence of experimentalism and its relations of power are therefore a hallmark of the technocapitalist paradigm.

The accumulation phenomena and their unfettered support for experimentalism are allowing technocapitalism to conquer facets of human and social existence left untouched by capitalism's previous incarnation. Thus, technocapitalism's attempt to conquer society through experimentalism is made feasible by the tearing down of restraints to accumulation, much as the elimination of obstacles to capital accumulation in the eighteenth and nineteenth centuries allowed the factory system of industrial capitalism to conquer craft work and the structures of mercantile society.[10] The collapse of these restraints, which are complex and involve myriad cultural and institutional factors, has made it possible to shift *power* from those who exploited the most important resources of capitalism's previous phase to those who now exploit the most important resources of technocapitalism.

Transfers of power, made possible by rapid accumulation, entailed the emergence of new technologies and organizational modes, and allowed paradigmatic changes within the general framework of capitalism in the past. Thus, power shifts driven by accumulation have provided capitalism with new leases on life during its two centuries of existence, but at the expense of major social pathologies. One such shift in the late nineteenth century involved the change from early industrial capitalism to middle industrial capitalism, as the factory system, using a vital set of technologies (steam generation and steel, for example) made way for mass production through new organizational arrangements (involving Frederick Taylor's "scientific management") that used a set of new technologies (electricity, petroleum refining, and internal combustion engines, for example).[11] As a result, exploitation of labor and the depersonalization of work processes catapulted to new heights and became major pathologies of this shift.[12]

Then, the shift from middle to late industrial capitalism in the later part of the twentieth century involved the change from mass production to flexible production, based on another new set of technologies (computers, electronics, and satellite communications, for example). Among its pathological effects were the elimination of entire occupational categories and the concomitant destruction of employment coupled with economic insecurity for vast segments of the working population.[13] At the same time, the transition period commonly characterized as "postindustrial" capitalism emerged as part of this shift.[14] So-called postindustrial capitalism was really only a component of late industrial capitalism based on the rapid growth of services that complemented the emerging sectors and industries of that era.

Services thus extended the "value chains" of the industries of late industrial capitalism to support unfettered consumerism (itself grounded in the new industries typical of that era). Ideas behind production in industry were often transferred to services, turning services into a sort of manufacturing process, for example, as fast-food services became an "industrialized" alternative to restaurants.[15] Another example, airline services, took up the characteristics of a manufacturing process as large-capacity aircraft operating under principles of industrial efficiency became a mass transport mode, replacing long-distance passenger ship and rail services.[16] The alienation and depersonalization of work that had become a signature pathology of industrial capitalism thus also became a part of service activities.

All these shifts were made possible by the *accumulation of capital.* Power was transferred from those who exploited old technologies and organizational modes to those who exploited the new technologies and organizations vital to the new incarnation of capitalism. In many cases, those who exploited the new technologies and organizations also helped dynamize the accumulation of capital by concocting easier and faster ways to secure capital.[17] Capital accumulation, the traditional accumulation process of capitalism, thus changed with every shift of power from one era of capitalism to another, securing the capital needed to extract value in ever faster and more effective ways.[18]

The long-standing process of capital accumulation is, of course, also a part of technocapitalism and of its experimentalist apparatus. Technocapitalism is, like its predecessors, dynamizing the accumulation of capital by concocting means to seize it in ever faster and larger quantities. One can easily see that already, in the rapid and unprecedented global flows of investment capital supported by innovations in software, communications, and electronics.[19] Thus, increased capital accumulation under technocapitalism is part of the transfer of power from late industrial capitalism's corporate behemoths, with their emphasis on production, to corporate experimentalism, with its obsessive focus on research. The new organizational mode of this incipient era of capitalism is the *experimentalist corporate organization*, which is often exclusively dedicated to research. As we see in later chapters, this peculiar organizational mode can be considered a new form of corporatism.

This new organizational mode thus displaces the old industrial corporation and its overwhelming focus on production. The growing importance of this new organizational mode is accompanied by the rise of new technologies. The vital new technologies representative of technocapitalism can be found, for example, in biotechnology and its related areas of genetic engineering, proteomics, bioinformatics, and biopharmaceuticals (among others); in nanotechnology and its many related fields, such as molecular computing and nanomedicine; in biorobotics; and in various other esoteric new fields that are closely related to experimentalism and its corporate apparatus.[20]

In addition to the ongoing process of capital accumulation that has always been part and parcel of capitalism, the emergence of experimentalism as a societal phenomenon is supported by *two other major processes of accumulation*. These accumulation processes are unique to experimentalism and to the larger phenomenon of technocapitalism in the sense that never before had they acquired the magnitude and influence they now have. While they may have been at work in some semblance in previous eras, their rising profile has been a hallmark of the last part of the twentieth century.

One of the two major accumulation processes supporting experimentalism involves the *accumulation of technological knowledge*. This process is crucial for creativity, the most precious resource of technocapitalism. The accumulation of technological knowledge involves society (broadly conceived) in the substantial, long-term buildup of experience with technology. This buildup must perforce occur through the generation of *new* knowledge. Implicitly, the accumulation of such knowledge is *power* for those who control it over those who lack the possibility of accumulating it in sustained and substantial ways.

The accumulation of technological knowledge at a societal level therefore carries the seed of power as it grows and compounds. It confers power to the societies that can accumulate faster, in both qualitative and quantitative dimensions. Today, this phenomenon accounts for the global technological supremacy of certain nations that feel entitled to impose their blueprints for most everything—from cultural values to governance and warfare—on other peoples who are regarded as "inferior" based on their technological capabilities, culture, and race. It is naïve to think that the power conferred by the rapid accumulation of technological knowledge stops at a nation's borders in this era of technocapitalism. The power conferred by this form of accumulation is *global* in most respects, and it is bound to become more so as obstacles to the power of technocapitalism are bypassed or taken down.

The accumulation of technological knowledge also confers power on corporatism. The capacity of corporate capital to tap accumulated knowledge is a major factor in the link between this process and the global reach of corporatism. Because of its focus on research and creativity, the experimentalist corporation is therefore primed to exploit the vast reservoir of knowledge provided through this accumulation process. However, one should not underestimate the capability of old-line industrial corporatism to tap this reservoir.

The marriage between textiles and nanotechnology is one such example. A mundane industry dating to the earliest industrial times stands to be reborn through one of the most technologically sophisticated sectors of our time, which is greatly symbolic of the new era of technocapitalism. A new textile industry is poised to flood markets with the likes of unstainable fabrics (pity the laundry business), extremely thin and light garments able to protect from the most frigid weather, and underwear packed with nanotech sensors that monitor various physiological functions along with the geographical location of those who wear it. Old industrial companies, along with capitalism itself, have therefore found a new lease on life through the accumulation of technological knowledge.

Evidence of the accumulation of technological knowledge can be found in the dynamic rise of invention patenting during the second half of the twentieth century. Invention patent awards, for example, increased fourfold in the United States during that period, while patent applications rose more than sevenfold.[21] Evidence from other rich nations (northwestern Europe, Japan) also showed substantial increases, despite devastating losses of skilled population and technological infrastructure as a result of the Second World War. Patenting, therefore, rose faster than ever since its inception as a property right. The accumulation of this vast stock of knowledge in such a short period of time reflected the growing importance of technological creativity as a major social and economic resource.

That virtually all of this rapid increase in patenting came about through corporate research points to the very close association between the accumulation of technological knowledge *and* corporatism. Patents assigned to individual inventors during the second half of the twentieth century thus stagnated, as invention was taken over by corporate research. Moreover, as the cost and complexity of invention increased, many independent inventors were either cast out of patenting or were absorbed by corporate research.[22] This situation in some ways reenacted the condition of independent craftsmen in the eighteenth and nineteenth centuries, who had little choice but to join the factory system of early industrial capitalism. Invention thus became *corporatized* in the second half of the twentieth century. A transfer of power from individual inventors to corporatism became a hallmark of this accumulation process, setting the stage for the eventual emergence of experimentalism as a major corporate endeavor.

Much related to the accumulation of technological knowledge was the rapid *massification of higher education* that occurred during the second half of the twentieth century. Access to higher education became a right, taken for granted by the populations of most every rich nation. Demands for dedicating public resources to open up access became an important source of political leverage. As a result, what had typically been a preserve of elites and the bourgeoisie became open to others between the 1950s and the 1980s.

The massification of technological higher education was of particular importance to the accumulation of knowledge during the second half of the twentieth century. In most every rich nation, numerous polytechnic universities were opened or expanded, enabling a level of access that would have been unimaginable at any previous time. The dynamic expansion of public university systems, comprising multiple campuses with strong science and engineering programs, had a very important effect on accumulation. These institutions generated successive waves of graduates who contributed to the increasing reservoir of knowledge. Quality was sustained by creating various tiers of public higher education with varying degrees of openness. And in many cases, public university systems acquired greater recognition than the private alternatives that had traditionally served elites.[23]

As might be expected, corporatism tapped intensely into the talent flowing from this remarkable expansion of higher education. Cutting-edge corporate research departments were created to expand corporatism's global reach and power over many aspects of society. There are too many examples to be cited on this phenomenon, but one of its immediate and most notable ones was the rise of so-called "high-technology" sectors during the 1980s, such as personal computing and microprocessors, which spawned a kind of "high-tech" corporatism that relied as much on production and distribution as on research.[24]

This surge of "high-tech" corporatism was an important stepping stone on the way to technocapitalism. It relied on talents cultivated by the massification of technological higher education that had started in the late 1940s. By the 1980s, a critical mass of highly talented technologists with corporate experience had formed, based on numerous waves of university graduates in the sciences and engineering. Thus, the massification of higher education and the larger process of knowledge accumulation finally began to show results after three decades of rapid and continuous expansion. The continuing and dynamic nature of these two related phenomena have been part of the platform from which technocapitalism is emerging.

The second major process supporting experimentalism involves the *accumulation of technological infrastructure*. This process also experienced great dynamism during the second half of the twentieth century in most every rich nation. Fundamentally, it comprised the construction of a vast array of laboratory facilities for experimental endeavors in the sciences and engineering. However, innumerable other kinds of infrastructure involving communications that supported experimentalism, such as the Internet and the Web and electronic and conventional libraries, were also part of this accumulative process.

Educational infrastructure directly related to technology and science, such as instructional laboratories and classrooms, were part of this phenomenon. Much of this expansive process was, of course, related to the previously discussed massification of education. Creating and expanding public university systems with multiple campuses, for example, required a substantial amount of construction. Therefore, it may not be surprising that total public spending on educational construction in the United States rose sixty-fold during the second half of the twentieth century.[25] Other rich nations experienced similar increases in educational infrastructure spending, providing a formidable support base for experimental endeavors.

This kind of support has been of great importance to corporatism. In a society where corporate power tends to decide or co-opt most any aspect of the public domain, the large historical cumulation of public spending on infrastructure was a boon to its power. The rapid accumulation of public technological infrastructure during the second half of the twentieth century therefore subsidized the power of corporatism, allowing it to become more effective in extracting value out of new knowledge. This kind of public subsidy for corporatism has arguably been more important than all the myriad fiscal "incentives" often cited in the media, such as tax breaks, export subsidies, and the often-corrupt loosening of regulatory controls. This is especially so because the effects of infrastructural accumulation are *long-term*, lasting over several generations, and tend to compound over time.

A critical mass of vital technological infrastructure has been the outcome of long-term accumulation. After decades of accretion and compounding this phenomenon, coupled with two other vital accumulation processes—technological knowledge accumulation and capital accumulation—created a formidable platform from which

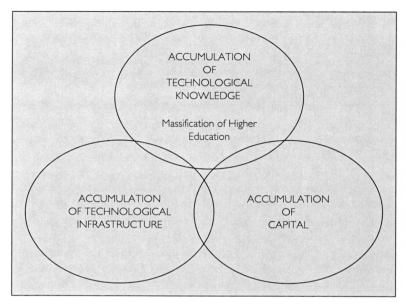

Figure 2   Processes of Accumulation

technocapitalism and its handmaiden, experimentalism, are emerging. These three phenomena, suggestively shown in Figure 2, are not independent of each other. They act together, and are entwined in the fabric of the new era.

Thus, the accumulation of technological knowledge is symbiotically related to the accumulation of technological infrastructure and the accumulation of capital. These accumulation phenomena, acting in concert, are a major support for experimentalism. The inherently social character of the accumulation of technological knowledge (which is essential for nurturing creativity) makes experimentalism a sociosystemic phenomenon, despite its essential connection to corporate power.

Experimentalism as System

The vast knowledge and infrastructure accumulated over a half century created the conditions to establish experimentalism as a system. The systematization of experimentalism is primarily organizational and is therefore closely related to corporatism. In this context, systematization involves the imposition of wide-ranging frameworks to manipulate research. These frameworks typically seek to program experimental endeavors so that they can be undertaken as continuously as possible to generate streams of new inventions and innovations.

Systematization is part and parcel of the inextricable relationship between experimentalism and corporate power. It is therefore a corporate construction, driven first and foremost by commercial objectives. Systematization is all about the exploitation of creativity, which is an inherently social, qualitative, and intangible resource. It is also a social phenomenon, within and outside the corporatist dimension, meaning that its operation depends largely on social relations that revolve around experimental research. And, systematization helps generate new organizational arrangements, tailored to the requirements of corporate power.

As we see in later chapters, systematization is at the core of a new kind of organization, spawned to serve the needs of corporate experimentalism. The scope of the new organizational mode is all about research. Creativity is its most precious and valuable resource. Extracting value from creativity through research, in order to generate commercial gain, is the uppermost objective. As might be suspected, this new organizational mode contains serious pathological tendencies, fostered by the antithetical interests of corporatism and the kinds of resources that are vital to experimentalism. The conflicting character of these interests and the pathological effects are dealt with in later chapters, but we should keep in mind that they are part and parcel of the larger phenomenon of technocapitalism and its corporatist underpinnings.

Although the systematization of experimentalism is still largely uncharted, there are several effects that can be observed at this time. All of them are entwined with corporatism, with its expanding reach over all things social and with its pathologies. To a great extent, they show how experimentalism is derailing long-running perceptions of technology and science, as technocapitalism's roots deepen and overcome social restraints.

The *first* effect involves a break with what has been perceived to be a long-standing driving force of experimentation. Traditionally, experimental research was driven by a need to solve "problems." The problems were usually related to one of two kinds of failings: the inadequacy of an existing technology to solve a certain condition *or* a lack of compatibility between existing technologies that required a new one to bridge the gap or replace them altogether.[26]

In the emerging era of technocapitalism, however, corporate power and commercial gain are the drivers of experimental endeavors. Although problem-driven experimentation does occur, it is being overshadowed by corporatism and its commercial imperative. Extracting commercial value out of research is therefore acquiring a higher priority than solving any specific technological problem. This is already obvious in the strategies of many research-driven corporations that place profit and market power above technological problem solving. Rendering their own products obsolete by replacing them with new ones that only provide marginal improvements, for example, has become a major preoccupation of corporate research, as sustaining profits becomes the main priority. Instead of targeting their resources to come up with breakthroughs that address major problems, their efforts tend to focus on tweaking existing technology to increase short-term returns. Profits therefore become the real "problem" to be solved, displacing technological problem solving to a lower plane.

Examples of this phenomenon abound among technology companies. Some large technology corporations such as Microsoft, for example, routinely make products obsolete in order to boost profits and "shareholder value."[27] The new products they unveil often do little beyond what the previous version did for most users, as occurred with Microsoft's Windows 95, 98, XP, and Vista software versions. Marginal improvements that are irrelevant to most users nonetheless promote sales, as many customers rush to buy the new product without any real understanding of its benefit over the previous version (benefits are often obscure or not widely known at the time the new version is introduced). Moreover, the company contributes to this situation by refusing to support old versions of the product. Customer service for the previous versions of the product is thus cut off, leaving users who do not buy the new version stranded (and thereby forcing them to buy the new product if they want any support at all). Similarly, other companies who depend on the Windows platform to sell their services to their own customers then have to pay Microsoft to have access to the new version or risk having their business severely damaged.

The systematization of experimentalism has made profits over problem solving possible by allowing greater control over research by corporate governance. Shifting away from problem-driven research to systematic tweaking is now easier than ever. Systematization has turned research units into appendages of corporate power and strategy, largely eliminating the autonomy they had to develop their own problem-driven agendas. Thus, it should not be surprising that profits and market power become the real drivers of research. By allowing greater corporate control over research, systematization has also sought to reduce risk by favoring short-term tweaking, which is perceived to have lower risk compared to problem-driven basic research. The latter, which often has a long-term scope, tends to be disfavored because it is perceived to be more uncertain and expensive.

Systematization has also made it possible to move away from problem-driven experimentation by making it easier to link research (and experimentalism, in general) to the vast resources provided by the two major accumulation phenomena discussed earlier. Systematization can, for example, channel accumulated knowledge to research by providing access to an extensive repertory of possibilities and resources. Such repertories can supply ideas whenever improvements on an existing technology are needed. Thus, the hard choices and commitments that often accompany problem-driven experimentation can be precluded. Such possibilities are also indispensable when surveys of past and existing technological characteristics must be compiled. Access to infrastructure through systematization can also offer opportunities for imitation, thus avoiding the large and uncertain investments required by problem-driven research.

A *second* effect of the systematization of experimentalism involves the blurring of boundaries between technology and science. Thus, the long-standing question of whether technology is driven by science or the inverse has become largely irrelevant.[28] Under technocapitalism, the overwhelming preoccupation is to extract value in whichever way is most effective.

As experimentalism becomes systematized, researchers therefore tend to ignore the difference between technology and science. In the laboratory, both are often practically the same, and questioning causality becomes a rhetorical waste of time in the experimentalist corporate setting. Experimentalist research activities seldom recognize any difference between them, since achieving results by any feasible means is what counts. Thus, for example, a nanotechnology research project is unlikely to try to sort out whether relevant knowledge from chemistry was derived from prior experience with materials engineering. Similarly, a bioinformatics project aiming to decode genetic data is unlikely to stir much debate on whether software applications are being driven by microbiological knowledge.

Erasing the bounds between technology and science is also partly a result of the accumulation phenomena discussed previously, and of the wide-ranging access that systematization allows. When so much knowledge is available, it becomes very difficult to determine causal influences. The complexity of the interrelations is often daunting as, for example, a given strand of technological knowledge may appear to have been derived from science, but the science in turn might have previously come from technology, and the inverse may have been the case before that. The question of whether technology had causal influence on a specific strand of scientific knowledge or vice versa can therefore become little more than a rhetorical nuisance in the context of technocapitalism.

The *third* effect of systematization is related to the social character of experimentalism. Systematization turns experimentalism into more of a social artifact as it improves its capacity to extract value. For value to be extracted, creativity must be exploited. As creativity is an intangible and inherently social quality, by facilitating its exploitation, systematization makes experimentalism more dependent on social relations. The social nature of creativity and its capacity to redefine notions of value is broached in the next chapter, but it should be kept in mind that it is the experimentalist context and its systematized organizational character that make it possible for this resource (creativity) to be exploited.

Social relations typically occur through networks. Networks, and the social mediation they provide, are vital for sustaining creativity and thus, indirectly, experimentalism. As we will see in later chapters, these networks operate largely out of the control of corporate governance (in its specific contexts), posing major challenges and dysfunctions to corporate power. The systematization of experimentalism facilitates access to these networks by establishing channels of contact, diffusion, and transaction. Thus, the frameworks imposed through systematization add to the socialization of experimentalism by facilitating social mediation outside the specific domains of corporate power.

Any notion that regards experimentalism, or its systematization, as being separate from society should therefore be quickly dispelled. Through its dependence on creativity and through networks, experimentalism is deeply embedded in society, more so than any other component in any previous phase of capitalism could claim to be. The new organizational mode it has spawned, the accumulation phenomena upon which it depends, and its corporatist identity guarantee its social character and its ultimate need to be accountable to society.

Conclusion

The advance of experimentalism threatens to turn society into the laboratory of technocapitalism. No aspect of human existence may be out of reach of this phenomenon if it remains unchallenged, especially as the link between experimentalism and corporate power grows stronger and tries to collapse most any obstacle to its reach. We have only just begun to witness the start of this new stage of capitalism, which is likely to be more oppressive and farther reaching than prior versions. The twenty-first century will tell the story of this trajectory and of the forces that manage to challenge its advance.

As in previous stages of capitalism, the emergence of technocapitalism is accompanied by a new organizational mode. Experimentalism is the vehicle through which the new organizations are constructed. The experimentalist corporation thus embodies the ethos of this new era of capitalism, much as the factory typified the spirit of industrial capitalism. And, corporate experimentalism is all about research. Creativity, an intangible and inherently social quality, is its most precious resource.

Two accumulation regimes, those involving technological knowledge *and* infrastructure, underpinned the rise of creativity as the fundamental resource of technocapitalism, along with the historical process of capital accumulation. As a social creation, experimentalism is therefore highly dependent not only on creativity but also on the accumulative phenomena that made it the most important resource of our time. These phenomena have been as vital to technocapitalism as capital accumulation was to industrial capitalism in the nineteenth and twentieth centuries. Only now, however, accumulation involves an intangible resource that is fragile, qualitative, and highly dependent on social mediation.

On creativity, and on its commodification and reproduction, therefore rests the edifice of technocapitalism. Corporate experimentalism, as the driving force of technocapitalism, must consequently find ever more exploitive ways to turn this vital resource into streams of new inventions and innovations. For, at its root, experimentalism is much about corporate power and its extraction of value from creativity. Commercial value and corporate power are therefore the ultimate "truths" for which experimentalism relentlessly searches.

As the twenty-first century unfolds, better perspectives on this new phase of capitalism are likely to emerge. At this time, however, the full impact and social dimensions of technocapitalism and of its driving force, experimentalism, are largely unknown. We must nevertheless grapple with the limited insights that are available in order to try to understand its profile and possible effects. And we must also seek ways to oppose its dehumanizing character and pathologies. The following chapters provide critical perspectives on other visible features of this phenomenon and the challenges that any opposition to its reach may need to consider.

Creativity as a Commodity

A major feature that sets technocapitalism apart from previous eras is the vital need to commodify creativity. The commodification of this most *intangible* and elusive human quality has characteristics separating it from the commodification of other resources in previous stages of capitalism. The distinctive character of this process and the features that underpin its role in the rise of technocapitalism are addressed in this chapter.

Commodification is defined here as the set of processes or activities through which the results of creativity are commercialized. Commercialization typically involves products or services obtained from the exercise of creativity. Reproduction is defined as the regeneration of creativity through social mediation. Reproduction allows creativity to be exercised such that it can generate new inventions and innovations. The social context and its relations are vital for reproduction to occur. In the context of technocapitalism, however, the exercise of creativity occurs in corporate organizations. Such organizations are typically in charge of commodification and its ancillary activities.

The pervasive commodification and reproduction of creativity to advance corporate power is a major aspect of technocapitalism. This new version of capitalism colonizes aspects of life and work that were left untouched by prior stages of capitalism. The overarching importance of creativity as a commodity can be found readily in any of the activities that are typical of technocapitalism. In any area of biotechnology, such as genomics, proteomics, bioinformatics, or biopharmaceuticals; in nanotechnology; in molecular computing and the other sectors that are symbolic of the twenty-first century, the commodification and reproduction of creativity are at the center of their commercialization. None of these activities could have formed, much less flourished, without the unremitting commodification of creativity that makes their existence possible.

The commodification of creativity is transforming the social relations of research in every field of technology. Industrial capitalism changed the social relations of work and rural life, force-fitting them into the mold of the factory system through the exploitation of labor. Commodification of capital and labor became part and parcel of this process two centuries ago. Today, technocapitalism opens new frontiers for capitalism by commodifying creativity in a pervasive way, sparing few efforts to extract value whenever it can do so.

Commodification involves the deliberate transformation of creativity for the purpose of commercial transaction. This transformation involves organizational modes that are specifically designed to generate inventions and innovations rapidly and frequently. Though it may be difficult to visualize, turning creativity into a commodity that can satisfy human wants and needs is common to all technocapitalist activities. However, as I discuss in this chapter, turning creativity into a commodity involves characteristics that are quite different from the commodification of other resources.

The commodification of creativity must disintegrate and reconfigure creative experiences into components from which value can be obtained. Value derived from these components can take various forms. It can, for example, take the form of new intellectual property, such as patents, or that of a new method, process, formula, service, or tool. However, disintegrating and reconfiguring creative experiences typically involves a great deal of compartmentalization. This compartmentalization of the creative process is fraught with risk and great uncertainty about its outcomes. The frailty of creativity and its qualitative underpinnings is such that the very process of commodification can destroy it. This occurs mainly because commodification is, in and of it-self, contrarian to many of the conditions that make creativity flourish.

Creativity versus Commodification

There is an underlying antithesis between creativity and commodification. Turning talent into a commodity can be a demeaning experience, but even when it is not, it is often at odds with creative endeavors or with the process of exercising creativity. Transforming creativity into a commodity can easily stunt imaginations and is often also the main source of alienation for creators, from the results of their talent *and* from their social context. As a result, the commodification of creativity often carries the seeds of its destruction. Only the social context can keep the raw, vulgar nature of commodification from turning creative processes into alienating experiences.

The conflict between commodification and creativity is mediated by society and its organizations in the technocapitalist era. But this does not mean that social and organizational contexts can dispel the fundamental contradiction that exists between commodification and creativity. Clever organizational arrangements may help soothe the alienation that accompanies the commodification of talent, but they cannot make it vanish. At best, the social and organizational contexts can make it covert, concealing its destructive character so as to allow the extraction of value to take place.[1]

Turning creative talent into a commodity is therefore a source of alienation for those who exercise creativity. Alienation, conventionally defined as detachment from one's social context, was a source of social pathologies throughout the history of industrial capitalism. From the early days of the factory system, the commodification of physical labor detached workers from their social milieu, dehumanizing their identities through production processes that extracted value by means of repetitive or mind-numbing tasks. Although research processes found in the technocapitalist corporation are very different from the factories of industrial capitalism, the nature and effects of commodification share a common effect: alienation. Scientists and engineers are not immune to this effect, if we take the words of prominent scientists Richard Levins and Richard Lewontin into account: "We see the commoditization of science as the prime cause of the alienation of most scientists from the product of their labor."[2]

The antithesis between creativity and commodification resides in the very nature of creativity. Its character sets creativity apart from other human endeavors in the technocapitalist paradigm, not to mention the fundamental resources of previous eras. Creativity is, *first* and foremost, an *intangible* quality. It involves the ability to absorb existing knowledge and transform it into previously unknown ideas, processes, methods, formulas, services, or tools. The role of imagination must be emphasized in this definition, for mere absorption of knowledge is not creativity. At the same time, as we see later, social relations and the social context in which creativity occurs are fundamental to its exercise and reproduction.

If the history of science and technology is any guide, creativity has a lot to do with imagination. Fertile imaginations were fundamental for the creation of most new ideas, processes, and tools. Imaginative thoughts were typically at the start of a creative search, being updated, affected, and shaped *through the social context.* The suggestion that imagination may be more important than knowledge has been voiced with some frequency, indicating that knowledge alone does not lead to creativity.[3] However, the fundamentally social character of imagination has often been ignored or downplayed.

Creative imaginations are shaped by their social relations and their social context. Social tolerance and encouragement of imaginative behaviors play a very important role in nurturing creativity. Far from being confined to schooling, social support for imaginative behaviors must reach into most every aspect of life and human experience. However, this context is often contrarian to the objective of commodification, which requires expediency and the extraction of commercial value in the shortest possible time, is intolerant of behaviors incompatible with those requirements, and ultimately generates alienation.

An example of how social relations and social contexts shape creative imaginations can be found in software research. Network-based social relations have structured one of the most supportive contexts for exercising creativity—the Open Source (Linux) software research network.[4] The social relations that occur through this network are grounded in the unfettered exercise of creativity through collaboration. All results must be freely posted for everyone in or outside the network to see, use, or improve upon, thus casting out property claims and profit-seeking schemes. Encouragement between participants, their sharing of insights, and the display of their creativity motivate others to exercise their own imaginations, thereby compounding collaboration. All the more remarkable is that this type of social context is not based on face-to-face contact, but is rather impersonal (and often anonymous).

Second, the social context provides the capacity for those who exercise creativity to think differently, breaking with preexisting dogmas, conventions, and precepts. Thinking differently is itself a product of imagination and subversion, and it often involves transfers of ideas between very different fields.[5] Such transfers typically involve social relations. Thinking differently is often supported by deep familiarity with the subject one seeks to be creative about, which also involves the social context and its influences. Only then can "thinking differently" result in new ideas.

New ideas are thought to be the main result of creativity, and this outcome is greatly influenced by social contact and its experience. In contrast, existing or codified knowledge often requires limited social contact to be tapped. Therefore, experience that leads to the creation of new ideas is itself a product of the social context. The result of these inherently social features of creativity is the possibility of discovering anomalies in existing ideas, or in their embedded methods, processes, formulas, services, or tools. Finding such anomalies is the key to overturning established paradigms, according to some philosophers of science.[6] However, the inherently social character behind the "finding" of the anomalies is often neglected.

There are different ways to come up with new knowledge, but all of them depend on the social context for support and survival. Imaginatively recombining disparate strands of existing knowledge is one of these ways. Extending existing knowledge to consider aspects it was not originally meant to regard is another. The social context supports these paths by making the wealth of accumulated experience available to a creative process and by facilitating the cross-fertilization of ideas and thoughts.

Commodification may, however, favor some paths and prevent others that are more intellectually rewarding from being explored, subject to calculations of value extraction, property claims, expediency, and financial considerations that are irrelevant to the creative process itself. This is often the case in most every area of research related to technology. Probably the most vivid examples can be found in the contrast between Open Source software creation, which is not commodified, and the commodified kind. The latter, most prominently exemplified by Microsoft and the design of its Windows operating system, limits the knowledge of in-house researchers to portions of the operating system's code to avoid leaks that may compromise the proprietary character of the software.[7] Conversely, Open Source software research is nonproprietary (and noncommodified) and requires all who contribute their creativity to post the results and make them freely available to everyone else (including those who are not part of the Open Source network).[8]

Third, creativity involves substantial experimentation, which itself often relies on social relations at the level of groups, organizations, and professional communities. Commodification, however, relies greatly on regimentation and compartmentalization in its quest to extract value from creativity. These two features of commodification frequently restrict or disable social relations, leading to greater alienation for those who provide creativity. Regimentation therefore often poses a major obstacle to the creation of new knowledge. The compartmentalization of creative processes that is part and parcel of commodification is also often inimical to free experimentation, which tends to be socially driven. Rigidities are often introduced based on cost, expediency, or proprietary considerations that constrain the free flow of experimental initiative by creators.

These constraints are an obstacle to experimentation and to the reservoir of curiosity that usually drives it. They also pose a serious obstacle to the openness to new experience that is very much a part of experimental creativity. Such openness is socially driven through networks of social relations that nurture creative curiosity. Experimentation, after all, often relies on a fascination with research tasks, in and of themselves. The social context nurtures these characteristic elements of experimentation by supporting various reinforcement mechanisms, such as the cultivation of a sense of worthiness, appreciation, and encouragement. The fascination, the openness to new experiences, and the curiosity that drives experimentation, however, become hostages of commodification and its penchant to regiment and compartmentalize. This antithetical situation can create considerable tension between commodification and the experimental nature of creativity. It also leads to the social alienation of those who contribute creative talent, from the results of the creativity and from the larger social context that must be tapped to sustain their talent.

Examples of this condition can be found in any of the corporate organizations and sectors that are symbolic of technocapitalism. In genomics, for example, those who decode genetic information are not at liberty to share their findings with researchers outside the corporate organization that employs them. Legal contracts and coercive measures are put in place to keep any research findings from being shared with others outside the corporation, in order to secure appropriation (through patenting, for example) and every possible advantage in marketing a new product. Even within the corporation, new research findings are often compartmentalized within a research group or unit to prevent them from being shared with others (in the same corporate organization) who might leak them to outsiders. In this manner, alienation is institutionalized in the corporate setting, cutting off those who provide creativity from the social relations that nurture their talent. The sharing of new knowledge and insights with the larger professional community of which they are part is also often foreclosed. At the same time, the strictures imposed by the regimentation and compartmentalization of external (or even internal) contacts tend to detach the providers of creativity from the results of their talent, thus introducing another dimension to their alienation.[9]

The constraints imposed by commodification are also at odds with another important characteristic of experimentation. Typically, experimentation requires much persistence and an inordinate attention to research work and related activities. Persistence and attention are time consuming and cast off other concerns not related to the creative process. They are often at odds with the objectives of commodification, where timeliness, economic realism, proprietary concerns, and rapid shifts of commitment based on commercial calculations are the norm. These objectives of commodification, therefore, often constrain attention to research and the free development of creative curiosity, leading to greater social alienation for those who provide creativity. At the root of this antithesis is the fact that commodification is all about material benefit, whereas experimental creativity is often inimical to material gratification.

This antithesis between creativity and commodification is usually not resolved by schemes of co-optation. Co-ownership, partnership, shareholding, and the like often do little or nothing to resolve the divergent natures of creativity and commodification. Such arrangements can, at best, only temporarily cover up the loss of free initiative to experiment or create, artificially concealing the social alienation that commodification imposes. Also, the relations of power imposed by commodification are often compulsory and therefore authoritarian. They usually require the provider of creativity to submit to their regimentation; not doing so often has adverse effects on employment and careers.

Fourth, unlike tangible resources, creativity is not exhausted through usage or application. Moreover, the exercise of creativity tends to create possibilities for more creativity to be exercised. This occurs because the knowledge gained serves as a stepping stone to more creativity and, most important, because of creativity's inherently social character. Creativity begets creativity, adding experience to imagination, along with new perspectives on how to exercise it in better ways. All of these characteristics depend intensely on social relations and the social context.

Commodification, however, is most effective when it exploits tangible resources. Dealing with a resource that is not exhausted through use or application poses major problems for commodification because it is difficult to estimate the commercial value of a resource that gains intangible qualities as it is exercised over time. Commodification is oriented toward the here and now, what can be immediately measured, assessed, and exploited. Dealing with a resource that is not exhausted, can gain quality over time, and cannot be easily measured defies the main objective of commodification: to extract commercial value as speedily as possible from resources based on known quantities and qualities.

Fifth, creative processes usually incur great uncertainty in terms of outcomes and the possibility of benefiting from them. Uncertainty here applies not only to economic and social outcomes but also to social and psychological ones, often with serious personal repercussions for creators. Further, great uncertainty is also typically accompanied by substantial risk of an economic and professional nature. Stigmas often attach to failure, and failure is often a product of risky experimentation (stigmas are, after all, a social creation).

Uncertainty and risk account greatly for vast qualitative differences in the exercise of creativity in the corporate context. They often end up limiting the scope of creative processes by, for example, causing researchers to be constrained to using existing knowledge rather than developing new ideas. In other cases, limitations on the scope of creative processes may result in a menial reinterpretation of existing knowledge, thereby foregoing an important breakthrough. In either case, socially driven perceptions of risk and uncertainty can determine how freely creativity is exercised.

The highest expectation for a creative process, namely pushing out the boundaries of existing knowledge in a revolutionary way, is often abandoned when risk and uncertainty are considered. Commodification (and corporatism in general) tends to be averse to much risk taking, especially in experimental projects whose ultimate outcomes are unknown. Pushing out these boundaries is the riskiest proposition for any important research project, since it involves finding major anomalies in existing paradigms so that their rules can be violated. Only these anomalies can start a truly revolutionary cycle in technology such that a "paradigm shift" can occur. The extreme uncertainty of these endeavors is often out of the scope of resource-conscious risk takers, however, who expect to "program" the creative process as they would a factory routine, ignoring the fact that such routines would negate the very nature of creativity.

Great uncertainty and risk are therefore enemies of commodification. Moreover, the high uncertainty and risk of most creative endeavors make it impossible to simulate or model creative processes, except in the most general ways. This impossibility of anticipating outcomes with any degree of certainty can make the impulse to compartmentalize and regiment all the more urgent in any process of commodification. However, compartmentalization and regimentation are often futile in reducing the uncertainty of creativity, and usually end up shortchanging the exercise of this most precious resource.

Utility and Value

The main objective of corporatism in commodifying creativity is to generate *market value* (or exchange value) such that a surplus (or profit) can be obtained. However, market value is not the only kind of value to be found. There is also *use value*, or the utility (usefulness) that may be derived from the commodification of creativity. This dichotomy between market value and use value follows the parameters established by Marxian political economists over many decades.[10] As we see later, however, new aspects are introduced by the social character and intangible quality of creativity.

Obtaining market value typically involves exchange through the sale of a product or service that results from the commodification of creativity. Fundamentally, the exchange must generate a surplus such that its benefit exceeds the total cost of commodifying creativity (including, for example, personnel salaries and benefits, experimental hardware, and the range of other costs incurred). This calculus is the main basis for the corporate commodification of creativity. Obtaining *surplus value* is therefore a major force in the corporate commodification of technological creativity. Surplus value can therefore serve as an indicator of profit. Only corporate actors have the resources to commodify technological creativity in the context of technocapitalism and obtain surplus value (or profit). This is due to the expensive and complex array of talents needed in research, the high cost of experimental hardware, and the high risk and uncertainty that characterize experimentation.[11]

Market value is itself socially mediated. It would be a fantasy to think that markets are separate entities from society; they are, in and of themselves, both a reflection and a result of the relations of power in society, particularly corporate power (in the context of technocapitalism). Other social aspects reflected in markets are, for example, class relations, inequalities, and the regulatory power of government. However, corporatism can be considered to be the most important force in markets today, given its reach into every corner of society. For corporatism, market exchange is an essential element of its power, even when markets tend to be competitive (or nonoligopolic). The hope and objective of corporate power, therefore, is to derive surplus value from the commodification of creativity through market exchange, regardless of the form that exchange happens to take.

Use value represents the utility (or usefulness) of any result of technological creativity. These results can encompass a wide range of possibilities, such as a new tool, idea, organism, process, formula, method, or service. Use value is not entirely dependent on market value; it often exists even when the market value of a product is very low.[12] The history of technology provides many examples of obsolescent products that continued to serve their users long after their market value practically disappeared and new replacements were introduced.

In this book, use value is redefined as *social value*, which implies a broader definition. Use value all too often refers to utility (or usefulness) to individuals, and therefore tends to have a narrow scope. This aspect is subsumed in the term social value, but the objective is to consider that utility has a much broader scope when creativity is placed in the social context.

Social value therefore includes all possible forms of utility that result from technological creativity *for society at large*, including communities, organizations, groups, individuals, and all other socially identifiable entities. Social value may not be dependent on market value (as noted previously in the case of use value) and may be entirely independent of surplus value. Thus, the results of technological creativity may be of benefit to society, even when they have no surplus value and practically no market value (as occurs when they are not exchanged).

Numerous examples can be found in the history of technology (especially medical technology) on this situation. Vaccines that were not or could not be profitable, and were not marketed, nonetheless saved many lives and thereby had considerable social value. This has been important for many poor nations, where lifesaving vaccines such as those for poliomyelitis and diphtheria were distributed by government agencies free of charge.[13] Selling them would have excluded most of the population, thus defeating the main objective of public health. Many medications for rare diseases are in a similar situation. To extract surplus value, the price charged by the manufacturer may be so high that practically none of those who need the medication may be able to purchase it, in which case the medicine will have no market at all (and, consequently, no surplus value). However, there is social value for such medications because of the lives they can save or the health improvements they provide.

Similar conditions can be found in software design. New software code created on an Open Source framework and posted freely on the Web has no market value since it is not sold or exchanged (and therefore has no surplus value). However, such software can have much social value when it helps many people solve their processing problems.

Similarly, invention patents that are never used will have no market value, but they may have social value if the ideas they contain help build up skills or contribute to technological education. For social value to exist, therefore, the results of technological creativity must satisfy a *social need* (broadly defined). Without a social need there can be no social value, even when market value exists, as in the case of fraudulent products whose only purpose is to provide surplus value to the seller. Thus, the question of whether market value can be justified at all when there is *no* social value is posed here. From a critical social perspective, market value that is not grounded in social value has no basis at all. Or, put another way, *social value is the basis of all market value.*

Technological creativity must therefore generate results that have social value if those results are to have any market value (and the chance of capturing any surplus value). Otherwise, the results of creativity would be fraudulent, in the sense that they would have no real utility, and their only purpose would be to generate some gain for the seller through deception. The actual social utility of the results of creativity are myriad and can include, for example, saving lives or preventing illness; facilitating learning; collapsing the cost, time, effort, or space required to accomplish most any task; or making human existence and nature more sustainable. These results of technological creativity typically involve new technologies.

In the context of technocapitalism, however, these results are typically appropriated by corporate actors. Thus, in a certain sense, social value tends to be controlled by corporatism, as the results of creativity must perforce be made to have market value (and, ultimately, surplus value or profit) if they are to sustain corporate power. The path to capture such market value (and, ultimately, surplus value) must be created through the commodification of creativity, which, as noted earlier, is a process fraught with major contradictions and great risk. For commodification to be successful, the social value of any results of creativity (such as new technology) must therefore be held hostage by corporate power, through appropriation (by means of a property right, such as a patent) and through the market power of the corporate actor as reflected in its capacity to obtain market value (and, ultimately, surplus value). As corporatism holds the results of creativity in its power, and therefore also their social value, it sets the stage for the pathological character of technocapitalism, as we will see in subsequent chapters.

The need to consider social value as a more general form of use value (as noted earlier) in the context of creativity and technocapitalism stems from various features that are distinctive (or in some ways unique) to creativity. One of them is the *inherently social character of creativity* as a socially mediated human quality, as discussed previously in this chapter. Another feature is the *intangible* nature of creativity, which makes it *separable* from its results. The same applies to many results of creativity, which are themselves separable from their uses. Results of creativity, such as patents, software code, proteomic network analyses, or mathematical formulas, for example, are separable from the uses made of them, simply because they are intangible. They are therefore *not* embodied in a product (physically), even if the product happens to be based on the knowledge they provide. As a result, their utility can be very diverse, encompassing individuals, organizations, communities, and societies. The multiplicity of benefits therefore needs to be framed and understood as a social phenomenon that transcends any narrow (or individual) conceptualization of use value (in the conventional meaning).

Another feature is the *inherently qualitative character of creativity*. Accurate quantification of creativity is often impossible, partly because of its *separability* from its results, as noted earlier. This makes most any quantification of the use value of creativity (and even its results) narrowly defined, difficult, or even impossible. Using the broader conceptualization of social value in place of use value seems better attuned to this feature for, after all, if narrow quantification is very difficult or impossible, understanding the *qualitative* dimension would have a better chance if it is done broadly, from the standpoint of the social context or of society at large.

This aspect may not be very clear, but the contrast between creativity (the prime resource of technocapitalism) and the main resources of industrial capitalism can provide some perspective. Under industrial capitalism, the raw materials, physical labor, and capital expended in production were quantifiable and led to precise formulas to measure and exploit them, such as the piece-rate system, or units of weight, volume, and output, for example. Those resources greatly influenced the use value of any manufactured product, and such value could be estimated quantitatively. Those estimates were done in fairly narrow fashion, for example, on the basis of the utility derived by anyone who purchased a manufactured product. However, these estimates of use value are often practically impossible to do in the case of creativity, which is neither a physical input (as raw materials are, for example) nor an output (in the sense of a manufactured product). Creativity is an intangible, qualitative resource (grounded in experimentation and research) that is used for many activities (even when narrowly confined to technology). Most of these activities are in no way similar to industrial production or to the factory processes that were a hallmark of industrial capitalism. This makes creativity much more socially mediated and socially diffuse than any of the tangible resources of industrial capitalism.

Another distinctive feature of creativity that supports the broader conceptualization of social value (in place of use value) is that the utility of any of the intangible results of creativity *tends to increase when they are shared*. This characteristic contrasts with the case of tangible resources (such as raw materials), whose utility is usually diminished when they are shared. This condition is rooted in their tangibility (measured through weight or volume, for example) and the fact that any reduction in their tangible measures usually also reduces their utility to users. Creativity, however, being qualitative and inherently social, requires social mediation, interaction, and social relations (all of which are means for sharing). Without them, creativity cannot flourish. Therefore, using the notion of social value (in place of use value) seems better suited to the inherently social nature of creativity.

A related feature is the fact that creative processes and their results often increase their utility through their relations with other creative processes. In other words, new ideas, methods, processes, formulas, or services can become more useful when they interact with other ideas, methods, processes, formulas, or services. This feature is apparent in network relations between creative processes. The extent and scope of network relations can therefore increase social value through interaction and the sharing of insights and knowledge.

This condition can be observed in networks that involve much creative activity. In Open Source networks, for example, the utility of software code is usually influenced greatly by the extent of the network of programmers who contribute their talent.[14] Without a large number of participants, the utility of the software developed would likely be more limited as the possibilities for testing and improvement are reduced. Similarly, genetic decoding achieved through parallel research networks is influenced by the extent of participation in the network. The kind of utility obtained in isolation (outside the network by individuals working alone) is likely to be much less than that obtained through the network.[15]

Reproduction and Commodification

The importance of social value and the inherently social character of creativity complicate its commodification greatly. In contrast with the commodification of the main resources of industrial capitalism, the commodification of creativity involves *not* a tangible resource that can be easily appropriated, quantified, or measured, but a socially mediated *intangible* resource that is qualitative and defies measurement.[16] The commodification of this most vital resource of technocapitalism is also complicated by the social nature of its reproduction. Social mediation of reproduction is essential if commodification is to succeed in its objective of extracting market value.

The meaning of *reproduction* used here is derived from Marxian political economy.[17] In the context of technocapitalism, the reproduction of creativity is a recurrent process whereby the providers of creativity regenerate their talent. In this sense, the conditions for creativity to be exercised are re-created. This is vital for commodification to have much chance of success. The reproduction of creativity is conditioned by the three accumulation processes discussed previously in this chapter. The accumulation of technological knowledge and technological infrastructure are of particular importance, as they provide a platform upon which learning and access to knowledge occur. These accumulation phenomena, along with the unavoidable accumulation of capital, must be seen as structural supports for reproduction in the technocapitalist paradigm.

The reproduction of creativity is sustained, however, through the social context which comprises social relations and their networks. The social context and, more broadly, the mediation of society at large are fundamental for nurturing the ideas, imaginations, motivations, knowledge, and experience through which creativity is regenerated. Social nurturing also involves, for example, the provision of stimuli to expand the ability to imagine, to think differently, to experiment, and to understand the risk and uncertainty that are part and parcel of experimentation. The social context also supports the absorption of codified knowledge through social relations and their motivational influences. Such knowledge is usually prerequisite for generating new (uncodified) knowledge through experimentation.

Three dimensions are of particular importance in society's mediation of the reproduction of creativity. One of them involves *networks* and the myriad ways in which they facilitate access to tacit knowledge, as well as to intangible qualities such as experience, counsel, collaboration, and sharing, all of which are vital for reproduction. As we see in later chapters, networks also offer the possibility of increasing the social value of intangible qualities through sharing.

Digital networks, a result of new technologies that helped the emergence of technocapitalism, have supported reproduction greatly. Digital networks are the backbone through which many of the interactions that support reproduction occur. Widespread access and the diffusion of new knowledge are now possible in ways and at speeds that would have been hard to imagine in previous stages of capitalism. The scale and scope of access provided through these networks have also been instrumental in the spread of capitalism and its pathologies around the world.[18] It seems appropriate, therefore, to note that in no previous phase of capitalism were networks as important as they are in the emerging technocapitalist era.

A second dimension in society's mediation of reproduction involves *legitimation*. Social legitimacy can be an important influence on the reproduction of creativity to the extent that it supports the motivation to regenerate creativity. In this sense, social legitimacy involves support from a professional community, from influential groups within it, or from society at large for a research project, a given talent, or results thereof. There are myriad ways in which legitimation can support reproduction. One of them, for example, involves the formation of communities of allies to provide advice and support during controversies and performance reviews, to facilitate contracts or grants, or to overcome bureaucratic hurdles.[19] Blocs organized to generate mutual support and reciprocity often become mechanisms for legitimation. Joining them often helps gain acceptance from peers in a profession or discipline.

Social mediation to provide legitimation is usually related to diffusion and political influences. Obtaining favorable reviews of research results for publication is a common example of diffusion-related influence. Forming coalitions to lobby for government funding is a case of how legitimation can influence the politics of institutional support. The formation of a coalition is often in itself a vehicle for legitimacy in technology and science, particularly when the coalition's objective can be translated into political gains for legislators. The success of this kind of social mediation often enhances the reputation of a specialty.

A third dimension of social mediation can be considered at the individual level. The reproduction of creativity also involves social influence on how individuals work, on their attitudes and dispositions toward others in their field, and toward society at large. Mentorship and counsel are examples of social mediation that influence attitudes and creative outlooks. Some of the outcomes of this kind of social mediation at the individual level are, for example, persistence in the face of adversity, greater discipline, and methodical approaches to research.

Institutionally, organizations that promote education and research are part of the social mediation mechanisms operating through this dimension. They are a social mediation instrument that inculcates certain habits and ways of approaching creative tasks that can be used in experimentation. In some cases, they can initiate ideas that become experimental projects in their own right. In the context of technocapitalism, this kind of institutional mediation is often part of a diverse infrastructure of training and education that prepares individuals to provide talents for the commodification processes that are part and parcel of corporatism.[20]

Other social mediation mechanisms—institutional or not—that attempt to regenerate individual creativity involve promoting craft work (hobbies) and temporary sojourns from the pressures of commodification (sabbaticals or leaves). Craft work or "craft-love," in particular, tends to temporarily redirect individual creativity away from commodification, to pursue an interest for its own sake rather than for commercial ends.[21] The typical strategy is for such interests to be directed toward fields unrelated to the ones involved in commodification. Providing a respite from commodification and its more intense creative tasks, and validating the self, are also strategic objectives of these programs.[22]

A diagram showing the functional components needed to extract value from creativity is appropriate at this point. Figure 3 shows the relationship between commodification, reproduction, and utility. Commodification is but one member of the troika. It cannot, on its own, turn creativity into a source of market value, much less surplus value, unless reproduction is effectively engaged. A major issue, to be discussed

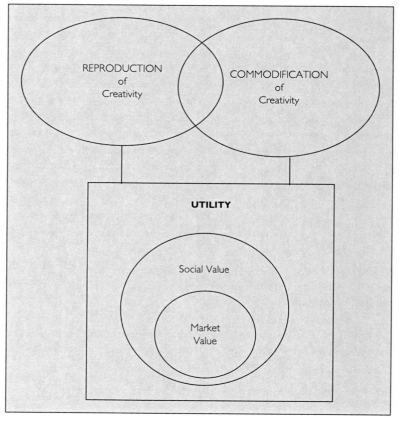

Figure 3 Fundamental Components

in later chapters, is that commodification is a corporate endeavor, used to obtain market value from a very elusive and intangible human quality. Reproduction, however, is a social endeavor that must necessarily occur through social mediation, externally from the corporate context.

Social value can therefore be considered an essential result of reproduction, since *both* are largely an outcome of social relations and support. As noted earlier, however, social value is the key to market value, and therefore eventually to surplus value. This fundamental aspect complicates commodification greatly, as it removes some of the components noted above from the control of corporate power. Thus, corporatism may control the process of commodification to a great extent, locating it within the corporate context, but it has very limited power over reproduction. As we see in later chapters, this cleavage is a source of major changes in the corporate structures of our time, and it is also a major source of pathology.

Commodification as Process

The commodification of technological creativity is accomplished through experimentation. Experimental pursuits are part and parcel of the process of commodification. Experimentation is as important to the commodification of creativity under technocapitalism as production and the factory system were to the commodification of labor under industrial capitalism.

The emphasis on experimentation as the means to commodify creativity is a distinctive feature of technocapitalism. The experimentalist ethos of technocapitalism seeks above all to obtain market value from any technologically creative pursuit. In an era when highest value accrues to technological creativity, no idea, organism, or tool that can collapse cost, time, effort, or space in significant ways over existing technology can be ignored. And we must recall that corporate organizations are the vehicle through which commodification occurs.

Trial and error, guesswork, uncertainty, and risk are intrinsic aspects of experimentation. They pose a major problem for any process of commodification. Commodification typically treasures certainty, foresight, and timeliness. High uncertainty therefore complicates the process of commodification by making it difficult to anticipate outcomes.

Through systematization, corporate organizations therefore try to reduce the uncertainty and risk of experimental processes, setting up ways for commodification to occur.

Corporate organizations typically comprise research departments, laboratories, and individuals engaged in the kinds of activities that are typical of technocapitalism, such as biotechnology, nanotechnology, genomics, molecular computing, proteomics, bioinformatics, and biopharmacology, among others. Thus, corporate organizations provide the context for transforming tacit knowledge obtained from experimentation in these activities into products and services. This is accomplished by appropriating the results of creative experimentation.

This unmitigated appropriation of the results of creativity usually involves standardization. New knowledge obtained through creativity thus becomes codified knowledge through the process of commodification. This transformation has the objective of turning any utility derived through creativity into market value. Market value and, eventually, surplus value are the ultimate objectives of this process. The logistics, scope, and strategy of commodification are therefore major functions in the corporate ecology of technocapitalism. As we see later, these functions require new organizations with distinctive characteristics of their own.

There are three general steps to the process of commodification. The objective here is to outline the basic features of the process and its steps rather than engage in a detailed discussion of their mechanics. The *first* step involves attention to the configuration of various aspects: design of experiments, testing, interpretation of results, elaboration of new paths, or combinations to experiment on, for example. The usual fragmentation and compartmentalization of these components try to lend an impression of certainty and order to what is essentially a very unpredictable process. The effort to compartmentalize them often reflects the insecurity of commodification, as it tries to reduce uncertainty and streamline the process as much as possible.

Systematizing creativity is an objective of compartmentalization, and it is part and parcel of the effort to streamline. The systematization of creative research requires standardization, control, and measurability. Through them, creative skills and creativity itself are viewed as disembodied inventory items. The regimen imposed through systematization typically aims at producing a continuous stream of creative results in the shortest time with the least possible resources. This in itself is a tacit tactic to reduce risk and uncertainty, especially in activities (such as biotechnology) where long testing cycles (that often last several years) and high failure rates are common.

Compartmentalizing and systematizing pose major problems for commodification, however. It is possible, for example, to lose sight of the whole and its qualitative dimensions. Compartmentalization often ends up dissipating personal and group associations that are the backbone of creative interaction. It can also introduce unnecessary and even harmful competition between the atomized components of a creative process. The tensions introduced by compartmentalization and systematization can, for example, wreck the cross-fertilization of ideas, place competition above collaboration when collaboration is most necessary, and diminish the intrinsic rewards of creative action.

Moreover, standardized methods imposed through systematization often reflect the relations of power between corporate governance and researchers. Corporate power may favor standardized (or established) methods in its quest to obtain market value as rapidly as possible. Researchers, however, may opt for new methods that require more of their creativity and that can potentially provide groundbreaking results, but which are also more uncertain and risky. Not using the standardized approach may make a researcher vulnerable to negative charges, undeserved scrutiny, or controversy. In the corporate context, departures from policy can lead to personal disadvantage or even loss of employment. Yet, breaking away from a standardized approach is often important for finding the anomalies that underpin major breakthroughs.[23]

Examples of the failure of systematization can be found in the research activities associated with technocapitalism. A common one involves debasing researchers' creativity by confining it to the objective of getting an experimental process "to work" so that it performs in "the right way." In corporate parlance, performing "the right way" typically has market value in mind as the uppermost priority. Getting the expected results narrowly and fast often trumps other alternatives in such cases, even when the latter are potentially more creative or humanly rewarding.

This kind of mind-set is antithetical to most creative processes. In software research, for example, the best creativity often comes from individuals who spend substantial amounts of time experimenting freely on their own, at their own pace, usually reaching outcomes that cannot be foreseen. To the most creative individuals in software, experimentation is practically a hobby, and it is often done for "fun" or for the thrill of finding something no one else has. Hacking, as this form of experimentation is often referred to, usually involves playful tinkering (as opposed to the criminal sort), but can lead to substantial breakthroughs.[24] Standardization would likely ruin the attraction that draws thousands to this sort of experimentation, which is characterized by free flows of creative concentration, time, and uncertainty. Those who experiment usually find uncertainty attractive, but it also complicates greatly any program to systematize their creativity.

Many experimental activities require exploration, trial and error, tinkering, and intuition. Narrowly fitting them into rule-bound channels can wreck the creative process. Narrow-channel approaches can work well when experimental tasks can be programmed in fairly rigid ways, which are most suitable for expert systems and artificial intelligence–driven programs. However, expert systems often encroach human creative involvement and can be counterproductive, whenever firsthand human experience can lead to significant breakthroughs.[25] Force fitting creativity into narrow roles often demeans it, and is a common problem with compartmentalization.

A major challenge for corporate power is, therefore, to try to compartmentalize the creative process without destroying it. Commodification processes that damage creativity become dysfunctional. Whenever this occurs, the prospect of obtaining market value and, eventually, surplus value can be severely compromised. Orchestrating a creative process to come up with results in cost- and time-effective ways is a daunting endeavor that the most experienced corporate managers often fail to achieve.

The *second* step involves the disengagement of the fragmented aspects of the creative process from their original context and from their authors.[26] The results of creativity are assembled as research products and take an existence that is independent from the creative process and from those who created or discovered them. This *alienation* of the result of creativity from the creative process often involves, for example, the transfer of an idea, method, or tool to a corporate entity that is typically impersonal and may have little interest in the creative process itself. Alienation thus usually entails the corporate takeover of ideas and intellectual property from those who create.[27]

Transferring the results of the creative process to corporate entities is typically necessary if production is to take place. Industrial-scale processing thus builds upon the alienation of the results of creativity from the creative process. The creators of an idea, method, or tool typically lose any possibility of maintaining control over the results of their work. Control here refers to the possibility of changing the nature and character of the results of their creativity, but may also include receiving professional credit for their efforts and obtaining fair compensation.

The separation of authorship from the results of the creative process is therefore characteristic of this second step. It implies potential abuse of authors or creators, as the results of their work are disengaged from their control. The effects go beyond such symbolic issues as, for example, the signing over of patent awards to a company.[28] Experiencing this kind of alienation on a serial basis can be detrimental to commodification in the long run. Low morale and resentment may result, thereby compromising creative processes and the possibility of obtaining market value and surplus value. This is where corporate governance, with its array of punishments and incentives, steps in to safeguard commodification and its appropriation of creativity.

The *third* step involves market exchange of the results of creativity. Using these results in production is often part of this step. The results of creativity therefore become a commodity, in the full meaning of the term, and are appropriated by the highest bidders. Their putative owners typically have no relationship to their creators or authors, making the results of creativity all the more disembedded from the creative process through which they emerged. Technological creativity is thus turned into a commodity to be sold and exchanged, and its ultimate objectives become obtaining surplus value and power for those who appropriate its results.

This third step is fraught with risk, however. Many ideas, products, and processes that are commercialized are often not profitable. Second-mover research, reverse engineering, and clever design-around tactics by competitors often prevent those who appropriate the results of creativity from realizing their hoped-for surplus value. Fraud and theft are as much a part of commodification under technocapitalism as they were in previous times, if not all the more so. Even when such problems are not encountered, the introduction of slightly better products by competitors shortly after a new product's market debut can doom any prospect of gain.[29]

The market value of the results of creativity can probably be more easily damaged than the commodities of industrial capitalism ever could be. Corporate strategies aimed at preempting competitors from gaining market value through predation or theft are more common than in the heyday of industrial capitalism, given the rapid flow of information and the global scope of corporate action nowadays. Competitive destruction of the market value of the results of creativity therefore poses a threat to the third step of commodification. This threat introduces higher uncertainty and risk to the process of commodification, leading to greater efforts to regiment creative processes. This is an important contradiction that, as we we will see in later chapters, turns commodification into a source of pathology.

Conclusion

The commodification of creativity is as vital to technocapitalism as that of capital or factory labor were to industrial capitalism. This complex process is at the root of the activities that can be considered symbolic of technocapitalism. The exploitation of creativity for commercial ends is therefore a hallmark of the emerging era. This means that the commodification of creativity in research is no more avoidable under technocapitalism than commodification in factory production was under industrial capitalism.

It should not be surprising that the commodification of creativity often fails to produce its intended results. Young as it is, the trajectory of technocapitalism is littered with the carcasses of failed attempts to commodify this most elusive and intangible human quality. And, given the complex and elusive nature of creativity, commodification under technocapitalism is much more difficult than its counterparts in previous phases of capitalism.

At the root of this difficulty is the fundamental antithesis between commodification and creativity. What in previous times may have been undertaken for its own sake, in search of joy and self-validation, must now be taken up for commercial gain. The fact that this undertaking is subservient to corporate power introduces major contradictions and pathologies to society and to the corporate context itself.

The possibility for contemporary society to remedy this antithesis is limited but not impossible, as we see in later chapters. Corporate power attempts to control the commodification of creativity, while society reproduces this vital resource. This cleavage is a major source of the contradictions noted in this chapter. The following chapters explore other aspects related to these contradictions and to the social pathologies they generate.

Networks as Mediators

Networks are the means through which some of the vital processes of technocapitalism are articulated. Phenomena related to creativity, its reproduction, and its value rely on social mediation provided through networks. The characteristics of networks, their mediation, and their contribution to the emergence of technocapitalism are considered in this chapter.

Features such as extent, hierarchy, modes of control, power, and inequity influence the roles networks play in this new phase of capitalism. These features articulate the quality and character of social mediation. The term social mediation here refers to the apparatus of relations that help reproduce creativity. These relations occur at multiple levels, ranging from the larger context of society to the level of groups and individuals. They are vital for regenerating creativity in all its forms and dimensions and, in this sense, are very important for the commodification of this vital resource.

Social mediation typically helps relate network participants to one another for common objectives. In the context of technocapitalism, however, network-based mediation plays a very important role. Reproducing creativity, diffusing knowledge, and promoting participation are some of the functions of network-based mediation. Other functions involve support for creative agendas, collaboration and sharing, and the articulation of exchange relationships. These functions are part of the social context, and their operation helps structure the relations of network participants.

The most important networks of technocapitalism are external to corporate organizations. These are the networks that help reproduce creativity. This condition contrasts with the reality of industrial capitalism, where the most important networks were usually internal to organizations and dealt with tangible resources. External networks were primarily for exchange of those tangible resources or their products. The factory systems of industrial capitalism could internalize *both* commodification and reproduction to a great extent. The corporate organizations of technocapitalism, however, must deal with *intangible* resources, which must be reproduced through the social context. Networks external to the corporate context are the main vehicle through which such reproduction occurs.

Networks can therefore be seen as mediating agents of technocapitalism to the extent that they help reproduce its most important resource. That resource, creativity, is at the root of all the activities that can be considered symbolic of the new era. The new sectors spawned by technocapitalism—such as nanotechnology, genomics, or bioinformatics, among many others—depend on creativity more than on any other resource. Their future advancement, if not the future of technocapitalism itself, rides on the quality and capabilities of this most elusive resource, and on the capacity of social networks to reproduce it.

Network Extent

The importance of networks to technocapitalism depends largely on their extent. *Network extent* is defined here as the array of qualitative and quantitative features that help reproduce creativity. The definition of extent includes *range*, which refers to the scale and heterogeneity of a network.[1] Range often has been closely associated with supportiveness. Thus, the larger the scale (or size) and the greater the diversity of participants (in terms of experience and knowledge, for example), the more supportive a network is likely to be. Range is therefore important for the reproduction of creativity and for the kind of supportive social mediation that a network can provide.

This definition of network extent also includes *accessibility*. Ease of access is very important for reproducing creativity. Social mediation depends greatly on the availability of participants gained through access. Open access is therefore a desirable quality of networks that involve social mediation. Contact, learning, sharing, and the diffusion of knowledge are largely functions of accessibility.

Accessibility also influences quality. The more accessible a network of creative researchers becomes, the more likely it is to attract other creative researchers. Quality often begets quality through accessibility; a more accessible network increases social mediation and the quality of opportunities available for enhancing creativity. Accessibility is therefore vital for reproducing creativity to the extent that it facilitates social mediation. More possibilities for developing relations that support the exchange of ideas, experience, and new knowledge are a logical outcome.

The definition of network extent used here includes *composition*. Composition refers to the kinds of interests, knowledge, experience, and creative aptitudes found within a network. It is closely tied to participation in terms of who joins, how frequently interaction occurs, and the character of relations. Composition affects greatly the quality of social mediation a network provides. Some creative interests are more likely to find support, depending on the composition of participants. However, networks that combine wider range with greater accessibility are likely to have deeper and more diverse compositions.

The definition of extent also includes technical features related to network structure. Complexity, redundancy, and interconnections (involving links and interactions) are some of these features. They are largely derived from range, access, and composition. Complexity, for example, is a function of network range, in the sense that larger size (or scale), greater heterogeneity, easier access, and a diverse composition are more likely to result in greater complexity. Similarly, greater redundancy and more interconnections are likely to result from wider range, particularly larger scale. These technical features are therefore a function of the previously discussed components of network extent: range, accessibility, and composition.

The importance of networks for reproducing creativity is therefore closely related to their extent. Greater network extent is very important for the reproduction of creativity. Limited extent detracts from a network, as it diminishes social mediation and the relations it encompasses. Thus, restricting the extent of any network of researchers would be counterproductive, since it would compromise the effectiveness of reproduction. Organizations that attempt to limit network extent (or any of its various features) are therefore likely to shortchange their own commodification processes and, eventually, the market value they hope to extract from creativity. This is a symptom of the antithesis noted in the chapter "Creativity as a Commodity" between the social nature of reproduction and the corporate character of commodification.

The relationship between greater network extent and greater benefit to reproduction defies a centuries-old principle of mainstream (or neoclassical) economics: the notion that value increases with scarcity. For hundreds of years, this simple rule has governed economic thought, becoming a normative precept among mainstream economists upon which numerous Nobel Prizes and tens of thousands of publications rest. Yet, the reality of network extent shows that abundance, rather than scarcity, increases the importance (or value, in a general sense) of networks in the context of technocapitalism.

The assumption of scarcity as a source of value (or benefit) may have had much to do with the long-standing association of mainstream economics with industrial capitalism. Tangible resources were most important during that phase of capitalism. The scarcity of tangible resources typically drove up their value. Limiting network extent was often desirable since it increased corporate control over resources and production.[2] Many of the tools of mainstream economics were built for the analysis of industrial capitalism, with its overarching emphasis on production, capital, raw materials, and factory labor. The "production function" is, for example, one of the more important concepts in the tool kit of mainstream economics. Initially intended as little more than a recipe to estimate capital and labor's association with the value of production, it became a do-all tool applied to most any situation.

The use of production functions to evaluate any activity shows how entwined mainstream economics became with industrial capitalism. "Knowledge production functions" have been applied, for example, to that intangible human quality, as if it could somehow be cobbled serially on some factory's conveyor belt. "Innovation production functions" have been devised as well, extending the factory analogy to research activities, and subsuming creativity to be a raw material "input" not much different from ore, coal, or crude oil. Most important, however, production functions and most every analytical tool of mainstream economics are unable to take network extent into account. Doing so violates the principles of general equilibrium and optimality upon which the theoretical edifice of neoclassical economics has been built. As a result, mainstream economics seems unsuited to consider networks, or network extent, and their vital role in the context of technocapitalism.

Marxian political economy, in contrast, provides a much better framework to consider the role of networks and creativity in the technocapitalist context. Its broad, critical perspectives are better suited to study the apparatus of capitalism than the reductionist, static frames of mainstream (or neoclassical) economics. Mainstream economics not only ignores fundamental social phenomena in the evolution of capitalist society, but its frameworks are ill suited to consider the role of networks and creativity in the context of technocapitalism. More ominously, the spreading use of mainstream economics precepts seems to be behind many of the emerging social pathologies of our time.[3] As we see in later chapters, some of the more serious pathologies of corporatism can be attributed to the practice of major theories supplied by mainstream economics.

The networks of technocapitalism are very different from those of industrial capitalism. Fundamentally, the networks of technocapitalism support *intangibles*, such as creativity and knowledge, which depend on social mediation. The most important networks of technocapitalism are external to organizations and are vital for securing these intangible resources. In contrast, the most important networks of industrial capitalism were internal to organizations and were an accessory of managerial control.[4] The networks of industrial capitalism targeted *tangible* resources. Network-based social mediation could be limited by industrial capitalists because its influence on the quality of tangible resources was often insignificant. The quality and quantity of those resources were often programmed and specified in contractual agreements, making such mediation marginal. Moreover, social mediation often stood in the way of greater corporate control over resources.

Production, above all else, drove industrial capitalism. The overarching attention to production and the labor process did not require much social mediation outside the factory to keep them going. External social mediation for a vital resource, labor, was curtailed by corporate power because it often led workers to organize, claim rights, or oppose management. External mediation for capital was typically contractual and was channeled through formal institutional contacts subservient to corporate power. Even for external exchange involving raw materials or products, limiting network extent often made sense in order to prevent actual or potential competitors from learning operational details. Commodification and reproduction were thus largely structured internally in the factories of industrial capitalism.

In the context of technocapitalism, in contrast, research is the main driver of corporate power and profit, *not* production. The overarching attention to research and its main resource, creativity, requires much social mediation *outside* the corporate context. The reproduction of creativity is an *external*, socially mediated function that depends greatly on network extent. Commodification remains an *internal* corporate function, however, that is subject to corporate power and governance. As we see in later chapters, this functional split between commodification and reproduction is a potential source of major dysfunctions and pathologies.

Limiting network extent and social mediation is therefore untenable for the technocapitalist corporation. Creativity cannot be reproduced without abundant social mediation. Reproducing creativity effectively therefore requires network-based social relations that can lead to new knowledge, enhanced aptitudes, and richer imaginations, for example. This condition is driven by the social nature of creativity and its intangible character.

Greater extent increases the importance of networks for reproduction in two major ways. *First*, the larger the extent of a network, the more dynamic and stronger the reproduction of creativity is likely to be. Larger extent is fundamental to achieve greater social mediation. And, the more social mediation there is, the greater the quality of reproduction may be. Therefore, the reproduction of creativity cannot occur in isolation as would, say, the processing of a raw material in a factory. Under technocapitalism, network extent and its social mediation usually defines the quality and effectiveness of reproduction.

The fact that creativity is not exhausted by usage or application, unlike tangible resources, means that greater network extent and social mediation are essential for reproduction. Any resource that is exhausted through usage would likely be devalued by exposure to larger network extent. *However, not only is creativity not exhausted but it is also actually enhanced by greater network extent and more abundant social mediation.*

Open Source networks provide an example of how network extent supports the reproduction of creativity. These networks thrive on the sharing of ideas and results between participants. The exercise of creativity through them is subject to pervasive social mediation. In the case of Open Source software research, for example, everyone can benefit from any improvements to software code, since results must be made freely accessible to anyone.[5] And, everyone is a volunteer who freely contributes creative talent through the network. Market exchange and surplus value (or profit) are therefore not the driving forces of these networks. Rather, they are driven by the possibility of reproducing creativity, which is sustained greatly by network extent since the larger the range, the greater and more accessible participation becomes, and the more diverse and deeper the composition, the more important the network's social mediation is likely to be.

Because the results of creativity in Open Source networks are made freely available to anyone outside the network further increases network extent and helps draw more participants. Making it freely available to anyone who wishes to download the latest improvements, regardless of whether they participate in the network, ensures that the results of collective creativity will be put to use and tested by a larger population than that of network participants. Such use or testing in turn provides further insights that generate more creativity within the network. These compounding effects render the reproduction of creativity more dynamic and qualitatively richer, while increasing the possibilities of collaboration and interaction.

Also important in Open Source software research networks is the fact that they allow creativity to be reproduced outside any process of commodification. The freewheeling exercise of creativity outside commodification that these networks provide enriches the possibilities for reproduction. Freeing participants from the strictures and conflict that pervade commodification therefore supports the free flow of ideas. Moreover, making all results freely available to anyone can create legitimacy for those who contribute creativity by displaying their talents to everyone and making it possible to share ideas at a personal level.

Personally sharing ideas often leads to the building of social relations that transcend specific tasks and projects.

Network-based social mediation also confers higher quality to Open Source software over the proprietary alternatives. Network extent and social mediation in Open Source software networks therefore not only support the reproduction of creativity but also contribute greatly to the quality of the results. The fact that higher quality can occur entirely outside any process of commodification dissipates the notion that creativity must be tied to commodification and its commercial objectives in order to provide reliable results. The alternative to Open Source (Linux) software, Microsoft's Windows and Vista, which are developed through the commodification of creativity and the corporate appropriation of its results, are often thought to be of lower quality.[6] Microsoft retains property rights to its software code and must therefore keep it secret in order to keep generating surplus value. One of the effects is that appropriation restricts greatly the possibility of testing Microsoft's code widely and openly, thereby contributing to lower quality.

Open Source networks are proliferating in sectors other than software. One of the more conspicuous applications has involved encyclopedias. A free, Open Source online encyclopedia (Wikipedia) is now the world's most frequently consulted source of information.[7] In all cases where Open Source networks occur, network extent and social mediation enhance the reproduction of creativity and increase the importance of a network to participants. In biotechnology and in medical research, for example, Open Source networks involve the sharing of all improvements to a technique with everyone.[8] Such sharing promotes further improvement. Creativity is reproduced as interactions generate new ideas and provide insights through the social medium supported by greater network extent. In bioinformatics, Open Source involves the sharing of databases and computational results among participants. Sharing of results and databases in turn leads to the reproduction of creativity through interpretation of results, exchange of ideas related to new tests and data, and the buildup of professional relations.[9]

Greater network extent has a *second* important effect on the reproduction of creativity. This involves the possibility that greater network extent will enhance the *social value* of creativity by making reproduction more effective. Social mediation through greater network extent can be the key to this effect. Such mediation can provide greater exposure, review, and diffusion, for example, thereby improving the effectiveness of reproduction and (ultimately) the results of creativity. For instance, effectiveness may be related to how well those results collapse cost, time, effort, or space (or save lives) over existing technologies.

As previously defined in the chapter "Creativity as a Commodity," social value comprises the utility that results from technological creativity for society at large through the satisfaction of a social need. Network-based social entities, such as communities, groups, organizations, or individuals are potential beneficiaries of the social value of a new invention or innovation. Discussions in the previous chapter noted that social value is a prerequisite for market value to occur. Therefore, market value cannot occur without social value. Only through fraud or deception can market value be obtained for a product or service that has no social utility. Greater network extent that enhances social value can therefore ultimately lead to greater market value, if the results of creativity are commercialized.

Examples of the importance of network extent for reproduction and social value can be found in various cases relevant to the technocapitalist context. Open Source (Linux) software research networks are a prime example of how network extent leads to social value by making reproduction more effective. Open Source network extent helps provide better quality through participation and collaboration. Free access practically guarantees that the results of reproduction will find social utility. Moreover, the social value of the results occurs *outside* any process of commodification. Such networks are therefore completely outside corporate control. Social value occurs without obtaining any market value (or surplus value). *Social value can therefore exist without market value when network extent and its social mediation make it possible to occur.* In the case of Open Source software research, network extent contributes to social value and a more effective reproduction of creativity through larger scale (or size), open (and therefore greater) accessibility, a deeper and more diverse composition, and social mediation founded on nonproprietary collaboration.

Parallel experimentation networks provide another example of how greater extent can enhance social value by making reproduction more effective. These networks involve simultaneous experimentation by researchers in various parts of the world, performing activities that might otherwise be scheduled sequentially or that cannot be carried out within a single laboratory.[10] The greater the network extent for parallel experimentation, the more likely that additional data and findings will become available. And, the greater the availability of data or findings, the more participants and creative talents will likely be attracted to the network.

Substantial savings in cost, time, effort, or laboratory space create social value for parallel experimentation. These savings can then be channeled back into research, thereby expanding the means to support experimentation. Greater network extent can therefore help research become sustainable by saving resources that can help make the reproduction of creativity more effective. A more effective reproduction of creativity in turn enhances any potential social value, as it allows more expansive sharing or collaboration. More sharing and collaboration can then lead to wider uses for the results of creativity, or to greater quality, thereby enhancing social value.

Another example of how network extent enhances social value by making reproduction more effective can be found in distributed computing.[11] Harnessing the power of interconnected desktop personal computers, distributed computing networks have made costly (mainframe) supercomputers unnecessary for many research activities. There are hundreds of millions of desktop personal computers connected to the Internet in the world, but the fastest supercomputer in existence only produces maximum computing power equivalent to about sixty thousand personal computers. Thus, a distributed computing network comprising several hundred thousand desktop personal computers would provide many times the power of the fastest supercomputer in existence. Since most personal computers typically use less than 10 percent of their total computing power at any given time, and none when they are idle, a distributed computing network can amass substantial computing power by simply interconnecting as many personal computers as it needs. Individual owners of personal computers have, in many cases, volunteered to allow their machines to be used in such networks.

Greater network extent can help distributed computing reproduce creativity more effectively by reducing computing costs. Lower computing costs have social value in themselves. Computing is essential for reproducing creativity because it supports many activities through which this resource is regenerated. Sharing or analyzing data, carrying out Open Source collaboration, or engaging in parallel experimentation are some of these activities. In bioinformatics, for example, distributed computing networks can be used for decoding genetic information, thereby eliminating the high cost of purchasing and maintaining supercomputers. In so doing, they support the reproduction of creativity through sharing, collaboration, and interaction.

Distributed computing networks can be used for experimental simulation in nanotechnology research to determine how different molecular structures behave under changing environmental conditions. Another use of distributed computing networks involves Web search engines, updating directories that would otherwise need supercomputing power to be done in a timely way. In public health, distributed computing networks can be used to develop vaccination strategies for vulnerable populations. These activities generate social value since they are necessary to advance well-being. They have social value even though the results of the creativity they reproduce might eventually be commodified and commercialized. And, their social value exists even when the results of creativity are not commercialized, as in the case of Open Source software research networks, noted earlier.

Beyond reproduction and social value, greater network extent can also significantly enhance market value. Market exchange is the last step in the process of commodification, as noted in the previous chapter "Creativity as a Commodity." The benefit of greater network extent has become vividly obvious to many companies whose business models depend on market exchange through the Web and the Internet. In many such cases, network extent seems to have become the single most important means for obtaining market value (and, ultimately, surplus value).

Microsoft, for example, has pursued greater network extent most aggressively over the years, even at the cost of attracting antitrust prosecution in the United States and Europe. Years ago, Microsoft bundled its main product, the Windows Operating System, with various free services such as e-mail, a Web browser, and word processing, in order to capture greater market extent. Its clever strategy of offering such services for nothing had the ultimate objective of obtaining as much market value from its main product as possible. The key to its strategy was expanding network extent through users and applicators. Capturing greater market extent made Microsoft the richest corporation on earth.[12] And, it did this by ignoring the centuries-old precept of main-stream economics, which assumes that greater market value can be attained by making a necessary product scarce.

Examples of how other companies have tried to capture higher market value through greater network extent are numerous. Netscape freely gave away its Internet browser to try to capture greater network extent by attracting more users. Having more users made Netscape more attractive to advertisers.[13] Attracting advertisers through greater network extent was the key to the company's market value. Sun Micro-systems provided the Java software freely, to try to achieve greater network extent by having more users and more applicators who based their business models on it.[14] Later, Sun charged applicators for up-grades, thus capturing market value for its services. The applicators, in turn, had more potential customers since Sun had given away the basic software. Similarly, millions of copies of the McAfee antivirus software were initially distributed freely in order to achieve greater network extent. McAfee then later charged users for updates. Paying for up-dates became unavoidable when the company made its software unus-able after a preset time limit.

Other examples of how network extent enhances market value can be found in the proliferation of for-profit distance-learning (e-diploma) companies, such as the University of Phoenix. Distance learning is a new frontier of the massification of education. It expands the boundar-ies of access beyond the trend that saw the creation of public higher education systems and open universities, starting in the late 1940s. Through diverse course offerings and degrees, distance-learning com-panies have expanded their network extent, which, in turn, increased enrollment and thus the market value of the business. Greater network extent thereby provided more revenues and more market recognition, attracting more online students. Also, the fact that distance learning collapsed overhead costs by eliminating the need for brick-and-mortar facilities made greater network extent all the more attractive for that business model.[15]

Hierarchies and Control

Networks and network extent can dilute hierarchies and their control structures. Fluidity, bottom-up regulation, and much social mediation are characteristic of networks that reduce hierarchy. Their diminished hierarchy often provides an impression of lack of control or direction. However, controls are very much a part of the networks of technocapitalism, and they are often elusive to grasp. In contrast with industrial capitalism, where control was typically hierarchical and depended much on bureaucracy and face-to-face contact, the controls embedded in many of the networks of technocapitalism tend to be loose and fluid. Bottom-up controls, often referred to as "self-organizing," are typical of these networks. This means that controls can be changed as participants reconfigure their contact through network extent and social mediation.

The term hierarchy here refers to control structures that use a network and its participants for a given objective. Hierarchies typically involve several levels of authority, with a division of labor that enforces control over various functions and creates specialization. Social mediation is necessary to achieve control through hierarchies, particularly when participants have the option to exit the network. However, *social mediation is also necessary to dilute any hierarchy and its control structure.* Social mediation, therefore, has a dual function in this regard.

Many of the networks that reproduce creativity involve significant dilutions of hierarchy. Whether a hierarchy is diminished depends on the quest of some participants to exercise control over others, and on the others' capacity to oppose the established control structures. This dialectical relationship is by no means static. The social relations that make hierarchical control possible can become fluid, with outcomes that may be difficult to anticipate. Such uncertainty is a distinctive feature of diminished network-based hierarchies.

Networks often dilute established hierarchies by making it possible to bypass them. This possibility is mostly a result of network extent. Greater network extent and social mediation create alternatives. Alternative links, nodes, flows, and social relations are important for bypassing established hierarchies. Such alternatives are essential to dilute a hierarchy, and they often contain the seeds of frequent systemic change.

Alternatives dilute authority and the tendency of hierarchies to force specific roles on participants. Alternatives often result from redundancies introduced by great network extent and its social mediation.

Redundancies mean that more than one satisfactory outcome can be obtained. As a result, there is not "one best way" to obtain a satisfactory result, but alternative ways that lead to acceptable outcomes. These alternatives can therefore neutralize the control that some levels in a hierarchy exercise to impose their power upon others.

Control is, however, by no means eliminated when a hierarchy is bypassed or diminished. Control can emerge *from the bottom up* rather than from the top down, as in a conventional hierarchy. In other words, control can be self-imposed by participants in a network, even when little or no hierarchy exists. Regulation of the Internet, for example, largely emerged from the bottom up.[16] Contrary to what many believe, this "network of networks" is highly controlled by rules set by organizations such as the World Wide Web Consortium (W3C) and the Internet Engineering Task Force (IETF), both of which control operational standards, and the Internet Corporation for Assigned Names and Numbers (ICANN), which controls the domain name assignment system. These organizations were largely *self-created* and *self-governing*, to the extent that they have open membership and usually make decisions on a consensual basis.[17] Curiously, and because of this bottom-up kind of control, the Internet is often viewed as unregulated or even anarchic.

In biotechnology and medical research, for example, Open Source networks can control the sharing of techniques by requiring peer reviews before any contribution can be posted.[18] Once posting occurs, network controls require that new versions or improvements be shared with everyone. This opens any contribution to further testing and verification, which will in turn be subjected to the controls established by the network to keep all results open and available to members and the public. The controls are themselves elaborated by participants, who can suggest modifications at any time, subject to approval by consensus from network participants.

Similarly, controls in Open Source software research networks typically require that preselected participants review all contributions before they are posted. Such controls ensure conformity with the objectives of the network and try to prevent malicious code from being posted. Nonproprietary controls require that rights be signed over to the network, to preempt property claims for any contributions. Control in Open Source software networks also comes from the participants themselves, as they review and modify each others' work relentlessly, posting all new versions for anyone to freely modify, download, and use. This sort of collectivist control for a creative endeavor is distinctive of the Open Source software movement and its experimentalist ethos.[19]

Bottom-up networks can benefit the reproduction of creativity greatly. Their collectivist controls provide flexibility to individual participants and can cut down the entry barriers that are often found in hierarchical structures. They are therefore easier to join, participate in, and exit, and the choice of roles that participants play can vary. Leadership roles such as creating a community of allies or a power bloc, or forming lobbying coalitions are relatively easy to articulate when they resonate with other participants. Social relations can be more easily developed as barriers to acceptance found in hierarchies are diluted. Bottom-up networks can also reduce the oligarchies and vested interests that entrench themselves in order to impose their priorities on others.[20] As a result, for example, the social utility of an invention or innovation can be enhanced when rapid diffusion makes it known to network participants.

Another feature of bottom-up control is that trust tends to underpin a network's social relations. Without trust in those who articulate control and in the network's larger community itself, a network will find it difficult to survive. When hierarchies are diluted, it is all too easy to exit, or to join or form a rival network. For this reason, networks that help reproduce creativity often seek to preserve participants' trust by relying on such mechanisms as consensual decision making, easy access, participatory discussion, and open debate.[21] These measures do not work all of the time, but the feeling of trust they provide, even if not well justified, helps sustain a network's control apparatus.

The dilution of hierarchy can also induce a devolution of functions to the base. This may involve a fragmentation of decision making or the means of control, and it can also spread risk among participants. Various localized nodes of control can develop in a diluted hierarchy that check one another's control and provide some balance within the network. Greater autonomy and a fragmentation of control can therefore be outcomes of devolution. However, while they may work out well with bottom-up regulation, autonomy and the fragmentation of control can pose serious problems for organizations.

As discussed earlier, the networks that help reproduce creativity are *external* to organizations. This contrasts with the organizations of industrial capitalism, for which the most important networks were *internal* and where hierarchy and centralized control were often essential. The networks that reproduce creativity are, however, external and therefore rely on social mediation. This means that the technocapitalist corporation cannot hope to survive as an island, isolated from the larger society and from other organizations, even competitors. Therefore, the technocapitalist corporation cannot be self-sufficient when it comes to reproducing creativity.

The technocapitalist corporation thus faces a major dilemma. It can open itself to external networks and risk losing control over creativity, which would jeopardize its appropriation of that precious resource and the chance to obtain market value. *Or* it can limit its external network relations, thereby foregoing the benefits of greater network extent. In that case, it risks shriveling its most precious resource, creativity. This outcome would compromise the survival of any technocapitalist corporation.

The fate of most technocapitalist corporations rides on how this difficult dilemma is addressed. This is an unfolding dialectic whose full profile and trajectory are difficult to visualize at this time. Some organizations have chosen to cope with it by establishing network-based alliances with other companies and then embedding a research unit to research unit (R2R) network within the larger network.[22] Thus, an implicit hierarchy is created within the general network of the alliance. This tactic can provide the benefit of some (network-based) social mediation, albeit circumscribed. However, it forces organizations to forego the benefits of greater network extent. It is therefore a difficult compromise whose effectiveness depends on circumstantial factors, such as the kind of research being undertaken, its talent requirements, the nature of the alliance, government regulation, and the competitive dynamics of the sector in which they operate.

In other cases, the choice might be made to segment research units and turn them into autonomous organizations with freedom to network externally on their own, independently of the main organization. The "spin-offs," as they are referred to in economic jargon, can provide an impression of independence from the larger organization, even when little of it actually exists. Spun-off units can be part of a larger modular strategy of organizational reconfiguration, where some research units become autonomous "modules" in the organizational apparatus.[23] Modular strategies typically attempt to improve the performance of some research units by freeing them from sclerotic organizational structures where hierarchy impedes networking and rapid adjustment.

A modular strategy is, however, difficult to articulate and poses serious risks to many large organizations. That is why many organizations scale down this strategy and allow some research groups to operate autonomously on a temporary basis to network independently with other organizations for specific projects. The software company Sun Microsystems, for example, allowed a group of researchers to set up an autonomous unit to experiment outside the company's direct control and to network with other companies and their researchers.[24] As the company's hierarchy and control were brushed aside, it was possible to improve their research creativity through external networking and come up with the Java software in a short time. Similarly, the biopharmaceutical corporation GlaxoSmithKline split its research department into several centers to loosen up the company's internal hierarchy and allow each center to network externally on its own.[25] This tactic went as far as to induce each center to compete with one another for resources both inside and outside the company by networking with many other firms (including competitors).

Most technocapitalist corporations therefore find themselves with no recourse but to tie into external networks and their social mediation. The strategic subterfuge with which such tie-ins are executed, using spun-off proxies, pseudoautonomous groups, and satellite companies, is a reflection of their often desperate need to sustain research creativity through external networks. As technocapitalism unfolds, it is not too difficult to imagine that the growing importance of external networks could make conventional organizational structures obsolete. If or when that occurs, a revolution of the organizational ecology of research-based businesses could radically change many current views on corporate organization.

Power and Inequity

Networks can be *dualistic* in their scope and structure. Some networks dilute hierarchy, possibly reducing disparity, while others can concentrate power and generate inequity. Both sides of this double-faced aspect of networking depend on social mediation. *Social mediation can therefore promote the creation of bottom-up, collectivist networks that have little or no hierarchy, or it can support the formation of oligarchies that accumulate power and sow the seeds of disparity.* This dialectical character of social mediation permeates network relations and affects many aspects of technological creativity, including reproduction, commodification, and market exchange.

Dualism is therefore an important characteristic of networks and their social mediation. The definition of dualism used here refers to *both* hierarchy and inequity. Figure 4 outlines some of the features of network dualism, the characteristics of the hierarchical and nonhierarchical modes, and their potential outcomes on inequity. The features

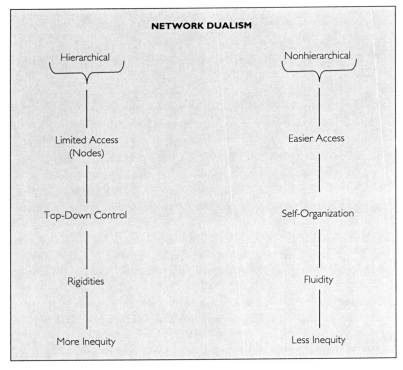

Figure 4 Network Dualism

noted in the diagram take into account previous discussions on hierarchy in this chapter. Underlying each of the dual modes is the role of social mediation, which encompasses both, in a dialectical sense. Social mediation, therefore, can be either a vehicle for greater equity or it can serve the opposite effect, depending on the relations of power found within a network.

Social mediation can lead to major disparities in the accumulation of creative resources within a network. Participants—whether individuals, groups, or organizations—that become more proficient in the accumulation game can be empowered over those who lag behind. The dynamic of many networks is such that this tendency can be exacerbated when little or no redistributive checks exist. Even bottom-up networks, despite their collectivist tendency, can be susceptible to this condition when accumulation becomes a dominant objective.

In networks that help reproduce creativity, inequities perceived to be unjust can be quite damaging. Dysfunctions in social mediation can be an outcome, leading to a loss of trust among participants. Loss of trust can result in doubts about many participants' reliability, sincerity, or reciprocity, for example. Inadequate commitment to the network and its objectives is another possible outcome. In such cases, some or many participants may exit the network, leading to loss of morale among those who remain and further erosion of their social relations.

The networks most likely to develop great inequities are those that retain some measure of top-down hierarchy, which typically empowers some nodes or participants over others, developing differences of influence and control. The result is that, as inequities in the relations of power become pronounced, the more powerful participants impose their prerogatives on those who cannot check their power. This game of accumulation, power, and inequality is part and parcel of the dynamics of technocapitalism, as predatory tactics or coercion drive some participants to impose themselves on others. This condition is found, for example, in supply-chain networks that comprise large corporations and their smaller suppliers.

The empowerment of some nodes or participants over others, and its consequences, comprise several aspects. *First*, empowerment of a few occurs when many network members link or relate to those participants. The parties that accumulate connectivity then become "hubs" as more participants link to them. Larger network extent can compound this process. With larger network extent, new entrants may decide that linking to the most powerful is desirable, simply because most participants already in the network have done so.[26]

This sort of selective linking can provide advantages to those who connect to the most powerful. These advantages, for example, can be greater effectiveness in their own activities as they use resources that the most powerful have accumulated, and that cannot be obtained elsewhere. Another advantage can be higher status and legitimacy over other participants, gained by relating or linking closely to the most powerful members of the network. The perception, often illusory, of being able to exercise power and coercion over others less well linked to the most powerful also can be a perceived advantage. And the ambition, all the more illusory, of someday being able to take the place of the most powerful within the network by linking to them, also must be taken into account. All of these perceived advantages play on human desires for efficacy, social vanity, domination, and lust for power, and it would be unrealistic to think that they can somehow become less important under technocapitalism. If anything, technocapitalism stokes these desires like no other social system did before. Researchers, technologists, and scientists are, after all, human.

Second, the dynamic of empowerment of a few over the many often leads to *linkage dependence*. This means that most participants become dependent on the most powerful members or nodes of the network for certain resources. These can be intangibles such as creativity, knowledge, or experience, or they can be tangible resources such as equipment and financing. As a result, future decisions end up being determined by decisions made in the past, simply because those that become dependent find it hard to break away from their tie to the most powerful.

The word "choice" is often used to describe how linkage dependence takes hold, as it is assumed that those who become dependent can select who they will become dependent on. In reality, however, often there is no choice. Participants become bound to a given experimental method or concept imposed by the most powerful, and there is no viable alternative. They stay with the method or concept as it evolves and can be taken for granted by those who own it and have the most power within the network. And, for those who became dependent, the cost of breaking up and switching may be too high or altogether prohibitive. In this calculus of the situation, the cost of breaking their dependence may not be offset by the short-term benefits of switching, and the long-term benefits may be too uncertain or too difficult to anticipate.

An example of this condition can be found in research units using computer equipment and software for laboratory experiments, for which there may be very few suppliers. At the level of the computer system, linkage dependence begins when very costly hardware is purchased, as with supercomputers. Purchasing another kind to replace the hardware would entail substantial cost; then the software would likely have to be changed, adding to the cost, time, and effort of having to learn a different system. Social relations might also be impaired as contact with the previous supplier and its technical support are broken off, and links have to be established with new suppliers that require trust building and the sharing of operational knowledge. Moreover, the new system may be incompatible with others already in use or with those of partners. As these details are assessed, the linkage-dependent research unit may decide that the costs and disruption of switching do not justify the benefit that it could bring, adding to this calculus the possibility of rapid obsolescence of computer and software.

Third, the empowerment of the few over the many can result in substantial inequity within a network. As the powerful gain more power, they are likely to accumulate it; then, sustained accumulation by a few leads to an oligarchy. And, as the oligarchy exerts greater influence and force over the other members of the network, inequity can be compounded.[27]

To use statistical parlance, this dynamic results in the connectivity of participants *not* being distributed normally around a mean (in other words, not randomly). Instead, a skewed distribution of connectivity and relations will occur, and the distribution will be highly biased toward those who accumulated the most power within the network. In the context of networks, this is the winners-take-all or rich-get-richer outcome of the empowerment of the few over the many.

An example of this dynamic can be found in the development of the World Wide Web. Although it is not a dedicated research network, the Web can be used for that purpose. Moreover, the Web is external to organizations, which depend on it for many resources, including creativity. Creativity is, in any case, very much a part of the Web's development, since "content" pretty much decides whether anyone will link to any given site. Connectivity in the Web, despite its substantial network extent, follows a skewed distribution.[28] A relatively small proportion of sites or nodes accumulates most of the links and flows that occur in the Web. This condition was not intended by the Web's inventor.[29] Thus, despite its seemingly freewheeling character and the unintended outcome, with connectivity being voluntary and the large variety of choices available, the Web provides one of the best examples of the kind of inequity that can be sustained through network extent and social mediation.

Another example of network-sustained inequality can be found in the relations between academic researchers and for-profit publishing companies. Such networks are also external to corporate organizations in the publishing business. The networks are limited in extent, scope, and structure, but show great inequity between the two main categories of participants: publishers and researchers. Researchers typically hand over their manuscripts, which incorporate the results of their creativity, to publishing companies for free. The publishing companies then sell back those contributions, at substantial prices, to (nonprofit) academic institutions and other researchers in the form of subscriptions to journals or as books. Contributions may undergo peer review, to check on quality and identify mistakes, and to legitimize the work with comments that can be used to attract sales. The cost of the peer review process, which usually does not compensate reviewers at all, amounts to a very small percentage of subscription cost or book price.

Clearly, researchers could organize themselves to take over the review, publishing, and distribution of their work. The publishing corporations control the entire process and reap all the profits for creativity given to them for free. This situation goes on despite the fact that, technologically, it has become easier than ever to publish and distribute. Distribution makes up a corporate publisher's largest cost, yet the Web reduces such cost to almost nothing, making it harder to explain why researchers have not taken publishing more into their own hands.[30] The publishers, on their part, pay only a pittance to authors in the form of minute royalty percentages in the case of books, and nothing at all in the case of journal articles. High sales do not change this situation much, as any academic researcher whose work sold well can attest to.

However, the oligarchy of for-profit corporate publishers confers legitimacy upon the work they publish because of their distribution networks and recognizable corporate names. As the process perpetuates itself, this oligarchy accumulates more power over authors, most of whom are all too willing to sign over their rights and agree to most any condition set before them. And they agree to it in order to gain some intellectual legitimacy through, paradoxically, those who are really just concerned with commodifying the result of their creativity to obtain market value (and surplus value).[31] The network-supported inequality generated through empowerment of the few over the many thus has a way of sustaining itself, as long as power can maintain its hold on those who cannot check it.

Change over Change

Networks can generate change systematically. Imbalance and disequilibrium usually accompany systematic change. In the context of technocapitalism, where the most important networks are external to organizations, change and disequilibrium tend to be systemic. This means that network-based change is usually not confined to one participant, but typically affects other participants within the network. Thus, the trajectory of participants, be they individuals, groups, or organizations, is not entirely dependent on each one's creativity and merits, but also depends on the trajectories of the other participants.

The character and quality of network-based change can be very diverse. Change in research-oriented networks, which are symbolic of technocapitalism, can range from the incremental to the revolutionary. Revolutionary change typically overturns established paradigms, leading to major disruptions in the status quo. However, the more common type of change tends to be incremental, achieved through organizations' research and development (R&D) units. Both incremental and radical change can be induced by "first-mover" research, where the organization that actually comes up with a new idea, process, formula, method, service, or tool gets to obtain market value from its invention. However, much incremental change is of the "second-mover" type, where a company mainly takes advantage of other organizations' findings, either legitimately or surreptitiously. Second-mover research, therefore, may also contribute to change, but its spread is greatly responsible for the explosion of litigation over intellectual property that plagues corporatism.[32]

Systematic change and disequilibrium are intrinsic to the networks of technocapitalism. These networks are typically *external* to organizations and can dilute control, especially when there is little or no hierarchy. Change is therefore expected and accepted, if not taken for granted, whenever networks and their social mediation play a role. This situation contrasts greatly with industrial capitalism, where change was usually viewed as a threat, and the possibility of it occurring in networks external to organizations was regarded as something to be avoided. Many a corporation under industrial capitalism went out of its way, at great cost to itself and its shareholders, to acquire other companies, neutralize their strategies, or drive them out of business altogether, in an effort to prevent change in its external relations.[33]

Systematic change and disequilibrium do not translate into an absence of control, however. Instead, control in networks where systematic change and imbalance occur is usually fluid and flexible. This permanent state of change is quite unsettling to those who expect networks to provide a proverbial rock-solid stability for relations.[34] The networks of technocapitalism are often unstable and quite susceptible to the risk and uncertainty caused by experimentalist trial and error, unexpected results, and controversy.

Networks with conventional hierarchies or oligarchic control might experience slower change than the bottom-up type, but this situation is far from certain. It may depend a lot on whether control is oriented toward impeding change or supporting it. However, change is difficult to impede by hierarchies and any oligarchy in the context of technocapitalism, mainly because there are many forces affecting networks that are external to organizations. Given the global scope of invention and innovation, it is not too difficult to find alternatives to bypass oligarchic situations and embedded hierarchies, provided social mediation can be enlisted for that objective.

It is possible, nonetheless, that if network-based hierarchies and oligarchies can impede change, its arrival may be all the more convulsive when it comes. An example can be found in the case of financial analysts and forecasters who develop similar opinions and strategies by networking with one another frequently. Such individuals and their organizations often have significant power over their fields of research and can exclude those "not in the loop" of their strategies. A small group of powerful individuals in those networks can become a de facto oligarchy that influences other participants, even though there may be little hierarchy within the network. Then, when an event which they did not foresee occurs, they can be destroyed financially. Their network relations made them underestimate the probability of its occurrence, since their strategies were similar. The history of technological disasters is also filled with such cases of network-generated biases.[35]

The disequilibrium inherent in the networks of technocapitalism is at odds with one of the best-known theoretical assumptions of mainstream (or neoclassical) economics—the notion that transactions and relations tend toward some sort of equilibrium, normatively speaking. This equilibrium assumption is vital for general equilibrium models, which are the most important conceptual tool underlying mainstream economics, and allows mainstream (or neoclassical) economics to operate logically and mathematically. Without the assumption of equilibrium, the models would become unworkable, and most of the theoretical edifice of mainstream economics would have no basis to speak of. This very important assumption and the vested interests it creates prevents mainstream economics from abandoning the assumption of equilibrium as a normative condition. At the same time, the equilibrium assumption prevents mainstream economics from considering networks adequately.

It is difficult to understand how equilibrium could be considered a standard characteristic of any economic or social process, even when a generous amount of imagination can be summoned. The workings of networks and of technocapitalism, if anything, indicate that equilibrium states in the economy and society are about as rare as meteorites crashing into cities. Notions of "equilibrium" apparently became part of conventional economic thinking because of the discipline's tendency to borrow terms from the physical and natural sciences. Such borrowings were part of an effort to legitimize economics as a "science," hoping that it could attract the kind of social prestige and recognition that the physical and natural sciences attained in the early and mid-twentieth century. The fact that "equilibrium" had little or nothing to do with economic and social reality was apparently lost on those who adopted it.

However, the notion of equilibrium was also of interest to industrial capitalism as it tried to make production, commodification, and the exploitation of labor more predictable. The fiction of equilibrium in mainstream economics was therefore as much oriented to legitimize the discipline in the eyes of the physical and natural sciences as to calm the anxieties of industrial capitalists. Change, disequilibrium and uncertainty were considered threats to the interests of industrial corporate power. As mainstream economics had previously tied in to industrial capitalism through analytical tools, such as the production function, so the notion of equilibrium gave it greater legitimacy with industrial corporate power. However, the fact that the idea of equilibrium is antithetical to the workings of networks has marginalized networks in the tool kit of mainstream economics. Now, when networks are impossible to ignore in the technocapitalist dynamic, mainstream economics seems ill-suited to consider this emerging phenomenon.

Network-based systematic change and disequilibrium are influenced by various forces. *One* of them is network extent. Rapid expansion or contraction of extent is a powerful force for change and imbalance. These changes can be a product of network switching by participants, as different networks vie with one another for new members. Typically, the addition of many new participants, or their departure, has substantial effects on network extent and the quality of its social mediation. The resulting changes and imbalance can be constructive, as they often act as catalysts for creativity and new knowledge. In Open Source software networks, for example, a rapid expansion of extent can increase creative interaction substantially, enriching the opportunities to reproduce creativity for participants, new and old.[36] Greater network extent can also provide many new opportunities for experimentation. More participants will likely translate into more experimental events that can address the interests of an expanded membership base.

A *second* force for change within networks is the rapid obsolescence of new inventions and innovations. Waves of inventions that collapse cost, time, effort, and space (or save lives) in close succession to one another are a destabilizing factor. Corporate survival often rides on whether a new product or service will have market permanence. A major question is whether the new replacements are revolutionary or not. Modest collapses of cost, time, effort, and space may not have the same disequilibrating effect as the revolutionary ones. In some cases, the waves of new invention or innovation might be so frequent that they become expected. In semiconductors and magnetic memory disks, for example, the pace of innovation is such that their capacities have doubled about every eighteen months since the 1960s.[37] Every doubling of capacity has provided significant possibilities for new computing and software applications. Wireless telephony, handheld computers, and animation software are but a few examples of how these possibilities were turned into products.

Rapid obsolescence is often driven by competition in research. Cutthroat competition in some sectors has been behind most of the "second-mover" research strategies adopted by businesses as they try to sustain the market value of their products and commodify creativity in ever faster ways. Short-term horizons for invention and innovation have therefore become the norm, as businesses strive to compete fiercely to establish a market niche that may become obsolete in a matter of months.

Rapid, short-term change often means that organizations must "unlearn" what made them successful, researchwise, and try new and uncertain research programs. The outcomes of new research programs would be unknown, but might hold promise for coming up with that new process, formula, method, service, or tool that will make the difference whether a company survives or is driven under by its competitors. Unlearning established ways has therefore been suggested as a tactic for recomposing corporate research in an environment of rapid change.

A major conflict with this aspect, however, is that corporate strategy has traditionally been oriented to *not* discard what made it successful in the first place. In large corporations typical of industrial capitalism, such as those found in the automotive industry, for example, strategies built around the development and marketing of the internal combustion engine prevented the development of alternative motive technologies, despite their feasibility.[38] Even the most effective management training programs find it very difficult to convince executives to disown what made their businesses profitable and follow what is uncertain and unknown. The result of "unlearning" past success is often disequilibrium through uncertainty and distrust, leading to changes in network participation, alliances, and partnerships, as research requirements change. For most corporate executives of the industrial capitalist era, this approach would have been considered nothing short of mad, and it would likely have been discredited. The organizations of industrial capitalism prized stability and moving along the known road above most anything else. In the technocapitalist corporation, however, such change and imbalance, and the uncertainty, risk, and distrust that they breed must be taken as a "normal" business condition.

A *third* force for change within networks is weak embeddedness of many participants. Weak ties can make it easier to change relations or exit a network altogether. However, weak ties do not necessarily mean that social mediation will be less important.[39] Social mediation can be important even when weak embeddedness exists, if the temporal scope of research projects is short-term and links between participants shift and change. Such shifting and changing has to rely on a lot of social mediation, which is vital to create social value and regenerate creativity, even when weak ties are the norm.

Parallel experimentation undertaken simultaneously in different laboratories around the world provides a frequent example of weak embeddedness. Individual researchers located in different continents may never get to know one another personally, and their interactions may be limited to dealing with narrow research tasks. However, the social mediation that makes all of the labs and personnel come together and collaborate across great distances will have to be strong if their coordination and collective creativity are to bear any fruit.[40]

Finally, the dynamics of network development are another force for change. Change can occur slowly during the early times of a network's formation, when extent is limited and the direction of relations is uncertain. This period of incubation can be followed by a shift toward rapid growth, as new participants join and network extent grows large very quickly. The shifting of stages can introduce substantial change and disequilibrium as new links, nodes, and modes of control are formed.

In Open Source biotechnology research networks, for example, a shift toward rapid growth would make it feasible for the network to multiply its electronic publishing outlets. This would become possible because larger extent would allow the creation of a division of labor where some of the outlets specialize in certain areas, such as bioinformatics, genetic decoding, or proteomics. As these changes occur, the reproduction of creativity could become more dynamic. Then, as a result, it may be expected that users of the new, freely shared knowledge would grow. That, in turn, might lead to a quantum leap in the network's extent as new participants join, attracted by the visibility and quality of freely shared knowledge. The leap in network extent could then cause drastic changes in the internal hierarchy and modes of control by, for example, moving toward a bottom-up condition where regulation becomes consensual and any preexisting hierarchy is diluted.

Conclusion

Networks are vehicles for social mediation and agents of change. The most important networks of technocapitalism are those that help reproduce creativity. They are usually external to organizations and are greatly influenced by social mediation in their modes of control, hierarchy, and relations of power.

Extent is possibly the most important feature of networks in the context of technocapitalism. It influences greatly the quality and quantum of participation, its composition, accessibility, and the range of a network. Through social mediation, network extent also influences the quality of reproduction, and possibly the social value of any results of creativity. Indirectly, network extent can influence market value, surplus value, and the dynamics of market exchange.

It is difficult to draw comparisons between the networks of technocapitalism and those of previous stages of capitalism. Nonetheless, the most important networks of this emerging form of capitalism are inherently *social*, they help regenerate *intangibles* without which commodification cannot take place, and since they are *external* to corporate organizations, corporate power has little influence on the external networks that help reproduce creativity.

In contrast with these features, the networks typical of industrial capitalism were either internal to, or were greatly dependent on, corporate power. The reproduction and commodification of vital resources were therefore primarily a corporate function and occurred mostly under the control of corporate power. In the context of technocapitalism, however, reproduction and commodification are split. Reproduction necessarily occurs outside the corporate context, while commodification is mostly a corporate function. As we see in later chapters, this condition is a source of major contradictions and pathologies for society, and for corporatism itself.

Given the complex nature of network-based social mediation, it may not be surprising that the reproduction and commodification of creativity pose formidable challenges. Corporate power is more limited than ever in its capacity to reproduce this vital resource, despite its hegemonic designs over technology. The next chapter provides an overview of the changing character of corporatism, and of the contradictions and pathologies that are emerging as corporate power tries to grapple with the network-grounded cleavage between reproduction and commodification.

Decomposing the Corporation

The decomposition of the corporation is a major phenomenon of technocapitalism. Network-based decomposition shifts power away from corporate organizations toward society. Virtually all aspects of the reproduction of creativity and other intangibles depend on this power shift toward networks and the social context. The distinctive nature of this phenomenon, the role of networks, and their effect on corporate power and its pathologies are addressed in this chapter.

Decomposition is the dismantling and externalizing of functions that were traditionally under the control of corporate governance. Networks and their social relations are the vehicles of decomposition, an emerging phenomenon whose full dimensions are still unknown. It became noticeable during the last decade of the twentieth century, and may become as important in corporate history as the introduction of mass production or the factory system were in earlier times. Decomposition is likely to affect most every corporate organization, whether typical of technocapitalism or not. In essence, therefore, the emergence of technocapitalism can be spawning a phenomenon that no corporate organization may be able to evade.

The corporation was an icon of industrial capitalism. For much of the past one hundred years, we have lived in a corporate society.

Corporatism touched most aspects of life and work, as its power spread over institutions, culture, governance, and the media. The corporation has been more representative of the kind of society we have known than the much trumpeted "consumer society." After all, consumerism itself was a product of corporate power and its influence over society.

Decomposition makes it impossible for corporate organizations to view themselves as separate from society or, in other words, to focus narrowly on their self-interest. Pursuing their self-interest without regard for society results in contradictions that turn decomposition into a dysfunctional and pathological process. Much of the corporatist psychopathy we witness today can be traced to schemes that deny the social context of this phenomenon.

Making corporations more accountable to society and viewing them as a product of their social context can be part of the phenomenon of decomposition. This phenomenon could be accompanied by a democratization of technology and science, if we seek greater social accountability from corporatism. As we see in later chapters, this possibility is not out of reach, despite the overwhelming influence wielded by corporate power in contemporary society.

Denial of the social dimension in corporatism may be considered an inheritance of industrial capitalism. The vital resources of that stage of capitalism were tangible and were reproduced and commodified internally under the control of corporate governance. The factory system of industrial capitalism and its labor processes made it possible for reproduction and commodification to occur internally. The *intangible* nature of the vital resources of technocapitalism, however, makes it impossible for the corporation to detach itself from society, mainly because those resources can only be effectively reproduced through the social context.

Networks versus the Corporation

Networks are subverting the corporate structures inherited from industrial capitalism. Their subversion is part of an unfolding phenomenon that is reconfiguring the place of corporations in society and the way they capture resources and obtain value, along with the very logic of corporate organization. At no previous time in history were external networks and their social mediation as important or as disruptive for corporate organizations as they are under technocapitalism.

The subversion of corporate organizations through networks is most palpable for any activity that depends on intangible resources. The phenomenon of decomposition is driven by the need to secure those intangibles. The most precious intangible, creativity, is becoming indispensable for activities or sectors one could consider far removed from technocapitalism. Whether in automotive manufacturing, textiles processing, airline transportation, or fast food provision, intangibles are making themselves essential to sustain corporate power. Decomposition therefore affects the established industries of industrial capitalism along with service activities. No corporate organization in our time can be considered immune from this phenomenon.

The corporations of industrial capitalism possessed hierarchical control structures. Significant vertical integration and in-house control of functions, especially those at the core of organizations, were typical of those structures.[1] In addition, those organizations comprised governance rules that enforced control over the hierarchies and their internal functions. Those structures are now coming apart, as network-based decomposition disassembles much of the internal apparatus of corporate organizations.

Networks make decomposition distinctive from other deconstructive processes, such as vertical disintegration. Decomposition goes beyond vertical disintegration, to change the basic premises of corporate governance through networks and their social context. The control structures and power of corporate governance were sustained through vertical disintegration because tangible resources, such as raw materials, capital, and labor were involved. Also, vertical disintegration usually did not occur through external networks, but rather through bilateral arrangements that were under the control of corporate power.[2]

Vertical disintegration typically involved production rather than research. Moreover, the rationale for vertical disintegration was usually based on narrow cost considerations related to tangible resources. The cost calculus dictated that corporate functions should be disintegrated until the cost of doing so became greater than the cost of keeping them vertically integrated. This simple principle became entrenched in the theory and practice of managerial economics during much of the twentieth century. With intangible resources, however, corporations usually have no choice but to externalize functions and reach out through networks for the intangibles they need. There is usually no alternative way to access those resources, since corporations cannot reproduce them on their own. As we have seen in the previous two chapters, the inherently social character of creativity, the most important resource of technocapitalism, places it outside the control of corporate power.

The split between the corporate commodification of creativity and the socially driven reproduction of this vital resource is therefore at the core of decomposition. Figure 5 illustrates the elements of this contextual split, where reproduction is a function of networks and their social mediation. Networks thus play a major role in the phenomenon of decomposition through their influence on the reproduction of creativity. Through reproduction, networks also affect the commodification of creativity, and the generation of social value and market value.

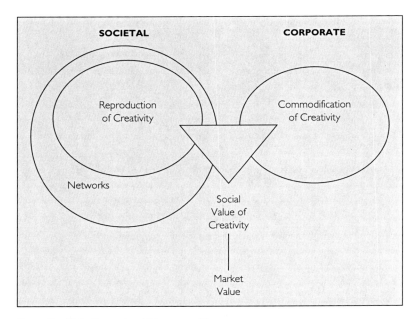

Figure 5   Main Elements of Decomposition

Decomposition through networks results in part from the inade-quacy of corporate organizations to reproduce the vital resources of technocapitalism. Although decomposition is a complex and multifac-eted phenomenon, its existence can be explained by four major aspects affecting corporate organizations. All of these aspects are influenced greatly by the qualitative nature of intangibles and the peculiar char-acter of networks, as noted in previous chapters.

First, corporate organizations cannot accumulate and marshal *in-ternally* vital intangibles, such as creativity, in any complete sense. The corporate structures of industrial capitalism were effective for produc-tion and related functions, but are not well suited for accessing, repro-ducing, and commodifying the intangible resources required by this new phase of capitalism. There are two major reasons for their inade-quacy. One of them is limited resources to reproduce the vital intan-gibles, given their social character, along with their effort-intensive and time-consuming characteristics. The most precious intangible, cre-ativity, requires enormous persistence, long-term commitment, and costly arrangements to reproduce and sustain. In addition, securing that intangible often involves relational ties that money alone cannot buy, even when it is generously available. All too often, that intangible re-source is not marketed and can only be found outside organizations.

Another reason is the complexity of talents needed to reproduce creativity and generate new knowledge. Multidisciplinary talents and experience are essential if creativity is to be reproduced and sustained. This complexity is compounded by the acceleration of technological change, which typically results in shortened product cycles, greater specialization, and short-life market niches. Old-line industries and sectors typical of industrial capitalism are particularly vulnerable in this respect, since they usually lack the resources needed to deal with that complexity, whether in research, production, marketing, or distri-bution. It is therefore very difficult, if not impossible, for most corpo-rate organizations to internally assemble the multidisciplinary talents needed to reproduce the vital intangibles that this new phase of capi-talism requires.

Examples of these features can be found in both the old-line cor-porate organizations that were typical of industrial capitalism and in the new sectors spawned by technocapitalism. In the automotive in-dustry, for example, design was historically undertaken internally and treated with much secrecy.[3] However, automotive design has been decomposed from conventional corporate structures and is often performed by independent design companies that orchestrate the entire process and network their ideas with industrial engineering specialists, who often are also independent. The engineering specialists, in turn, network with independent safety experts, and the design, engineering, and safety specialist organizations together network with independent marketing companies that try to anticipate consumer attitudes on new designs. The diverse expertise involved is simply too complex to be undertaken internally by the auto manufacturers given their limited resources.

Similarly, the design of microchips is being decomposed from manufacturing organizations, despite the risk of leaks and predation by competitors.[4] Independent microchip design outfits network with specialist outfits that can include electronic engineers, physicists, biologists, computer scientists, mathematicians, communication experts, graphic artists, software specialists, and linguists. The diverse and complex expertise is necessary as microchip design outfits try to anticipate potential uses for a product. This sort of complexity is often beyond the means of microchip companies to sustain internally. Even when the financial resources exist, internally reproducing the diverse and complex forms of creativity needed is usually out of reach for microchip corporations.

Second, networks are *more effective* than corporate organizations in reproducing intangibles—most of all, creativity. Their effectiveness is multifaceted and qualitative, and its precise dimensions may be hard to grasp. However, even a sparse understanding of their operation can show that networks and their social mediation are better suited to deal with rapidly changing conditions than the rigid structures that often characterize corporate organizations. Usually governed through tight control and authoritarian command, corporate organizations are deficient when they try to deal with the need to reproduce intangibles and adjust to rapid technological change.

Adding to their problems is the fact that the corporate organizations inherited from industrial capitalism have tried to detach themselves from society as much as possible, in order to appropriate resources, exploit them, and obtain market value.[5] Their logic, governance, scope, scale, and resource exploitation were based on this premise. In contrast, external networks and their social mediation are more effective for dealing with intangible resources and rapid change. Being part of society is precisely what is required to deal with the context of technocapitalism and its ever-pressing need to have creativity reproduced. Detachment from society is the wrong path to follow in this emerging new era, yet that is just what corporate power has often tried to do throughout its history.

Moreover, the social context of networks provides governance structures of their own that stand in contrast to those of corporate organizations. In networks, interaction, diffusion, and access to intangibles often occurs through preferential or reciprocal arrangements. Network participants are often interdependent, and the benefits of sharing intangible resources tend to lead to collective governance arrangements. These governance arrangements tend to be flexible, can adjust quickly to change, and are often dynamic in the way they cope with situations. Governance that provides these features, even when asymmetries in power exist, tends to be more effective for dealing with intangibles than corporate hierarchies and command-and-control management.

Their governance arrangements, therefore, tend to make networks better suited to reproduce creativity than corporate organizations. Networks also tend to stimulate learning more strongly and diffuse new knowledge faster than corporate organizations. This is made possible by the web of reciprocities, interdependence, and experience built up over time through social mediation. Since learning is a fundamental ingredient of creativity, its rapid regeneration can confer much advantage to network relations over corporate management.

A comparison of the main features of networks and corporate governance, shown in Figure 6, can provide an overview of contrasts. The preferential, reciprocal, and voluntary character of network-based relations and governance can be considered a result of interdependence and sharing, as the web of social relations deepens or enhances individual talents. These features, which are indispensable for reproducing creativity, contrast with the command-and-control, authoritarian character of corporate governance. The main concern of corporate governance, beyond commodifying creativity, is with obtaining market value and, hopefully, surplus value, such that corporate power can be sustained. Its priority is therefore immediate, short-term, and often

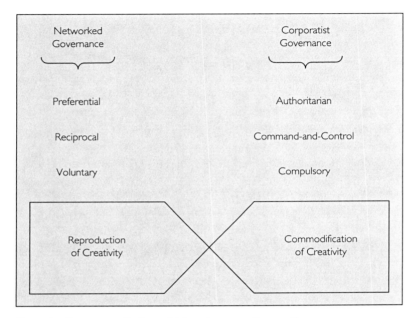

Figure 6 Governance Features: Networks versus Corporatism

results in incomplete knowledge of the complex, qualitative nature of creativity.

New knowledge gained through network-based social mediation is often deeper and more complete than what can be obtained through corporate organizations. New (or tacit) knowledge obtained through networks and their social mediation is usually not marketed or traded, nor is it effectively communicated through corporate hierarchies. That kind of knowledge is often derived through fluid, open-ended contacts or long-standing relations that have been built up over time with persistence, trust, and reciprocity. In these respects, networks embody the experimentalist ethos of technocapitalism more than any corporate organization, and they reflect the fact that the reproduction of creativity cannot occur in isolation from society.

The importance of decomposition through networks is becoming noticeable in many sectors and activities. In services, for example, large airlines are letting go of in-house functions, such as aircraft maintenance and cargo and passenger ground services, to let independent, specialized organizations handle them. Frequent-flier programs are being "spun off" as independent companies. Airlines are also forming network alliances for flight code sharing, passenger transfer, and frequent-flier benefits that are based on reciprocity, despite the impersonal and contractual nature of those arrangements. This has allowed many airline companies to extend their route systems, gain a global scope, and attract more passengers. Networking with other carriers also allows a dimension of creativity on new service concepts that they would not otherwise be able to provide on their own.

In the pharmaceutical industry, functions such as research, testing, marketing, distribution, or manufacturing that were previously held internally are now being handled through networks of independent companies.[6] Old-line pharmaceutical corporations are thus finding a way to learn biotechnology applications by letting the networks, which are usually made up of small new companies, do the kind of research that they cannot do as effectively. This phenomenon is not occurring for lack of financial resources at the pharmaceutical giants, but rather because their own corporate organizations cannot do as well in research as the smaller and younger organizations in those networks. Similarly, networking with independent, specialized companies for marketing, distribution, and manufacturing allows the large pharmaceutical companies to learn new ideas and techniques, and to benefit from operations that are more effective than they could perform on their own.

Another example of industrial capitalism, the large automotive corporations are likely to turn into little more than customer financing and distribution companies. Manufacturing and design seem destined to be performed by networks of companies specialized in specific parts of the value chain. The use of business-to-business (B2B), Internet-based networking to secure supplies has made it clear how much more effective network-based links with suppliers can be, not only in terms of cost reduction but also in quality, speed, and learning.[7] This is occurring despite the impersonal, competitive, and contractual way with which most automotive B2B networking has been handled. The B2B networks have also allowed many small independent companies to join the bidding processes of large automotive corporations, thereby breaking down entry barriers that would have been difficult to penetrate before. Some large automotive corporations have found B2B networks so effective that they have tried to collude and form a vast, common B2B network for parts procurement despite the risk of antitrust prosecution.

Third, networks are more effective for *reducing uncertainty* on intangibles than corporate organizations. This occurs because interdependence, reciprocities, and collaborative arrangements embedded in networks tend to be based on trust built up over long periods of time. Relational links, over purely contractual or competitive ones, are often an outcome of those arrangements, and are both product and drivers of long-term trust. In contrast, corporate structures tend to reduce uncertainty only over the short term, if they can do so at all, and usually in a compulsory or authoritarian way. Whatever trust occurs in corporate structures often results from fear. More often than not, corporations undermine themselves by promoting a culture of competition that ends up destroying whatever trust they might create internally. This basic contradiction has been at the core of much internal strife in corporate organizations throughout their history.[8]

Networks can also reduce uncertainty on intangibles because the arrangements they create may discourage opportunism, which typically has short-term horizons, often conflicting with the long-term investment of effort and time that are the basis of network relations. Opportunists' network participation is usually short and difficult, mainly because their behavior cannot elicit trust or nourish the kinds of relations upon which the reproduction of creativity depends. Interdependence, reciprocity, and collaboration are at odds with opportunism, which is often accompanied by deceit, predation, or fraud. Network participants who have invested considerable effort, time, and money in securing trust and reducing uncertainty often reject opportunistic behavior, partly because it reduces their own investment in the network.

Trust gained through network-based social mediation can also reduce uncertainty by helping resolve contingencies faster or by avoiding them altogether. The rapid adjustment that is characteristic of many networks can diminish the sources of contingency. Moreover, the kind of social mediation that creates trust often prevents contingencies from occurring in the first place. Information technology may also help resolve contingency by finding solutions to problems quickly. In contrast, even the competent use of information technology in corporate organizations often cannot resolve contingencies fast enough to compare with what networks can do. This occurs mainly because the rigidities introduced by corporate hierarchies tend to prevent rapid resolution. In some corporations, a culture of dwelling on contingencies has also been common, often prolonging and compounding problems. An example of how networks reduce uncertainty can be found in Open Source software design. Open Source networks provide a way for programmers from around the world to voluntarily contribute their creativity by designing software that anyone can use or improve upon. Such software is not proprietary and must be made available to everyone within and outside the network.[9] Posting all improvements and making them freely available to anyone allows flaws to be recognized and resolved quickly, compared to software designed in-house by corporate organizations. Corporations such as Microsoft, for example, design all software internally under tight proprietary rules.[10] Comparing quality between Open Source and Microsoft software can be an enlightening experience. The troubles caused by flaws in Microsoft's software have created untold pain, time losses, and monetary cost, as most any long-term user of the Windows operating system can attest to. Working through networks, in contrast, helps Open Source software reduce uncertainty by providing greater reliability.

Networks also reduce uncertainty and create lasting value through Open Source–type research in biotechnology and medicine. Results of experiments can be posted quickly for anyone to scrutinize or replicate. Making those results freely available allows parallel experimentation to occur around the world, through simultaneous testing and comparison of findings. The ongoing review and verification that occurs allows problems affecting health to be caught early.[11] The reduction of uncertainty obtained through network-based experimentation may therefore prevent complications and save lives since problems are detected quickly as compared to the closed-door, proprietary experimentation that typically goes on in corporate organizations.

Fourth, networks can *reduce transaction costs* on intangibles. This is more likely when trust, reciprocity, and interdependence are established through a network. The arrangements involved can facilitate transactions and reduce cost. They make it possible, for example, to avoid costly safeguards against contingencies that result from opportunistic behavior, such as deceit, fraud, or equivocal tactics. Avoiding costly insurance or litigation when performance is below agreed levels (or when delays and damages occur) can be one of the benefits. Similarly, reciprocity can make talents available when they are urgently needed, as in periods of high demand (or with short deadlines), thereby saving on recruitment and training.

Even in contractual or competitive situations, networks can make it possible to reduce costs over conventional bidding. Business-to-business (B2B) supply networks are an example of this situation.[12] Such networks can result in competitive bidding from numerous potential suppliers. If all bids are posted and can be checked by everyone, iterations of the bidding process can result in bidders undercutting one another until the process is ended. This game is often played by corporations soliciting bids through networks. It allows organizations that solicit bids to extract lower costs from suppliers, while at the same time letting smaller companies join the bidding process. This process can remove barriers to entry for smaller suppliers while reducing costs for the corporations that solicit bids.

It is therefore not necessary to engage in relational arrangements to reduce transaction costs through networks. Open Source software networks are not, after all, truly relational in the sense that the vast majority of participants never actually get to know one another personally, or ever have any face-to-face contact.[13] Also, the reciprocity that exists is not compulsory, as any participant can simply withhold contribution, although the collaborative relations that are built through the network may discourage it. Nonetheless, Open Source software research networks reduce costs by making participants agree to the convention that all contributions be nonproprietary and that they be made freely available to anyone. In this way, transaction costs related to appropriation, which typically underlie most intellectual property litigation, are avoided. Similarly, making all contributions freely available for modification or improvement by anyone reduces transaction costs for flaws or performance shortfalls.

Networks can therefore be more important for reducing transaction costs than corporate organizations. However, there may be more important concerns than transaction costs when dealing with intangibles like creativity. Unlike manufacturing and service production, where cost minimization might seem highly desirable, qualitative aspects are far more important for intangibles. Those qualitative aspects are probably best understood not by narrowly targeting quantitative indicators such as transaction costs, but by looking into the network-supported social context where the reproduction of creativity occurs. It may also occur that some long-standing precepts held by mainstream (neoclassical) economists and organizational experts regarding transaction costs are irrelevant when dealing with intangibles. In particular, the notion that organizations externalize functions until the cost of doing so equals or exceeds the cost of keeping them in-house becomes questionable when dealing with an intangible like creativity.[14] Organizations have little choice but to recur to external networks if they are to reproduce or access vital intangibles such as creativity. To focus on quantitative cost considerations and neglect the qualitative dimension would likely be disastrous for any corporate organization that depends on intangibles, most of all creativity.

This is where the calculus of much mainstream (or neoclassical) economic and organizational theory breaks down in the face of technocapitalism. For many decades, mainstream economists and organizational analysts have focused on either markets or corporate organizations to try to understand corporate capitalism.[15] Organizations were regarded as an alternative for markets in the face of uncertainty and were thus considered indispensable when functions and transactions could not be confidently undertaken through markets. This view neglected the importance of networks and their social context in structuring economic processes and corporate activities.

Part of this historical neglect was driven by the notion that corporate organizations are somehow *separate* from society. By focusing narrowly on the internal hierarchies of corporate organizations, the larger, network-supported social context was therefore ignored. Corporations were treated as isolated entities, with society considered only as a backdrop or not at all, in the theories of mainstream (or neoclassical) economists and organizational experts. Those theories were legitimized, despite their shortcomings, by some Nobel Prizes in economics and thousands of publications that claimed to provide knowledge on how corporate organizations function. Whenever their assumptions or adequacy were called into question, a common evasion was to refer to the theories as "normative," and to assert that they provided an ideal rational guide to how corporate organizations *should* function.[16]

The "normative" subterfuge has been a common response when-ever the shortcomings of neoclassical economic models were pointed out, along with their long-standing neglect of networks. Unrealistic (if not ridiculous) assumptions about human behavior and decision mak-ing, such as the notions of perfect foresight, complete knowledge, opti-mizing behavior, the absence of uncertainty, and the supposed benefits of pervasive competition, among others, worked their way into organi-zational models that are now taught in business schools around the world. Business school curricula were, in effect, colonized by neoclas-sical economic models during the past three decades. Those models worked their way into corporate organizations and are now taken as "best practice" managerial routines in the business world. More broadly, routines derived from the models are all too often taken as "recipes" of "what to do" in most any situation in organizations, work, communi-ties, and even in individual lives. Their practice has caused consider-able harm to those who must exercise creativity, leading to oppressive management, unsustainable risk, destructive hedonic decision pat-terns, and antisocial practices. At the core of those models, their pre-cepts, and their practice, is a neglect of networks as a major social and organizational force.

The neglect of networks by mainstream economists and organi-zational experts has also resulted, in part, from the widespread use of general equilibrium models. All of the assumptions noted before are part of these models and are indispensable for any general equi-librium model to work. General equilibrium models have been the staple of mainstream economic analysis, and contributed greatly to legitimize the discipline as a "science" during the second half of the twentieth century. Thus, they are not easy to forgo. Optimization is an essential component of those models. Networks, however, usually defy the kind of optimization assumptions prescribed by general equilibrium models. Networks' redundancies, alternative paths, and multiple satisfactory outcomes are impossible to take into account by any model that must depend on an optimal outcome (or just one best way) in order to work, as general equilibrium models typically do. The models' optimality assumption, therefore, poses a formidable block to understanding networks. As a result, the conceptual tool kit of mainstream economics seems inadequate for dealing with net-works. This may explain why the discipline has often attempted to downplay the importance of networks. Understanding the organizational character of technocapitalism thus seems out of reach for mainstream economics.

Decomposition and Power

Decomposition is shifting power out of the corporation toward external networks and society. This phenomenon is a major feature of technocapitalism and it reflects the rising importance of intangibles and networks. This shift presages a reconfiguration of the relations of power between corporations and society, and within corporate organizations themselves.

A consequence of this power shift is that the corporation is perceived *less* as being *separate* from society, and more as its outcome. The result is a socialization of corporatism that marks the rising importance of intangibles and the networks that sustain them. Corporatism's long-cherished dream of "laissez-faire" from society therefore seems far removed from the reality of the emerging technocapitalist era. Being left alone to pursue its own interest is a pipe dream that is farther from realization today than it ever was in the heyday of industrial capitalism. At the core of this power shift is the urgent need to gain access to intangibles and to allow them to be reproduced such that market value can be achieved.

The shift of corporate power toward society and its networks raises the need to democratize corporatism and to make it more socially accountable. Examples of this tendency can be found in many corners of contemporary society. Hardly a day goes by without some notice of public action against corporate wrongdoing, even when impropriety does not violate any laws. Corporate governance is currently undergoing greater public scrutiny than at any previous time in history, despite the overwhelming power of corporatism in contemporary society. At the core of this trend is the perception that corporations are social entities with obligations to society and a duty to comply with social expectations.

Seeking fairness, providing transparency in accounts and decisions, and taking responsibility for negative consequences are a few of the motives behind the plethora of legislation and prosecutions intended to socialize corporatism. Misdeeds such as intellectual property theft, accounting fraud, and manipulation of stock trading are eliciting greater penalties in courtrooms and have become the target of more legislative efforts and prosecution.[17] It may be surprising that this is occurring at a time when politics is under great influence from corporatism, despite its negative effects on public governance.

Another consequence of the power shift is that networks are creating new relations of power in their own right. The relations of power that occur within networks are fluid. Games of domination are counterposed by the need for accommodation and collaboration such that the reproduction of intangibles can occur. The result is that power relations within networks tend to lead more toward collaboration than competition. Collaboration usually relies on a buildup of trust over long periods of time, which can be damaged by the strategies of domination that often accompany competition.

In part, the new relations of power created by networks result from their reduction of "friction." Friction here refers to situations that vest power in corporate organizations, making it possible for them to dominate others, such as customers, suppliers, economic sectors, or institutions. Friction is common and can occur, for example, through ignorance of alternatives, or through the inertia that results from misperceptions of the cost needed to pursue alternatives. Ignorance and inertia are often mistaken for "loyalty" by naïve corporate agents. However, the easier knowledge of alternatives that networks provide to customers can now reduce such complacency.

Lock-in (or dependence) based on the bundling together of services is a common example of friction. Networks are a prime vehicle for eliminating such friction. Media and Web-based networks, for example, have unbundled television advertising and entertainment, as well as auto manufacturing, sales, financing, and maintenance. Another important example of friction is the reliance on face-to-face contact as a requisite for many transactions, such as banking, financing, or the purchase of major items like autos and homes. Networks have increasingly rendered face-to-face contact unnecessary for many such transactions. This is often neglected by those who believe that networks are a prime tool for fostering face-to-face contact. Open Source software research networks are, for example, not based on face-to-face contact, yet they are one of the most important examples of network-based research collaboration in our time.[18]

Distance provides another example of friction that has been rendered less important by networks, in research, education, communication, and many other activities. Similarly, friction rooted in local monopolies is being reduced by networks. Newspapers that have long held local monopoly power, for example, are being vanquished by Web logs and online media. Similarly, oligopolistic brick-and-mortar retailers are being driven out of business by online commerce. These examples of the reduction of friction by networks usually involve significant collapses of cost, time, effort, or space. Those effects make friction reduction an attractive strategy for many new companies that aim to capture market niches quickly through networks. Online retailers are among the best examples of these companies.

The new relations of power created by networks are also challenging the community ties of corporate organizations. Communities are tending to redefine themselves more by common interests than by accidents of geography or history. This phenomenon is more obvious in places that concentrate the most valuable intangibles of technocapitalism, such as creativity. Networks in such places are reducing the dependence of employees on corporate actors, as the community of talented individuals becomes more important than any group of corporations.[19] As a result, corporate organizations tap into the community for the talents they need, rather than trying to "own" employees or force-fitting them into a corporate hierarchy. Talent then tends to become more important than seniority, and talented individuals owe more loyalty to their creativity and to the community than to any corporate entity. The result of decomposition at this level is that corporate organizations must become embedded in the local social context rather than being mere providers of jobs and income.[20]

The fluidity of network-based power relations is also obvious in the temporal character of associations between talented individuals and corporate organizations at the community level. Commitments of individual talent to corporate organizations tend to be temporary and are often based more on mutual benefit than loyalty. Talented individuals tend to become more "free agents" than salaried employees. The community's social context and its networks allow them to follow their creative pulse rather than become part of any single organization. Corporate organizations thus have to learn to work and play within the local social networks if they are to attract the kind of creativity they require. This phenomenon, already obvious in places that have important concentrations of intangible resources, is representative of the power shift away from corporations and into networks and society.[21]

Another consequence of the shift of power out of the corporate domain is the creation of extraorganizational mechanisms to structure decomposition. These mechanisms attempt to break down and recompose the corporate value chain by creating a division of labor among various organizations rather than internally (through vertical integration), as in the past. This extraorganizational division of labor often leads to different specializations among participating organizations, staking out specific functional niches for them. Such arrangements can create a consortium of corporate organizations aimed at, for example, research, production, marketing, or distribution.

This development is obviously more than "vertical disintegration" in the sense that rather than disposing of activities or simply outsourcing them, the mechanisms in question attempt to form a relational arrangement. No matter how they are viewed, however, these mechanisms constitute a shift of power out of individual corporations toward the consortium of organizations. Whether such consortia can be viewed as networks is an open question, since access is circumscribed and their network extent is limited. Nonetheless, whether regarded as networks or not, they tend to reflect the power shift out of corporations that accompanies decomposition.

This situation would have been unimaginable under industrial capitalism, with its emphasis on scale economies and internal control of most every corporate function. It is a symptom of the rapid advance of decomposition that the old stalwarts of industrial capitalism seem to be the organizations most heavily engaged in this process, not out of calculated choice but rather because they have no other alternative for survival. Examples of this phenomenon are all over the industrial spectrum inherited from industrial capitalism, from automotive industries to steel, shipbuilding, textiles, and home appliances, for example. Corporations that were symbolic of industrial capitalism are therefore becoming ghosts of their former selves, vacating much of their internal structures to establish external arrangements.

The mechanisms structuring these external arrangements come in various forms. One version is the "strategic alliance," whereby several organizations pool their resources to address a shared objective.

Whether for research, production, marketing, or distribution, strategic alliances have become more common as corporate organizations find their resources more limited to secure the intangibles they need.[22] Although it might be assumed that strategic alliances can be relational, most alliances today seem to be of the "fast" or temporary kind, where the activities targeted are narrowly defined, the temporal horizon is short-term, and the parties involved stay narrowly focused on their self-interest.[23] Such alliances negate the character of a relational arrangement, with its expected long accumulation of shared experience, trust, and reciprocity. The fact that they are "fast" and temporary may be a sign that organizations only get involved half-reluctantly because they have no alternative to access the intangibles they need.

Strategic alliances can provide access to intangibles that an organization may not be able to obtain on its own. However, such alliances can be difficult to structure and are subject to manipulation, subterfuge, and theft as participants gain insights on the "secrets" of their partners. If rising litigation is a sign, alliances are a prime vehicle for the appropriation of others' intellectual property, trade secrets, or ideas, if not the raiding of talented personnel.[24] Thus, the shift of power out of corporate organizations through alliances is fraught with peril and potential damage from partners. Herein lies a source of conflict, as technocapitalism's insatiable need for intangibles makes it necessary for organizations to seek outside what they cannot do internally.

Another form of alliance is the research unit to research unit (R2R) partnership. The R2R alliance is a focused mechanism for interorganizational collaboration. It might involve collaboration on a single research and development (R&D) project or on several. These alliances can be important in securing access to intangibles that are not well marketed or that are complex and expensive. Commodifying creativity obtained from researchers in various disciplines is a common objective. Examples can be found in various sectors associated with technocapitalism, such as biopharmaceuticals, nanotechnology, and bioinformatics, for example, but it can also involve research in old-line industries such as automotive design, home furnishings, textiles, and garment design.

"Spinning off" units as autonomous entities is another mechanism used to shift power out of the corporate domain. The units might remain part of a corporate organization, but the hierarchy of command

and control may be relaxed to allow greater initiative. In some cases, such units may be independent enough to enter into partnerships or joint ventures with other organizations on their own. In other cases, they might be spun off as companies legally independent of the parent corporate organization, with the latter nonetheless owning much of the new unit. These schemes in effect create subsidiary organizations, but can mislead the unknowing into believing they are "independent" companies when, in fact, they are not. Such tactics can be helpful for enticing other companies to enter into collaboration with a spun-off unit, which they might not be willing to do with the parent organization that owns the unit.

The compartmentalization of the value chain into "modules," where units or independent companies perform highly specialized activities, is another mechanism used to shift power out of a corporate core. Modularity may occur by setting up several autonomous companies that coordinate specialized functions, such as research or production.[25] Modular operations are often closer to outsourcing than to strategic alliances, although neither of these two mechanisms is exclusive of the other. Modularity may therefore overlap with other ways used to shift functions out of the corporate domain. In that regard, it can be seen as a way of accommodating to the power shift, by externalizing functions but retaining some control over them.

In the automotive industry, for example, it is possible to find modular operations where some companies manufacture transmissions, others produce engines, different companies supply the electronics, and others provide the remaining parts for the vehicles. In the heyday of industrial capitalism, all these activities would have been part of a single corporate organization. Vertical integration was the means of control. With modularity, vertical disintegration can be deepened substantially. Modular units using the Internet and Web, for example, can be easier to coordinate. Modularity can therefore be adapted to take advantage of contemporary information technology to coordinate units and retain some control, despite their external character.

Finally, the power shift out of corporate organizations also affects the relations of power *within* corporate organizations. This dynamic is often accompanied by an internal shift of power, from production to research. Because production can be parceled out (or outsourced), it ceases to have the importance it once had for corporate entities. The new internal balance of power can then favor those who deal with the most valuable resource—creativity.

Under industrial capitalism, the most powerful corporate positions were often those in charge of production.[26] Production specialists, engineers, and labor managers typically rose to the top of the corporate ladder by using their knowledge of production processes to impress their bosses. An alternative to this corporate caste was the group of "bean counters" or accountants who kept track of corporate finances. The most ambitious of the accountants often impressed their bosses by finding new ways to increase profitability. Enhancing investment ratings and providing glowing impressions of corporate health and wealth, without overtly breaking professional norms or laws, were part of their professional advancement schemes. Throughout the era of industrial capitalism, corporate command usually shifted between these two managerial castes.

In contrast, researchers and research operations were often isolated from the corporate centers of power in the heyday of industrial capitalism.[27] Research units all too often suffered from the corporate version of the "odd person out" syndrome, regarded more as a vehicle to impress potential investors and visitors to trade fairs than as essential elements of corporate survival. It is telling that many research departments of industrial capitalist corporations were often physically isolated from corporate headquarters or were out of touch with the daily goings-on of corporate power. It is a distinctive mark of technocapitalism that researchers now often find themselves in charge of corporate power, which is perhaps decomposed to a great extent, but nonetheless in command.

This evolving dynamic is having an impact on internal corporate aspects. There are many effects, certainly more than can be considered in this discussion. Among the more important ones is the attempt to redefine work in a way that blurs the line between toil and play. Work, in this corporatist "reinterpretation," must be "fun" and as much a "hobby" as possible. The idea of work as fun and hobby implies that work can be turned into play and play into work, if only one can adopt the "correct" mind-set that will make it so. The hobbyist can work endless hours on his or her hobby-craft and never mind much the tiresome aspects of what is done. A hobby is "fun" in the sense that there is a compulsion about it that forgets any accounting of the time or effort expended. Such forgetfulness is all too attractive to corporate power, as it aims to distract employees from claiming their rights.

Behind this subterfuge is the urgent need to commodify creativity, such that its results can be turned into market value by corporate power. The mental twist that attempts to equate toil with play (and vice versa) reflects the imperative to overcome the previously discussed difficulties of commodifying creativity. At the bottom of it is an effort to cope with the shift of power out of corporate governance by redefining internal tasks and work itself, such that some measure of control can be retained, no matter how temporary it may be.

The corporate environment is, after all, often antithetical to creativity. The exploitive nature of corporate power and its detrimental effect on creativity therefore has to be disguised as imaginatively as possible. Whether those who contribute their creativity to enrich corporate organizations can be fooled long enough to forget where and who they are may depend much on circumstance, but the aforementioned effect is one of the ways in which corporate power tries to cope with decomposition. The fact that so many corporate organizations fall short in this endeavor reflects how difficult it is to manipulate the complex intangibles involved.

A diagrammatic view of the effects of decomposition on corporate power, shown in Figure 7, may help synthesize these ideas. Decomposition, through its power shift out of corporate organizations, makes the corporation seem more a part (or product) of society. External networks and extraorganizational links, made necessary by the character and nature of creativity and other intangibles, therefore turn the corporation into a social element. At the same time, major internal changes are affecting corporate power, as can be seen by the shifting emphasis from production to research. New efforts to reinterpret the nature of work also reflect the urgent need to maintain control, despite the complex, externally reproduced intangibles needed to sustain corporate power.

Despite the power shift out of corporations, one must not lose sight of the fact that the commodification of creativity must be carried out *within* organizations. Power over commodification must be retained internally if any market value is to be obtained. The reproduction of

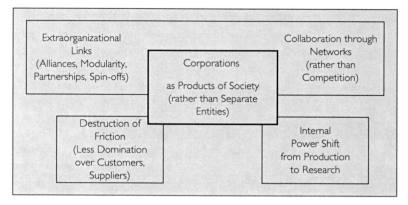

Figure 7 Consequences of the Power Shift from Corporatism to Society (and its Networks)

creativity, however, depends on external, network-based social mediation. Thus, while power over commodification is retained internally, corporate organizations nonetheless increasingly depend on external phenomena that are largely out of their control.

The power split between these two fundamental processes—commodification and reproduction—poses a major dilemma for corporations in the technocapitalist era. While power drifts out of corporate governance, organizations must nonetheless try to maintain control over commodification if any market value is to be obtained. This split is the source of much corporate dysfunction in our time, as will be discussed below.

Pathology of Decomposition

The power split between commodification and reproduction is at the core of the pathologies of decomposition. As power drifts out of corporate organizations toward networks and society, the conflict between the need to internally control commodification and the lack of influence over reproduction become a source of corporate dysfunction. Most contemporary corporate pathologies and their social effects ride on this conflict.

The frequent theft of intellectual property, as well as the predatory strategies, fraud, and other schemes aimed at taking advantage of those less capable of defending themselves are but a few symptoms of the power split noted above. The pressures placed on corporate organizations by this power split are substantial, if the pathologies are any indication, but they are not yet well understood. We may be observing only the tip of a deep and massive iceberg, whose consequences and future trajectory are still unknown.

A look back at industrial capitalism will reveal the absence of this fateful power split in corporate organizations. The corporations of industrial capitalism commodified and reproduced mostly *tangible* resources. The commodification and reproduction of those resources were usually undertaken *internally* within corporate organizations.[28] The corporations of industrial capitalism could therefore pretend to be *separate* from society, at least insofar as commodification and reproduction were concerned. External relations tied to reproduction never acquired the importance they have under technocapitalism. Consequently, the influence of external networks could be limited without damaging either the commodification or the reproduction of vital resources. This situation could be sustained because *both* processes were largely under the control of corporate power.

The pathological character of the power split between commodification and reproduction is therefore an important feature of decomposition and of contemporary corporatism. On the one hand, its split character forces corporate organizations to try to act as part of society in order to take advantage of networks and their vital role in the reproduction of creativity. But, on the other hand, it makes the need to maintain internal control over commodification all the more urgent, if any market value is to be obtained. The urgency of maintaining control over commodification cannot be ignored when technological invention and innovation proceed at a rapid pace. This means that lead times between a new product's entry and the introduction of rivals often decline to such a point that even the recovery of research costs becomes very uncertain.

Perhaps, then, it should not be surprising that so many corporate practices today seem psychopathic. The lack of a sense of moral obligation, the inability to understand fairness (especially at the social level), the obsession with extracting value to the exclusion of human and social needs, a prevalence of antisocial schemes and strategies, and the myopic attempts to maximize profits while shortchanging vital aspects of corporate life reflect the fundamental conflict between the external (the social) and the internal. Organizations that depend heavily on intangibles for survival are negatively affected by these psychopathic tendencies, given their conflict with aspects of external social mediation. At the root of this conflict is the fact that theories guiding corporate governance today deepen and compound these psychopathic tendencies.

Paradigm shifts are usually accompanied by new theories, but there are no new theories that can address the conflict between the external and internal power split of corporate governance. Instead, what one finds is a set of theories that is often poorly tailored to suit the corporate organizations of industrial capitalism.[29] These theories colonized business school curricula starting four decades ago, and they have left deep marks on the practice of corporate governance. Their pretense to be "scientific" has legitimized both the academic propaganda that supports them and their practice in corporate organizations. The prevalence of these theories today is at the root of the pathology of corporatism.

The practice of these theories has been widespread in most every area of corporate governance, and their maxims have been widely disseminated by the popular business media.[30] One does not need a management diploma to become familiar with their precepts. Their reach into the public's cognition has been such that it is easy for anyone involved in business to become familiar with their practice. Innumerable bits of practical advice and recipes can be found in every issue of any business magazine or newspaper. Practical individuals who think of themselves as not bound by theories or intellectual pursuits nonetheless become followers of their precepts. The widespread practice of these theories has effectively created the governance regimes that rule most every business organization today.[31] Their application has become accepted "best practice" in corporate management around the world. Their practice has been informally enforced in many ways, to the point that criticism of their precepts has often caused many a skeptic to be branded as incompetent or at least out of touch with "state-of-the-art" management thought.

An understanding of *how theories help determine corporate practice* (and the pathologies of decomposition) might be better understood if one looks at the situation from the perspective of the physical or natural sciences. In the natural sciences, theories do not determine outcomes. Outcomes are independent of theories and are not influenced by them. In biology, for example, a theory that assumes a given bacterium causes illness will change neither the behavior of the bacteria nor the illness in question. Similarly, in astrophysics, a theory that assumes a planet revolves around a certain star will not change the movement of either the star or the planet. This situation stands in sharp contrast with that of management theories and their practice.

Theories of management and corporate governance are usually self-fulfilling. This is because those who learn them adjust their behavior to comply with the prescribed conduct and precepts.[32] Thus, for example, profit maximization, which is at the core of management theory today (and is itself derived from neoclassical economic theories and models, as noted earlier), is taught as the primordial objective of corporate management. As a result, executives practicing the theory's tenets typically arrange all corporate functions to try to maximize profits, all too often obsessively, and all too frequently neglecting risk, damaging employee welfare, and disregarding ethics. The deep financial crisis that started in 2007 provided poignant examples of how the practice of such "optimization," which narrowly targets profits, can incur great risk in banking, not to mention the harm done to employees and to millions of people who stand to lose their money. Earlier on, the case of Enron illustrated how the practice of maximizing profits in any way led to the creation of shell companies to deceive investors, customers, regulators, and competitors. Such pathological applications of theories and precepts are all too frequent in corporate management today.

Thus, the practice of theories that on the surface may seem wise, harmless, or helpful often ends up becoming pathological in its substance and effects. The practice of game-based theories in corporate strategy has, for example, all too often degenerated into deceit of employees, customers, and the public at large. The fact that such practice often leads to better business performance then ends up serving as a model that others imitate. Subsequently, competitors who do not follow suit may end up shortchanging their own performance and otherwise harming themselves by becoming less competitive. Individuals who learn the theories and precepts (typically at business schools) and who may be quite honest at home or in their personal lives thus become part of the pathological apparatus of corporate practice, to the extent that their actions and decisions deceive or cheat others. They are, after all, simply using theories whose application is professionally accepted as "best practice."[33]

Self-fulfilling theories therefore modify the behavior of those involved in practicing them. Behaviors are adjusted because they are assumed to be instrumental in achieving a highly desirable outcome, such as higher profits, a more efficient extraction of value, or the appropriation of a kind of knowledge that leads to greater market control (as with important patents, for example). Self-fulfilling theories thus become "truth," whether they were right or wrong, as individuals modify their behavior to comply with the underlying precepts. In corporate governance, management is both consumer and controller of the practice of these theories, thereby eliminating most checks on their execution. As a result, the "truths" created by self-fulfilling theories tend to build on themselves, elevating what in the beginning might have been biased hunches into dogma and doctrine.

To the extent that theories are self-fulfilling, they are not scientific, and neither are management and corporate governance. The pretense of management and corporatism to be scientific in the same mold as the natural sciences is false, and their claim to be "science" seems to be little more than an attempt to legitimize what is actually propaganda and indoctrination. Unlike the natural sciences, where causal and functional explanations play important roles, in corporate governance, actions are guided by human *intent*.[34] Human intent is executed through behaviors *that can be adapted*. Indoctrination through the sort of "theories" commonly learned in business today often modify these behaviors on the basis of whether they are assumed to achieve the most desirable outcome, without adequate consideration of ethics, fairness, or moral obligation. Those who do not modify their behavior to suit these assumptions are regarded as less competent or, worse, as failures. Behaviors driven by intent, therefore, are based on precepts grounded in theory, whether or not one chooses to acknowledge it.

The pathology of decomposition and the psychopathy of corporatism are thus rooted in theories that are not only self-fulfilling and flawed, but which are also harmful in their application to corporate governance and its place in society. Many of the worst organizational pathologies and excesses of our time can be traced to them.[35] They can be particularly harmful to organizations that rely heavily on intangibles such as creativity. At some point, books may be written that will detail their wretched effects on the organizations and society of our time. For now, however, it is only possible to reflect on their role in a limited way, given the sparse information available and the obstacles that those who profit from their practice typically use to block this kind of discussion.

The theories in question have several common features. *First*, they support the conflict between the external and internal power split of corporate governance through very narrow views of how organizations should function. Their precepts typically single out one aspect (profit maximization being the usual one) and enthrone it as the most important objective of organizations, neglecting factors that may be more vital, particularly the intangible ones. *Second*, the context of the theories is typically *internal* to corporate organizations. Their practice and scope, therefore, is primarily a matter of internal corporate governance, and they tend to ignore the larger social context. In this regard, they are incompatible for dealing with external social relations, particularly those involving networks or their social mediation.

Third, any aspect of corporate governance that cannot be quantified is usually discarded or ignored. This tends to exclude creativity and other intangibles. Most qualitative factors share this fate. *Fourth*, the "scientific" claim of the theories allows them to adopt a fake functionalism that tries to mimic the physical or natural sciences. This creates the false impression that corporate organizations and their governance can be viewed as being separate from society, much as molecules, electrons, or cells in a laboratory setting. The theories' claim to be "science" also usually voids any consideration of ethics, fairness, moral obligation, or even legality. These considerations are all too often dismissed as "value judgments" that diminish the scientific clarity of the theories.

Fifth, the simplistic character of the theories makes them easy to teach and to learn. Simplistic theories are always easier to diffuse, learn, and understand than complex but more realistic explanations, particularly when the latter are intrinsically qualitative or defy easy quantification. The formulation of "recipes" for the widespread application of these theories is thus greatly facilitated. This can explain why business school curricula were easily colonized by them decades ago, and why the business media frequently uses them to provide recipes for action. *Sixth,* the theories are often inadequate for considering networks and tend to become dysfunctional or unworkable whenever this is attempted. This is partly the result of the general equilibrium models upon which most of them depend, and their unrealistic assumptions. In particular, the assumption of behavioral optimality is very crippling, but without it, general equilibrium models cannot be made to work. Since these models cannot consider networks or qualitative factors such as intangibles, fundamental aspects of decomposition (or of technocapitalism, in general) are ignored. Thus, reality tends to be pushed aside and ignored in favor of simplistic and unrealistic tenets.

Which, then, are the theories and how do they contribute to the pathology of decomposition? *Agency theory* assumes the maximization of "shareholder value" to be the sole objective of corporate organizations, where those in management are considered "agents" and shareholders are owners or "principals."[36] This theory draws heavily on the long-standing precept that corporate organizations have no social obligation other than to maximize profits for shareholders.[37] Agency theory was conceived to address what was regarded as the main problem of corporate governance: divergence between management's interests and those of shareholders. The alignment of those interests through incentives to management, such as stock options, was assumed to lead to the unfettered maximization of profits.

Agency theory neglects the role of those who contribute the vital intangibles that drive technocapitalism, such as creativity. Most of the time, those who contribute these intangibles are not "shareholders" to any significant extent, if at all. The theory is therefore biased in favor of those who contribute capital (the shareholders) over those who contribute the most valuable resource of our time—creativity. It is, however, usually easier for shareholders to sell shares or shift their capital elsewhere than it is for those who contribute creativity to claim their rights or change employers (or for their employers to replace them).

Moreover, shareholders are not actually "owners" of any business organization, as the theory assumes. They merely have a legal right to a portion of any profits made by a company. The assets of a company are actually owned by the legal entity that controls it, be it a partnership, corporation, proprietorship, or some other form. Such entities are *not* owned by shareholders in any legal way. Agency theory, therefore, discriminates against creativity, a resource that must be reproduced *externally* in favor of surplus value (or profits), which are instead mostly derived *internally* from commodification. This bias deepens the power split between the external (the social) and the internal by ignoring the former. It also makes organizations that depend on creativity very vulnerable if they follow the theory and ignore social aspects, such as networks or their social mediation, which are essential for reproducing creativity.

Given its flaws, it should not be surprising that empirical studies have found that the practice of agency theory often either fails or produces ambiguous results.[38] The theory, which dominates the practice of corporate governance today, is therefore being applied widely despite its apparent failings.[39] Since managers are both consumers and controllers of the theory, there are no real checks on its practice. Managers applying the theory want to "look good" to those who review their performance, and not practicing the theory would leave them with no other accepted tool to justify their actions. The theory's failings, therefore, are often covered up by blaming "exogenous" events or calamities, which usually have less importance than is claimed.

Agency theory partly keeps being taught and applied because it is supported by simplistic mathematical models (of the general equilibrium variety), which have been enthroned as "science" and are relatively easy to teach and learn. Unrealistic assumptions, such as the notion that agents and shareholders are perfectly rational, that employment markets are perfectly competitive and efficient, or that all parties involved have perfect foresight and invariably optimize their behavior, end up being mindlessly adopted regardless of the situation. Without those assumptions, the general equilibrium models that are the central pillar of the theory would become unworkable. Moreover, agency theory actually has little value for either explanation or forecasting.[40] The fact that this theory dominates both academic management thought and the practice of corporate governance today makes the latter dysfunctional when decomposition and technocapitalism are taken into account.

Competition theory is a second, widely diffused theoretical framework guiding corporate governance.[41] It is typically allied with agency theory and supports it by claiming that competition makes profit maximization essential for survival. Agency and competition theories therefore rely on one another to buttress their claims. Competition is, in and of itself, narrowly assumed to lead to greater benefits and value, regardless of its consequences. Thus, negative social consequences are either ignored or are implicitly assumed to be less harmful than the lack of competition itself. As a result, competition theory usually limits its scope to corporations and to their actions in the marketplace. For corporate governance, the theory and its practical weapon, competitive strategy, implicitly assume that *no one* can be trusted—not managers, employees, partners, suppliers, customers, or even shareholders.

Trust, a fundamental ingredient of networks and social mediation, is therefore practically cast out of corporate governance by competition theory. Perhaps, then, it should not be surprising that distrust, subterfuge, and predatory tactics characterize contemporary corporate competitive strategies.[42] The innumerable (and increasing) lawsuits over intellectual property, and the fraud, theft, and dishonesty that can be found in many aspects of corporate governance bear witness to the theory's antisocial character.[43] Distrust and predatory behavior therefore make competition theory and its practice fundamentally incompatible with social mediation through networks. The predatory behavior fomented by the practice of the theory would damage network relations, which are typically based on trust, reciprocity, and the long-term accumulation of goodwill. One could not find a better tool to poison the network-based, socially mediated reproduction of creativity than the strategic "recipes" provided by advocates of competition theory.

Competition theory was, in part, a product of the corporate structures of industrial capitalism. Competitive strategies are mostly *internal* to corporate organizations in terms of their formulation and execution. The narrow strategies that the theory spawns are typically formulated under the internal control of corporate management and are often implemented in a climate of secrecy and subterfuge. They therefore seem more appropriate to the time when vertical integration, mass production, and one-dimensional executives ruled the corporatist landscape.[44] Also, the strategies spawned by competition theory tend to be mostly concerned with the vital resources of industrial capitalism, such as capital, raw materials, or labor. The complexities of intangibles, their reproduction and commodification, not to mention the social relations upon which they depend, are too much for the theory's simplistic mind-set.

Competition theory makes decomposition dysfunctional to the extent that external ties such as alliances, partnerships, joint ventures, and outsourcing arrangements become subject to opportunistic or predatory behavior. Also, competitive strategies are *internally* based, with corporate self-interest as the uppermost priority. Internal control is especially important to competitive strategies because of its importance for execution. This exacerbates the split between the external and internal dimensions of corporate organizations in the context of technocapitalism.

An example of the negative effects of the theory and its strategies is the increasing emphasis on development work over research in corporate research and development (R&D) departments. This domination of development over research is largely a product of competitive strategies that value short-term, lower-risk, and "fast money" schemes over longer-term, higher-risk, but potentially more significant research.[45] The antisocial character of these strategies is often encapsulated by the term "second-mover research," meaning development work that can pilfer the work of other companies that invested in higher-risk (and potentially more significant) projects. Technological espionage today involves mostly second-mover research. Strategies involving second-mover research can range from the theft of ideas that are then used or sold as proprietary, to reverse engineering schemes aimed at copying new inventions in ways that cannot be legally challenged.[46]

Second-mover research often receives top priority when companies forego external research networks and their social mediation. Second-mover research, therefore, is usually completely *internal* to organizations and under the control of management. The authoritarian character of corporate governance tends to favor second-mover research, not only because it can be controlled but also because it tends to have lower risk, less uncertainty, and shorter time horizons than first-mover (or basic) research. After all, second-mover research helps avoid the higher expenses that the first-mover kind usually incurs, and lowering costs is a major concern for any profit maximizer. Since second-mover research activities are internal, it helps management avoid the sort of scrutiny that would occur through external networks, which would likely expose any pilfering of others' ideas or intellectual property, thereby raising the risk of litigation.

Paradoxically, however, networks and their social mediation can make companies more competitive, although not through the precepts or strategies espoused by competition theory. For example, companies that join business-to-business (B2B), Web-based supply networks can gain entry into sectors that might have otherwise been closed to them.[47] They can also establish relations with other companies, large or small, that would not have been possible without the networks. However, these networks tend to operate under principles that are quite different from the ones espoused by competition theory. In order to become competitive through such networks, companies must usually establish collaborative relations based on trust and reciprocity. Building trust is typically based on experience and interactions that occur over long periods of time, rather than the fast-money, predatory schemes that usually accompany competitive strategies.

Another instance of how external networks make business organizations more capable can be found in research collaboration. Organizations that do not have sufficient resources of their own to undertake some projects can only hope to be successful through such collaboration. To be successful, external research collaboration must rely on a division of labor between participants that is based on trust and mutual support rather than undermining each other, taking advantage of each others' weaknesses, and similar tactics found in competitive strategies. Collaboration through external networks and their social mediation may therefore make organizations more effective by providing an alternative to the toxic effects of competition theory and its strategies.

However, one should not lose sight of the antithetical character of collaboration and competition. External networks and their social mediation might make organizations more capable, but they do not resolve the antithetical nature of collaboration and competition. At best, a network might make its participants competitive with respect to organizations in *other* networks or with respect to stand-alone organizations not participating in any network, but competition in and of itself usually introduces negative tendencies, regardless of its mode. Unfortunately, competition theory typically does not address those tendencies or their cost to society.

Organizations and their strategies are therefore intrinsically conceived by competition theory to be *separate* from society (if not practically antisocial). Moreover, the separation of corporate organizations from society is supported by regulations that grant them all the rights of individuals, but few or none of the social obligations. Entities that have no obligation to society tend to have little or no understanding of fairness and morality. Their actions may thus turn out to be little different from those of wild beasts, where trouncing rivals, destroying them, or driving them into the ground become acts worthy of admiration, regardless of their human and social consequences.[48]

The third theoretical framework contributing to the pathologies in decomposition is *transaction cost theory*. This framework assumes opportunistic behavior to be the source of transaction costs.[49] The theory believes that opportunism creates uncertainty, and coping with uncertainty requires covenants. Transactions must, according to the theory, be based on contracts in order to contain opportunism. Transaction cost theory thus implicitly assumes that individuals and organizations cannot be trusted. Contracts then become the only means to make them fulfill their promises. And, in the theory's eye, corporate organizations are the best vehicle to contain opportunism, enforce contracts, and minimize transaction costs.[50]

Trust is practically cast out of transaction cost theory. This vital ingredient of networks thus becomes mostly irrelevant in the tenets and practice of the theory. Ethics, morals, social obligation, or questions of fairness are also implicitly discarded.[51] What count instead are corporate power and contracts, and the power of a corporate organization must be relied upon to lower transaction costs by enforcing contracts. Employees, partners, contractors, and even shareholders thus become little more than commodities to be distrusted and submitted by the power of corporate organizations. Corporate governance structures become the means to enforce contracts, but in order to do so, they must have control over all corporate functions.

The power shift from corporations to society therefore poses a major challenge for transaction cost theory. For decomposition and for the larger context of technocapitalism, the theory is not only dysfunctional but also pathological in its effects. Intangibles such as creativity are far more important than transaction costs for most contemporary corporate organizations, and contracts are not the only means to ensure that human beings live up to what they promise. Moreover, the reproduction of intangibles requires social mediation and trust to be effective.

The elimination of social mediation, trust, morals, ethics, and other qualities from the theory thus creates the impression that corporate organizations and their transactions are either *separate* from society or that their power must be imposed on society if society is to function. Transaction cost theory also tends to ignore networks as an alternative to corporate organizations in securing transactions. The theory thus assumes markets to be the *only* alternative to corporate organizations. However, markets are assumed to work only when transactions do not involve opportunistic behavior. When such behavior occurs, corporate organizations are believed to provide the only means of reducing transaction costs. This simplistic outlook leaves out the social vitality of networks for accomplishing collaborative relations that are not based on contractual agreements.

The theory's confinement to either corporate organizations *or* markets as the only vehicles of transactions also has its roots in the era of industrial capitalism. The internalization and control of transactions in corporate organizations were made possible by the *tangible* character of the resources that were commodified and reproduced. In other words, the most valuable resources of industrial capitalism were commodified and reproduced internally. Obtaining those resources required contracts whenever simple market transactions could not provide them fast enough or in sufficient quantity. Transaction cost theory could function and seem relevant as long as power could be kept within corporate organizations, vested in governance structures that could commodify and reproduce the tangible resources needed to obtain market value.

The theory's dysfunctional character therefore surfaces when the shift of power from corporate organizations to networks is taken into account. To the extent that networks are left out of consideration, the theory is inadequate for understanding the decomposition of corporate structures. As a result, transaction cost theory is unable to grasp one of the most important phenomena of technocapitalism. The theory's tenets thus become irrelevant to most activities that depend on networks, from Open Source software research to distributed computing, to the innumerable collaborative research webs that are part of the emerging technocapitalist era.

Transaction cost theory's tenets, taught and diffused widely through management education and the popular business media, have become self-fulfilling, much like the precepts of competition and agency theories. Those who are trained in transaction cost theory may come to assume that trust is a utopian aberration and that all parties to contracts must be regarded with suspicion. As trust, ethics, and other qualities are cast out and stripped of any role by the theory, dishonesty ends up being considered negatively *only* because it creates "inefficiencies," and its opposite (honesty) becomes desirable simply because it "saves resources."[52]

Transaction cost theory therefore shares the antisocial tendencies of competition and agency theories. Functionally, it also shares their narrow scope when it assumes that minimizing transaction costs is (or should be) the main objective of corporate organizations. In the theory's eye, costs are assumed to be subject to greater control than most any other aspect of corporate governance (including profits). Organizations that try to maximize profits usually do so by attempting to minimize costs. Since the theory views most activities under the control of corporate organizations as "transactions," minimizing transaction costs can fit in seamlessly with the analytical contraptions and profit-maximizing dictates of the other two theories. It should not be surprising, therefore, that transaction cost theory has become a staple of management education along with agency and competition theories.

Through their influence on corporate practices, the troika of agency, competition, and transaction cost theories are at the root of many contemporary corporate pathologies. At no previous time did theories influence corporate practices to the extent they do now. The practices they spawned deepen the power split between the commodification and reproduction of creativity that makes decomposition dysfunctional. Yet, there are currently no alternatives to their widespread influence on corporate practices. To the extent that these theories continue to be believed and practiced, decomposition, networks, and creativity will pose formidable challenges to corporate organizations.

Conclusion

The decomposition of corporate structures inherited from industrial capitalism is a major feature of technocapitalism. The corporation, an icon of industrial capitalism, faces a fundamental transformation of its governance and social relations. The external social context is becoming more important than ever, as corporate organizations find it impossible to reproduce vital resources on their own. The times when corporate organizations could consider themselves separate from society are therefore coming to a close.

As networks and their social mediation are the prime vehicles for decomposition, internal control is subverted. The corporation can no longer exercise the power over resources that it once commanded. Corporate organizations may be perceived more as products of society as internal structures are decomposed. Decomposition thus relies greatly on external network extent and the social mediation it provides. Reproducing the vital intangibles, enlisting collaboration, and reducing uncertainty therefore provide external networks with potential influence over corporate organizations.

The decomposition of power toward networks and society, however, poses a critical dilemma to the corporation. While networks take up a vital role in reproducing creativity and other intangibles, commodification remains largely under the control of corporate organizations. Therefore, the power of the corporation becomes split between functions that must remain internal and those that must become external.

The power split confronting the corporation and the rising importance of networks thus become a source of pathology for corporate power. Many of the psychopathic tendencies of corporate governance can be traced to this fateful power split. However, these tendencies are also rooted in theories and strategies that influence contemporary corporate practices. To the extent that corporate practices follow these theories, decomposition may deepen the pathologies that plague corporate power. Only by freeing corporate governance from their influence can decomposition spawn organizational forms that are accountable to society and serve human needs.

Experimentalist Organizations

The experimentalist organization is the corporate arm of techno-capitalism. Its aim, to control the commodification of creativity, is of paramount importance for this new version of capitalism. This chapter considers the distinctive features of this new form of corporatism, its external and internal relations of power, and the pathologies it generates.

The experimentalist organization is defined through its intense orientation toward research. It is a corporate form of organization that embodies the ethos of *experimentalism*, as discussed in an earlier chapter. The commodification of creativity is the most important function of the experimentalist organization. It is the means through which this organizational mode tries to come up with new inventions and innovations. The experimentalist corporation is, to a large extent, a *decomposed* organization. It must therefore rely greatly on external networks and society to reproduce its most important resource—creativity.

Research creativity is the lifeblood of the experimentalist corporation. Appropriating its results and obtaining market value are its main concerns. Its apparatus of power and control revolves around creativity, hoping to secure new inventions for commercial gain. The experimentalist corporation therefore lives or dies by research creativity. At no previous time in history has corporatism depended so much on this *intangible* resource to secure power and profit.

The nature of creativity, however, is antithetical to commodification, which requires elaborate organizational arrangements that often fail to provide results. Research creativity is risky, uncertain, and its results are usually difficult, if not impossible, to anticipate. Its qualitative, multifaceted, and dynamic character defies attempts to standardize it. Moreover, creativity typically requires a substantial, long-term accumulation of knowledge and experience to flourish.

The corporations of industrial capitalism, in contrast, lived by and for production. Factories were the icon of corporate power. The main resources of industrial capitalism were tangible and quantifiable; repetitive routines based on the use of raw materials, capital, labor power, and production hardware were fundamental for its existence. Its know-how was standardized, and operations typically required training and diligence but little creativity. Also, given the tangible nature of industrial capitalism's main resources, their commodification and reproduction could be controlled internally. This internal control often induced industrial corporatism to consider itself separate from society, with little or no obligation except to look after its own narrow interests.

The experimentalist organization, however, must confront the power split that accompanies the internal (corporate) and external (social) dimensions of creativity. This is a formidable challenge, given its *decomposed* organizational context. The construction of a peculiar organizational arrangement is required to try to control the commodification of creativity internally, while articulating the external relations that must reproduce this vital resource. This organizational arrangement, or research regime, attempts to oversee all matters related to research and is a major feature of the experimentalist organization.

Systematized Research Regimes

Systematizing research is at the core of the experimentalist organization. Systematization means that experimental research must always be the uppermost concern, undertaken without interruption (that is, continuously), as part of a general plan or framework that encompasses activities for which research creativity is fundamental. *A systematized research regimen is therefore an organizational structure constructed to manipulate research processes, such that creativity can be commodified.*

Unlike the corporations inherited from industrial capitalism, organizations operating under systematized research regimes are focused on research. In the conventional corporation, production, marketing, or distribution are balanced against research or will have more weight in the scheme of corporate governance.[1] In organizations operating under systematized research regimes, however, research may be the *only* organizational function. If other functions exist, research will dominate them in the scale of values of corporate governance. Under the systematized research regimen, all the avenues of corporate power lead to (or from) research.

Organizations operating under systematized research regimes tend to be overwhelmingly concerned with *intangibles*. The conventional corporation's preoccupation with raw materials, capital, supply chains, and other aspects relevant to production is a dangerous distraction for a company that operates under a systematized research regime. Corporate strategy and governance are therefore targeted to commodify intangibles. This is all very much in contrast with the companies typical of industrial capitalism, which targeted the exploitation of tangible resources, such as raw materials, capital, and labor power.[2]

The importance of research creativity for corporate survival often places research-grounded engineers or scientists in command of the experimentalist corporation. Intimate understanding of the intricacies of research functions is therefore valuable to those lusting for executive power in organizations with systematized research regimes. This characteristic stands apart from the corporations typical of industrial capitalism, where the reins of power were often in the hands of financial schemers, bean counters, or production specialists.

Evidence on systematized research organizations can be found in any of the sectors spawned by technocapitalism. Systematized research regimes are very much in evidence in gene-decoding companies, for example. The functions of corporate governance revolve around gene-decoding research operations, and little or nothing else. Gene decoding is but a stepping-stone toward appropriating the results of research creativity, as patents are sought for each and every decoded gene. Thus, life's most important feature is turned into property by systematically targeting research creativity to find new genes.

Systematized research regimes have turned companies such as Celera and Incyte into proprietors of new genetic knowledge, which they subsequently license or sell to pharmaceutical, chemical, or agroindustrial companies.[3] Their extremely profitable clearinghouse role, as owners and providers of genetic knowledge, is the result of an organizational model sustained by systematized research that targets the extraction of market value (and property rights) from research creativity. Nowhere in the corporate histories of industrial capitalism can one find an example comparable to this phenomenon—in the character and magnitude of its scope or in its overwhelming dependence on research creativity.

In biopharmaceuticals, systematized research regimes have generated some of the wealthiest corporations in the United States. Genentech, for example, the richest biotech company and consistently among the top twenty American companies in market capitalization, owes its position as the foremost example of biocorporatism to its systematized research regime.[4] The research regime was narrowly targeted to exploit research creativity related to oncology, immunology, and tissue repair compounds, in an attempt to reduce high uncertainty and risk. Ten or more years from the experimental stage to regulatory approval are often required for every compound tested, with rejection rates as high as eight thousand to one. The cost of turning out a single medication is often in the hundreds of millions of dollars.

At Genentech, systematizing research to reduce risk generated experimental processes that can yield multiple medications out of a compound. Alternatively, systematized research can yield single medications that can be used in diverse ways. The company licenses most medications to major pharmaceutical companies to sell or use, thus eliminating the dangerous distraction of articulating large production, sales, or distribution units. About one-third of revenues are consistently reinvested in research to sustain its research regime. Highly experienced researchers have always held the reins of corporate power. Genentech's systematized research regime is simply too important for the company's survival to be placed under the command of accountants, bookkeepers, or stock market wizards. Systematized research is therefore at the core of the company's extraction of value from scientific creativity.

Systematized research regimes are also very much in evidence in other sectors closely related to technocapitalism. In nanotechnology, bioinformatics, microchips, and software design, for example, corporate governance typically revolves around systematized research.[5] Even though functions such as production, marketing, or distribution may coexist with research, organizations that generate cutting-edge technology subordinate all operations to the research regime. This situation applies whether companies in those sectors are engaged in competition with similar organizations or whether they monopolize their sectors and customer markets. And, regardless of whether they compete or monopolize, the reins of power and decision tend to be firmly in the hands of highly experienced researchers.

The overarching concern of systematized research regimes with intangibles results in three distinctive features that are characteristic of their governance. These features mold the organizational culture of systematized research regimes, and they affect the internal relations of power that influence the commodification of creativity. The *first* and most obvious feature is the attempt to *manipulate* any and all aspects related to research creativity. *All* aspects of creative research are targets in the organizational culture of the systematized research regime, driven by the need to limit the high risks and uncertainty that affect commodification.

Attempts to control and manipulate research in the systematized regime revolve about creative power. *Creative power* can be defined as the potential for creativity of individuals and groups working under a systematized research regime. The exercise of creative power applies to any research activity where creativity is deployed for commercial gain. Creative power is what the systematized research regime attempts to harness in order to commodify research creativity.[6] Its results decide whether the process of commodification will succeed in overcoming uncertainty and extracting value from research creativity.

Providers of creative power part with any possibility of controlling its usage, effects, or value once the corporate organization appropriates its results through the systematized research regime. Once that occurs, the results of their creative power belong to them as little as, say, gold that has been sold belongs to the miner who provided it. This form of *alienation* is intrinsic to the commodification of research creativity through the systematized research regime. It seems unrealistic to believe that providers of creative power are adequately compensated for their exercise of creativity once its results are appropriated by corporate power. The annals of corporate history are filled with cases of misappropriation or outright theft from those who contribute creativity to corporate enrichment.[7]

The objective of creative power in the systematized research regime is part of this process of alienation. The objective of creative power is *to create value*. In contrast, the objective of the production regimes of industrial capitalism was to *add* value to raw materials, capital, or the labor process. Adding value was fundamentally important to the production regimes of industrial capitalism, given that commodification involved *tangible* resources, first and foremost. Creating value, however, is all about *intangibles* and it must fundamentally involve creativity in order to occur.

Creating value through intangibles makes it easier to alienate any results of creative power from those who provide it. This occurs because, under technocapitalism, the value extracted is *separable* from creative power (and creativity).[8] Thus, value can exist apart from any new ideas, processes, formulas, methods, or services after creative power is exercised and commodification occurs. The value of patents, decoded genetic data, formulas, or software code is therefore separable from those who contributed their creative power to make them happen *and* from the uses that are made of them.[9]

Despite the fundamental importance of creative power, it is difficult (and often impossible) to assess its worth to the systematized research regime. This occurs because creative power is essentially qualitative and its parameters (and potential) are very uncertain. Creative power is typically not marketed, partly because it defies quantification, but also because it is usually circumstantial to the organizational contexts in which it is embedded. The same individuals who provide it in one organization are often unsuccessful once removed from that context and its social relations. It is often very difficult, if not impossible, to transfer it from one organizational context to another.[10] Creative power, therefore, defies the sort of standardization upon which its marketing would depend.

This condition subverts the attempt to control all aspects of research creativity, which is a major feature of any systematized research regime. At the same time, it makes the intent to have such control all the more urgent, given the importance of creative power for the research regime. The urgent need to control it often damages the research environment, however, as it introduces authoritarian measures that regiment or stifle the very resource—creativity—that is at the core of creative power. It should not be surprising, therefore, that organizations often fail in their attempt to control creative power and end up resorting to theft or fraud in order to sustain their research programs.

A *second* feature of the systematized research regime is its recurring use of *artifices* to conceal the process of alienation discussed in earlier chapters, and the appropriation of talent that commodification entails. This feature encompasses a multitude of tactics, all of them targeting the concoction of creativity that reduces human actions to "recipes" that attempt to make alienation less noticeable. A quick glance at any business magazine or the many "how-to" management books published nowadays will reveal how much they have infiltrated management practice and education.

A fairly common artifice is the attempt to concoct research creativity through analytical templates, which provide a framework for making analytical choices and are mostly used for modifying products.[11] Through the templates, the functions of a product are deconstructed to try to understand them as relationships. The "relationships" are then changed, expanded, or contracted to see how and whether a new version of a product can be concocted. Clearly, this artifice to manufacture research creativity is quite rudimentary in its scope and possibilities. It cannot be considered a substitute for the reproduction of creativity. At best, it aims to support or enhance commodification by increasing the possibilities of tweaking a product in the hope that doing so will obtain more market value.

Template "creativity" typically fails to produce much research creativity (broadly speaking) and falls short of enhancing the larger element of creative power. Both of them encompass much more than the methodical deconstruction of existing products. This artifice is therefore unsuitable to the kind of creativity that results in technological breakthroughs. Most of all, it is inadequate for the highly complex, multifaceted, interpretive, and uncertain nature of research tasks in the research regimes of technocapitalism. Nonetheless, the pressure to commodify creativity by any and all means has led many corporations to use this artifice. By reducing the role of creativity to simplistic templates, this artifice supports (and trivializes) the alienation of researchers from the results of their talent.

Another artifice involves allowing autonomous initiative to a group of researchers within the systematized research regime. By subverting the internal status quo, this artifice usually tries to harness creative power for specific projects. It is often part of an attempt to establish a new research platform that will expand the research regime's scope and scale. This approach can be traced to the notion of "intrapreneuring," a management idea that was widely diffused during the last years of the twentieth century.[12]

The need to bring together multidisciplinary expertise on research projects often drives the autonomous initiative artifice. In most activities related to technocapitalism, multidisciplinarity is the norm. Nanotechnology research, for example, often brings together physicists, chemical engineers, computer scientists, physicians, mechanical engineers, biopharmacologists, electronic engineers, and microbiologists. Similarly, software research projects can require software designers, graphic artists, linguists, computer scientists, broadcasters, and electronic engineers to work together. Allowing autonomy can help such diverse groups of researchers pursue interests that are out of the scope of "normal" research regime governance. Relaxing control to permit these groups to self-organize or to work across research functions can enhance creative power, albeit temporarily.

The artifice of autonomous initiative may provide an illusion of control over the results of one's work. However, this scheme poses a serious problem for most research regimes. It is difficult to put an end to autonomous initiative when it is no longer needed, as usually occurs when a project ends or the research regime's priorities change. Once the genie of autonomy is out of the bottle, it may no longer be possible to tuck it back inside without some ruthless coercion. A return to authoritarian control, which is part and parcel of corporatist governance, may thus leave a bad feeling in the minds of those who operated under the illusion of self-governance that this artifice creates. Whenever this occurs, individual creativity and the creative power of the regime itself may be seriously impaired.

Emphasizing intrinsic over extrinsic incentives is another artifice commonly used by research regimes. Extrinsic incentives are grounded in traditional reward tools, such as salaries, promotions, or stock options. Intrinsic incentives, however, appeal to either altruism or self-esteem, such as the potential benefit of a research project to humanity, its importance to "science," eventual recognition from peers, or the legitimacy that might be conferred on researchers' credentials.

The intrinsic rewards artifice is based on long-standing behaviorist notions and on recent derivatives elaborated by some management specialists.[13] The fundamental assumption of this artifice is that research creativity can be enhanced if intrinsic incentives are emphasized over extrinsic ones. Its application may involve some loosening of the authoritarian control that is part and parcel of corporate governance. It may, for example, involve the "reconstruction" of a research unit as a "community" by lacing narratives and corporatist propaganda with selected intrinsic incentives that are then presented as "corporate values."[14] In its more ridiculous versions, it may also try to induce the members of a research unit to think of themselves as a "family." To promote empathy among the various echelons of the corporate "family," it may even resort to improvisational theatre in order to act out situations and enhance sensitivity.[15]

Appearances to the contrary, the intrinsic rewards artifice is a scheme concocted to make alienation and corporate appropriation more palatable to those who provide creative power. The top priority of the systematized research regimes of technocapitalism is to commodify creativity. Without it, market value cannot be obtained. The intrinsic rewards artifice can, at best, try to disguise alienation for those who provide creative power.

The integration of these artifices into contemporary management practice reflects the pressures under which systematized research regimes operate. As Figure 8 depicts, the aforementioned artifices are part of the effort to manipulate research processes (and those who provide creative power) such that commodification can occur. The articulation of these artifices in the systematized research regime has parallels with some measures employed by the factory regimes of industrial capitalism.[16] Among them, for example, were programs aimed at making workers purchase company stock to try to induce sentiments of co-ownership. Other, more evolved measures aimed to produce

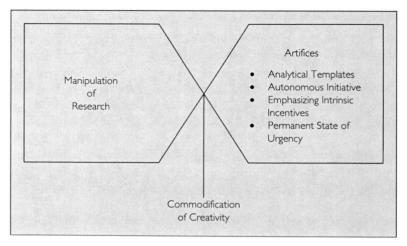

Figure 8   Artifices for Control

greater quality through peer pressure and teamwork. The artifices used in the systematized research regime are different in character and scope, but they nonetheless share a common objective with the ones used in the factory regimes of industrial capitalism. At the root of all these artifices is the attempt to reduce the alienation that is part of any process of commodification.

A *third* feature of the systematized research regime is its permanent state of *urgency* on all aspects related to the timing and speed of research activities. Urgency in the systematized research regime is bidimensional. It reflects the corporatist angst of preparing for the unexpected *and* it is also a symptom of an obsessive preoccupation to respond "fast" whenever the unexpected happens.[17]

On these two dimensions rides the culture of urgency of the systematized research regime. In contrast with the hierarchical governance of industrial capitalism and its "organization man" mind-set, the systematized research regime relies on "agents of change." These agents must forever rush to capture the next "great discovery" by articulating the cutting-edge creative power that will supposedly provide it. The usual mission of such "agents" is to implement controls over the researchers who must provide the creative power and (eventually) the "fast" research results. The "agents" must perforce be intimately acquainted with the projects they oversee and are themselves often involved in research.

But why is "fast" research needed? A major force driving the need for "fast" research is the race to create new technology. This race depends upon the rapid generation of new inventions and innovations and their usage in new products and services. Rival new products and services are being introduced faster than ever before, given the globalization of the technology race. Fending off unexpected rivals is therefore a major concern of the systematized research regime. Having to cope with serious unforeseen circumstances, or rivals, is among the most frightening in the gamut of "unexpected" contingencies.

The corporatist psychosis that results from the fear of preemption by rivals is a part of the systematized research regime. Preemption by a rival may foreclose the possibility of surplus value (or profit), not to mention the recovery of research costs. One of the common manifestations of this psychosis is, for example, the setting of unattainable targets or deadlines for research projects. For those who contribute creative power, meeting an unrealistic deadline often means having to meet equally (or even more) unrealistic ones later on. A climate of fear often accompanies this state of affairs, as failing to meet the target can provide an excuse for humiliation, demotion, or dismissal.

Another driver of the "fast" research syndrome is the obsessive corporate preoccupation with short-term financial performance, which typically requires a rapid stream of inventions and innovations that can be brought to market in the form of new products or services. Fast creative power, fast commodification, and fast market exchange thus become a corporate imperative. Short-term financial performance is fundamentally important for maximizing "shareholder value," which is the central tenet of agency theory, as discussed in the chapter "Decomposing the Corporation."[18] The "agents of change" in the systematized research regime therefore also become the "agents" charged with maximizing shareholder value. The narrow concern with short-term performance and the psychosis behind "fast" research itself are thus among the sources of contemporary corporate pathology, as we will see below.

A narrow focus on short-term financial performance can produce "fast" research, but it can also cause considerable harm to creative power. The bias of corporatism toward short-term performance can shortchange the interests of those who provide creative power, leading to their greater alienation, abuse, or demoralization. It is a tribute to the narrow-minded character of today's management education that short-term financial performance is usually touted as the uppermost objective of corporate governance. Its effect is to compound the climate of fear and anxiety that grips most research regimes by placing short-term gain over longer-term (and potentially more socially beneficial) results.

The need to compress research and development (R&D) time is another driver of the state of urgency. Compression of R&D time often leads a systematized research regime to configure sequential research or development activities in parallel.[19] Parallelism is widely used in biotechnology and biopharmacology, for example, to compress the time needed for clinical testing of new compounds. Similarly, in bioinformatics research, software code writing activities and testing are often done simultaneously in disparate parts of the world, using Internet- and Web-based communications to confer, coordinate, or test.

Another way to compress R&D time is to program research in a modular way. This requires setting up research groups or teams as "modules" to deal with a research project or its components.[20] Modularity can compress research time in situations where autonomy and a limited scope would speed up tasks, as in the case of parallel experimentation. In software design, for example, modular organization of research teams can allow subcomponents of a new software application to be designed simultaneously, following ground rules that allow the various parts to be assembled later. This organizational scheme has allowed companies such as Microsoft to come up with extensive software programs or applications in shorter time horizons.

Eliciting feedback or active cooperation from customers can also help compress R&D time. Schemes of "user involvement" in product development are a clever way for research regimes to use or even appropriate others' ideas without legal obligations or any sharing of profits.[21] Users freely surrender their time and creativity to "help" corporate power and profit, receiving nothing in return except the hope that perhaps the next version of the product they purchase might perform better than the last one. This clever stratagem can therefore shift some of the time and cost of development to customers. In the calculus of corporate power, this scheme can be supported as long as the trouble and costs of coordination are more than offset by whatever advantages are gained.

How far can the compression of research time go? Clearly, a reduction in research and development time can only increase the pressure for further reductions. The corporatist demand for "fast" research tends to be insatiable when viewed from the perspective of "shareholder value maximization" and the global race for new technology. It is unrealistic to imagine that the state of urgency that characterizes the systematized research regime can be relaxed as long as the pressure to commodify creativity exists. The pressure to commodify creativity is as fundamental a feature of technocapitalism as gravity is to everything on the earth's surface.

Collaboration and Power

The systematized research regime cannot resolve the fundamental contradiction between the internal (commodification) and external (reproduction) dimensions of creativity, addressed in previous chapters. The artifices, manipulation, and state of urgency that the systematized research regime resorts to cannot internalize the reproduction of creativity within organizations, no matter how efficient, clever, or ruthless the regime's governance happens to be. This is why *external* collaboration is essential if the reproduction of creativity is to occur. And, without the reproduction of creativity, its commodification cannot be sustained.

The reproduction of creativity must unavoidably occur through the social mediation that external, network-based collaboration allows. The complex, multidisciplinary stimuli, knowledge, and social relations required to reproduce creativity can only be accessed through networks and collaboration. Practically all the activities and organizations typical of technocapitalism (and their research regimes) rely on diverse talents and fields of endeavor. It is impossible for these organizations or their research regimes to secure all the resources needed to reproduce creativity internally. Research is indeed a complex endeavor in the age of technocapitalism, if not the most complex human activity of our time in terms of talents, knowledge, and hardware. Therefore, external collaboration through networks and the social mediation they facilitate is essential if the reproduction of creativity is to be sustained enough to allow commodification to occur.

This situation contrasts greatly with that of industrial capitalism, where the most important resources could be reproduced internally because the resources in question were *tangible*, whereas in the case of the experimentalist organization they are *intangible*. The organizations of industrial capitalism were also concerned with *production* first and foremost, while the organizations typical of technocapitalism live or die by their *research*. Also, reproduction could occur internally in the organizations of industrial capitalism because the tangible resources, and production itself, had limited complexity or could be standardized (and made serial or repetitive) and could be monitored by personnel who mostly required *training* but little creativity in and of itself.[22]

In the technocapitalist organization, in contrast, research creativity cannot be force-fitted into a standardized blueprint or operational mold that might allow it to be reproduced mechanically. The creativity needed by the systematized research regime is a resource that requires education in place of training, social mediation instead of isolation, new thinking rather than mechanical repetition, great persistence and reflection instead of mind-numbing routines, and a lot of complex, uncodified knowledge and experience in place of simple know-how. Creativity, the most important resource of technocapitalism, defies any attempt to be specified in how-to manuals, unlike the resources of industrial capitalism.

Moreover, creativity cannot be easily (if at all) marketed in any precise or quantitative sense, as were the tangible resources of industrial capitalism. There are no (and there may never be) standardized "creativity markets" from which the technocapitalist organization can draw the talent it needs, in contrast with the capital, labor, or raw material markets that were easily tapped by the corporations of industrial capitalism. In contrast with the capital, labor, or raw material markets upon which industrial capitalism depended, finding creativity through any market mechanism is a very uncertain and risky proposition.

The systematized research regimes of technocapitalism and the organizations in which they are embedded therefore face a fundamental dilemma. They can acquiesce to a dilution of their power over research and researchers through external collaboration *and* thereby risk losing control over both. *Or* they can constrain external collaboration, compromise the reproduction of creativity, *and* thereby damage commodification and the eventual achievement of market value. There is little room for compromise here, given the high uncertainty and risk that pervades the systematized research regime. It is often impossible for organizations or their research regimes to gauge how much external collaboration is enough—before (or even while) it is engaged—and efforts to constrain it may have negative consequences down the line that cannot be easily anticipated or controlled.

The systematized research regime attempts to deal with this dilemma, but cannot resolve it fully or permanently. Typically, schemes to either resolve or bypass it end up in failure or in dysfunctions to the research regime, to the organization in which it is embedded, or to the individuals whose creative power must be obtained if any commodification is to occur. At best, the research regime can hope to cope with this dilemma long enough to allow the commodification of creativity to take place until failure occurs. The failure then leads to changes and a repositioning of external arrangements until failure sweeps them off again. External arrangements articulated to avoid losing control over creativity therefore stumble from crisis to crisis, as the research regime finds itself unable to resolve this dilemma.

This state of frequent crisis is partly behind the systematized research regime's characteristic state of urgency, discussed previously. Urgency is usually bred by crisis or the fear of it. Stumbling from one crisis to another is hardly a recipe for stability, and stability is precisely what the experimentalist corporation lacks. Being so dependent on external collaboration for reproducing its most important resource, the systematized research regime is inherently unstable and prone to crises that it can neither control nor avoid.

An example of the kind of external, intercorporate collaborative arrangement set up by some research regimes is research unit–to–research unit (R2R) collaboration. This kind of collaboration is usually structured through an alliance. It is typically bilateral, but can in some cases include the research departments of several companies. Its main objective is to try to control the reproduction of creativity, while circumscribing external relations and knowledge sharing to a select group of participants. It is, however, usually plagued by opportunism and multilateral suspicion. Typically short-term and prone to disputes over intellectual property theft, external R2R collaboration can become an avenue for costly litigation or failure.[23]

A major problem with most external R2R arrangements is that they lack the kinds of advantages conferred by networks: in particular, large network extent with the myriad social relations, rich sharing opportunities, and the stimuli it provides, all of which are essential for reproducing creativity. The scope of R2R collaboration is usually narrow, highly targeted, and engaged mostly for a specific research project that the companies involved cannot sustain on their own. By foregoing (or attempting to replace) networks and their social mediation, R2R collaboration schemes often end up compromising the reproduction of creativity upon which commodification depends.

Another example of an external arrangement intended to control reproduction is the segmentation of research departments, granting them autonomy to establish relations with other companies on their own. This arrangement can be a variant of the R2R scheme considered previously, but it can provide the segmented units a measure of initiative in establishing their external arrangements. These arrangements might even lead to significant external networking that can bring in new ideas.

Segmenting and casting off research units as autonomous operations can also help conceal the umbilical cord tying the units to the parent company. This may provide an impression of independence to entice collaboration from potential rivals. As part of a covert strategy to capture new ideas and siphon them off to the parent company, this scheme may have some advantages, but its possibility of influencing the reproduction of creativity seems quite limited and short-term, at best. Once the opportunistic character of this scheme becomes known, it is likely to repel collaboration, or at least place it under a cloud of suspicion. This scheme may therefore carry the seeds of its own destruction, and it often adds to the climate of crisis surrounding the research regime.

The temptation to form (or link up with) external, intercorporate networks involving diverse companies that the research regime of a single company can neither control nor manipulate may nonetheless be too hard to resist. This may be the case where complex, multidisciplinary talents (or the convergence of new knowledge from various fields) are indispensable.[24] Without the network-based assemblage of these talents, it may be impossible to undertake some projects in the cutting-edge activities of technocapitalism, such as nanotechnology, proteomics, molecular computing, or biorobotics.[25] Short-lived and narrow as such network-based collaboration may be, it nonetheless presents serious challenges to a research regime. The challenges are derived from the relations of power (and inequities thereof) within a network.

The most important challenge has to do with the wielding of power by one or several network participants. Some of the companies that participate may use their power over others simply because they have more resources and therefore greater "weight" to impose research agendas. These companies may structure a division of labor within the network, where they acquire oligarchic power over less-powerful participants, who must then do their bidding if they are to remain in the network.

This situation creates *linkage dependence* that binds weaker participants to the most powerful ones as they seek a way to access the knowledge, insights, stimuli, and relations vital to reproduce creativity. The stronger participants may, in turn, need the weaker ones in order to have a critical mass of talent that they cannot muster or accumulate on their own. Such a critical mass may be crucial to generate the kinds of insights, stimuli, relations, and tacit knowledge that can influence the reproduction of creativity. At the same time, the weaker participants can become targets to be siphoned of any interesting new talents or personnel they may have. Linkage dependence may thus take up an *exploitive* function, as stronger companies extract vital talents and knowledge from the weaker ones.

Linkage dependence is therefore a vehicle for generating inequity and predation whenever companies (or their research regimes) network with one another. These networks are typically made up of a select group (or consortium) of companies collaborating on a research project that is too risky, complex, or costly to be undertaken individually by any one of the participating companies. Setting ground rules for cooperation often has little chance of containing predation by the stronger or richer participants, who can find a way to get around strictures by coercing or imposing on those with less power and resources. Predation and abuse are probably harder to do within a network than without it because of the erosion of trust that results, but the stronger participants may get away with it when there are no alternatives available to the weaker members. The only alternative for the weaker participants, which is to exit the network altogether, can lead to their disadvantage or failure.

Thus, in such cases, linkage dependence becomes a vehicle for abuse. However, even in cases where the stronger companies take advantage of weaker network participants, the power of the stronger members may be diminished when they join an external network. The social mediation provided by networking (even when networking is circumscribed) often tends to dilute power. The power of corporatism and of its research regimes may therefore be diminished by collaboration through external networks, even when such cooperation is ephemeral.

Pathological Pursuits

The pathologies and dysfunctions of the systematized research regime involve two dimensions. One is *external* to the organization and encompasses the research regime's relations with other organizations and with society at large. The second dimension is *internal* and involves the governance of the regime over the commodification of creativity. These pathological domains result from the split of corporate power, as the research regime seeks to reproduce creativity externally while attempting to sustain commodification internally, amid the maelstrom of high uncertainty and risk that pervades research.

The two pathological dimensions are branches of the systematized research regime's inability to resolve the fundamental contradiction between reproduction (the external) and commodification (the internal), along with the no less fundamental antithesis between creativity and commodification. The antithesis, grounded in the intangible nature of creativity and the social qualities that sustain it, is as much a part of the internal as of the external pathological domains. Creativity is, after all, shaped by the social context. Commodification, internal to the organization and in some respects antisocial, is all too often antithetical to unfettered human creativity.

Commodification's negation of the nature of creativity also affects the external, social context of reproduction, given its unavoidable connection with the internal governance of the research regime. The external social needs of reproduction are, after all, vital to the process of commodification, if commodification is to have any chance of obtaining market value. However, reproducing creativity in order to feed it to the process of commodification negates the joy and freewheeling curiosity that is vital to the spirit of creation. Creativity reproduced with the sole intent to commodify is about as free as salt from the seawater that carries it.

As commodification negates the nature of creativity, so the pathologies generated by the systematized research regime's *external* relations can co-opt those who, by function or circumstance, must articulate them. The antisocial influences underpinning the regime's pathologies are perhaps more obvious in the *predatory* strategies that have become a staple of its social relations. The fact that such strategies have become entrenched in managerial practice attests to the mean character of technocapitalism. At no time in human history were corporate subterfuge and theft as widespread as they are in this emerging new form of corporatism.[26]

The predatory strategies come in various forms and guises, but a major objective is to reduce the uncertainty inherent in the commodification of creativity. A way to reduce uncertainty is to appropriate the results of others' research creativity. Doing so can provide a shortcut to commodification, at a time when speed is of great importance to corporatism. Strategically, this form of theft can also preempt potential competitors from reaping commercial benefit from their own efforts at commodifying creativity. Thus, predation can serve the double purpose of enriching the corporate actor that undertakes it, while also reducing whatever advantage a potential competitor might have.

To consider the technocapitalist corporation and its research regime without realizing how important predatory schemes are becoming to its existence is about as realistic as expecting to swim without touching water. The most artful corporate thieves are those who can execute predation without leaving any trace of wrongdoing or any sign of illegality, at least not one that can be conclusively proven. Such stealth is, however, a very difficult task for even capable predators to accomplish, if the astronomical growth of legal disputes and court actions over intellectual rights is any guide. It is a sad testament to this state of affairs that intellectual property litigation is the most coveted specialization among aspiring legal students nowadays. Such an esteemed endeavor deals mostly, if not entirely, with corporate disputes and wrongdoing.

One of the more common forms of predation is espionage, which has become easier to carry out given the spread of research networks and the range of contacts they facilitate.[27] Advances in information technology, including the Internet and the Web, provide many opportunities to seek, bribe, or communicate vital information on most any aspect of research. The social mediation that networks provide is therefore often turned into an instrument of predation. What used to be cloak-and-dagger operations to, for example, steal ideas, performance data, or test results that can lead to a patent filing, have become easier to undertake and cover up. Similarly, network relations have often become a vehicle for setting up traps or tricks to induce others to reveal vital aspects of potential inventions.

How much predatory strategies have been institutionalized in the corporate apparatus can be seen in the proliferation of "second-mover" research activities aimed at stealing others' ideas. Such activities are quite diverse and can include, for example, reverse engineering of competitors' inventions, tweakings of stolen ideas or projects, or the surreptitious modification of formulas and processes devised by others.[28] "Second-mover," a term initially coined to define research that follows (or tweaks) existing inventions, has become an important tool of corporate predation.[29] Second-mover research is now an important corporate strategy in research-intensive organizations. Its main attraction is that it allows the systematized research regime to expedite the commodification of creativity.

Through predatory, second-mover research, the regime may also reduce the uncertainty inherent in the reproduction of creativity. Since the reproduction of creativity typically occurs externally through networks and their social mediation, it is mostly out of the control of corporate governance. However, second-mover research can restore some corporate control and provide a welcome relief to the angst and uncertainty that surround this fundamental process of technocapitalism. It can provide this control by appropriating others' ideas, which may expedite the predator's commodification of the purloined idea. It can, at the same time, reduce the advantage of the competitor from which the idea was stolen, while improving that of the predator.

However, predatory second-mover research subjects corporate power to another kind of risk—litigation—if it is found out and contested. Assessing one kind of risk against another is often a difficult if not impossible task, given the uncertainty involved. But predatory second-mover projects, being primarily internal and thereby under greater corporate control, are all too attractive to forego in an era when companies live or die by their research. Considering the two sets of risk, it is not surprising that corporate power often chooses the second-mover avenue of predation. The rationale may be that it is better to take a risk on what it has more control over, than what it does not control at all (or very little). Should it be surprising, then, that second-mover predation is turning into a major operational vehicle for corporatism and its research regimes?

Another form of predation may be referred to as *malicious opportunism*. This strategy seeks to manipulate partners engaged through intercorporate networks (or alliances) so as to benefit from their capabilities without reciprocating the terms of collaboration.[30] The objective, to take advantage of partners, can be done in different ways. A common one is to relegate partners to subordinate roles in the division of functions that emerges through the network (or through a multi-party alliance), such that the more risky or uncertain activities can be imposed on them. In this way, partners can be held responsible for the more difficult components of a project. Malicious opportunism thus serves the purpose of reducing the risk of commodification and reproduction by reallocating it to partners.

Examples of this strategy can be found in several forms of external (intercorporate) collaboration. In parallel research projects involving substantial experimentation, for example, a partner that takes over coordination can relegate other participants to do the riskier components of the project. The coordinative role then empowers the corporate actor that seizes it to delegate research assignments that benefit its competitive position vis-à-vis other companies engaged in the project. Such empowerment may, for example, allow the "coordinator" to gain vital insights into important ideas that are then purloined. In other cases, the coordinator can use its position to gain knowledge on a partner it may consider a takeover candidate. In such instances, the knowledge gained may be used to weaken the takeover target's bargaining position, allowing the suitor a negotiating advantage it would not otherwise have.

Another example of malicious opportunism involves undermining one or more partners to place them at a disadvantage with respect to other participants. This approach can include misrepresentations with the intent of causing a loss of confidence in the targeted partner. Among its objectives may be to dislodge the targeted partner from the network or alliance, or to cause others to commit more of their own resources, such that the opportunist can hold back and preserve its own for more valuable endeavors. "Wasting" others in this fashion is not an unpopular strategy among intercorporate network participants whenever much advantage can be gained or the targeted partner is considered to be a potential up-and-coming competitor.[31]

Considering the antisocial nature of these predatory strategies, it should not be surprising that *trust* is a scarce quality in the systematized research regime's external relations. The lack of that precious quality, which is so important for healthy social relations, underpins the external pathological dimension of the research regime. Trust cannot be manufactured through covenants, no matter how detailed or comprehensive those might be, particularly when *intangible* resources are at play and when the activities are as uncertain and risky as those involving research creativity. It is a fiction to think that contractual arrangements can restore trust when predation seems so ingrained in the corporatist ethos of the regime. When predation and might vanquish truth and honesty in order to gain advantages, in an era when "winning" the research race is everything, trust can become a disposable nuisance.

The lack of trust means that the systematized research regime's external relations tend to be *short-term* and volatile. When partners are seen as potential targets to be taken advantage of (or worse, eliminated) as the opportunity arises, one cannot expect external collaboration to last long. For this reason, most intercorporate collaboration is limited to specific projects, narrowly defined, and is intended to last only long enough for a project to be completed. However, since no one can be sure that the creativity obtained will not be used in other noncooperative projects by any of the partners involved, collaboration may end up shortchanged. This is part of the reason why the systematized research regime stumbles from crisis to crisis, unable to reproduce creativity adequately even when external collaboration occurs.

The building of trust, which requires fairness, honesty, and constructive reciprocity accumulated over long periods, is often viewed by corporatism as a "cost" that the systematized research regime cannot afford. Thus, the cost of predation, with all its risks and the possibility of disputes and litigation, may be preferred over the "cost" of building trust. This shortsighted perspective is one of the failings of technocapitalist corporate governance. It is fueled in part by the characteristic state of urgency of the systematized research regime, by greed, and by the predominant dogma on competition that is taught in management schools and diffused by the popular business media.[32] The business media all too often views competitive strategies as inadequate unless they destroy rivals.[33] Thus, it should not be surprising that the classic "large fish eat small (or weak) fish" adage can be used to characterize some of the systematized research regime's external pathologies.

In contrast with the external dimension, the *internal* pathologies of the systematized research regime are grounded in its governance of commodification. The most important internal source of pathology is related to the regime's attempt to manipulate any and all aspects of research creativity. Attempts to control can become obsessive because of the high risk and uncertainty inherent in the commodification of creativity, which often result in crisis and failure. Thus, much of the internal pathology of the research regime revolves around its attempt to reduce risk and uncertainty through manipulation schemes, which are often harmful to creativity.

Examples of this set of pathologies can be found in the governance of many research organizations. Having researchers work in machinelike ways is a common one, based on the belief that it makes commodification more predictable and therefore less risky. It usually tries to streamline the process of commodifying research creativity in the hope that it will be easier to manipulate so that market value can be obtained faster. This scheme also often seeks to establish greater control over specific research tasks and over how researchers exercise their creativity.

Inducing researchers to think and work in machinelike ways is attractive to corporate power because it is at the core of *mechanistic systematization*, as in the case of "expert systems" that automate what were previously human-performed analytical procedures. These systems, now widely used in such activities as blood analyses and genetic testing, for example, can save resources while eliminating the uncertainty and risk that often accompany human initiative. Mechanistic systematization is also at the core of "artificial intelligence" projects, which seek to replace human judgment and creative initiative.[34] Systematizing research in this manner would allow the regime to internalize much of the reproduction of creativity within the corporate organization, thereby establishing internal control over *both* commodification and reproduction. Thus, the prospect that machinelike thinking might lead to this sort of systematization is very attractive to the corporatist mind-set.

The regimentation fostered by the mechanistic approach is antithetical to creativity, however. One of its effects is to induce greater alienation among those who provide creative power to the organization. Alienation here involves not only the separation of researchers from the results of their creativity, as previously defined, but also the detachment of their initiative from the very process of creation, as "blueprints" of mechanistic systematization are imposed on them. Being induced to think mechanistically about creativity can also demean the dignity of those whose toil and lives are devoted to research. Given the authoritarian nature of corporatism, refusing to submit to mechanistic approaches can make a researcher a target for humiliation, if not demotion or dismissal.

Beyond its effects on alienation and human dignity, the mechanistic approach can reduce creativity and increase dysfunction within a corporate organization. The dysfunctions it introduces, which tend to show up in demoralization and mistakes (if not accidents), can damage the social medium of creativity. Creativity usually relies on trust, not only between management and researchers but also among researchers themselves. Imposing the mechanistic approach might lead to crises within the corporate organization, in its governance of commodification and in the conduct of research itself.

Another example of the internal pathologies found in the systematized research regime involves the appropriation of inventions from those who contribute creative power to the organization. Besides the fact that researchers are seldom adequately compensated for the results of their creativity, the theft of their ideas by legal (or extralegal) means is a pathology of corporatism.[35] After all, why should researchers who contribute creative power (and are directly under corporate control) be spared from predation by corporate governance, when corporations practice it externally, and especially when such predation is practiced on companies that have much greater power than any of the organization's own researchers?

The prospect of litigation cannot be much of a restraint on corporations that are used to frequent legal disputes, and all the more so when such organizations have the resources to mount formidable obstacles to those who challenge their internal practices. Individual employees who challenge corporate interests and expose their wrongdoing have reason to be fearful for their careers in an era when companies live or die by research. Moreover, the emphasis on "winning" the technology race—to market inventions before rivals—is such that ethical restraints tend to turn into disposable nuisances, even when their violation is exposed. Can the threats of litigation or negative public exposure be serious constraints on corporate power when corporatism seems as accustomed to them as fish are to water?

Although the relations of power between researchers and corporate management are quite asymmetrical, the practices noted above can nonetheless have negative consequences for corporate power. Among the most important ones are a decline in productivity, demoralization and distrust of corporate governance, and the possible loss of the most talented researchers to rivals. The loss of talented personnel, who might carry with them much of the research regime's memory and secrets, can restrain predatory schemes, at least on selected individual researchers. Nonetheless, even when internal predation is practiced carefully, the pathological climate of discouragement and ill will it creates can be costly to the research regime.

Why, then, does corporatism pursue internal schemes that have nefarious consequences? Beyond the overarching motive to reduce the high risk and uncertainty inherent in research, there is an important factor to consider. It is very difficult to manage research environments where creative people are treated as human beings and are given ample leeway to exercise their creativity.[36]

Such research environments require the effective *empowerment* of those who exercise creativity. However, such empowerment would reduce the control of corporate governance over commodification, effectively transferring control from management (and, indirectly, shareholders) *to* those who exercise creativity. This possibility is antithetical to current management dogma, as taught in most every business school and diffused by the popular business media. The teachings of "agency theory," a staple of contemporary management education, for example, place the empowerment of shareholders as the supreme concern of corporatism.[37] From its perspective, therefore, agency theory assumes management to be no more than "agents" of shareholders. Those who provide the most important resource of our time—creativity—are left out of consideration by the theory's simplistic perspective.

These difficulties, and the lack of simple recipes to guide the empowerment of those who provide creativity, add to the internal dysfunction of the systematized research regime. In an era when management dogma neglects or ignores those who provide the most precious resource, the research regime is left adrift as it tries to cope with the perils of commodification. Its internal control schemes not only tend to generate pathology but also prevent the regime from coming to grips with the exercise of creativity in humane and socially constructive ways.

The inability of the systematized research regime to empower those who provide creativity then compounds the fundamental contradiction between the internal (commodification) and the external (reproduction) dimensions of corporatism. As discussed previously, that contradiction poses a major dilemma to the technocapitalist corporation: It can allow its power to be diluted through external collaboration in order to reproduce creativity and risk losing control over this vital process, *or* it can try to retain control internally and thereby shortchange *both* the reproduction and commodification of creativity. Now, however, the need to empower those who provide creativity poses a further dilemma, which is primarily *internal* in its scope and effects.

This is the new dilemma: The systematized research regime can empower those who provide creative power, and risk losing control over the process of commodification itself, *or* it can ignore the need for such empowerment and thereby make the commodification of creativity a source of internal pathology. Given the authoritarian nature of corporatism, the difficulties involved, and the lack of recipes to guide such empowerment, the second alternative is the one most likely to be followed by corporate governance. This outcome can be expected because losing control over the commodification of creativity is a frightening prospect in an era when research creativity (and its commodification) makes all the difference to corporate survival.

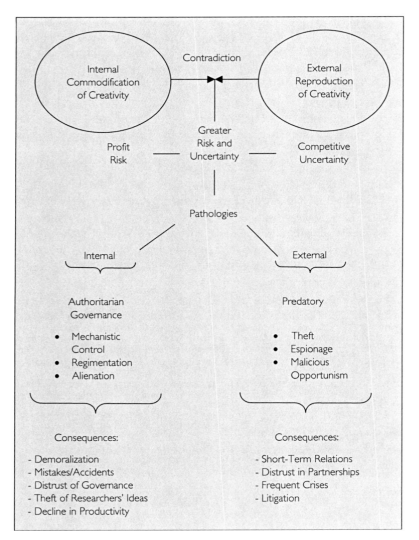

Figure 9 Contradiction and Pathologies

Since losing control over commodification is simply not acceptable to corporatism, the internal pathologies generated by the systematized research regime may persist or worsen. However, as the pathologies continue, they tend to sow the seeds of the regime's crises. Thus, internally, the regime is torn between the urgency to commodify creativity in order to extract value *and* the difficult problems that its pathologies create for commodification. The pathologies, therefore, introduce an additional level of risk and uncertainty to the research regime's already perilous existence. Most of all, they make commodification more difficult by undermining the social medium of creativity, which rests on qualities they negate—trust, fairness, reciprocity, and human dignity.

The internal and external contradictions of the experimentalist corporation and its systematized research regime raise many troubling questions. Although it is impossible at this time to know the full profile of the pathologies involved, the scope and depth of the contradictions indicate that their effects may be with us for a long time. A synthetic outline of the contradictions and pathologies, shown in Figure 9, indicates their likely internal and external impacts. Although their broader social implications are not easy to foresee, it may not be too far-fetched to imagine that the twenty-first century will bear the effects of these pathologies. The factory system of industrial capitalism, after all, generated pathologies that are still very much with us, in many aspects of culture, society, and nature. The pathologies of technocapitalism and its corporate organizations promise no less in their impact on this century. Our best hope for humankind is that the pathologies of the experimentalist organization can be checked through social accountability and through a democratization of decision making on technology.

Conclusion

The experimentalist organization is as representative of technocapitalism as the industrial corporation was of industrial capitalism. The features and pathologies of this new form of corporatism are likely to be as much a hallmark of the twenty-first century as the factory system and mass production were of the nineteenth and twentieth centuries. Its effects, although still largely unknown, are likely to be both very troubling and durable.

The systematized research regime, the main instrument of control for experimentalist corporatism, is unable to resolve the fundamental contradictions between the internal dimension of corporate governance, which revolves around commodification, and the external, social, and collaborative one that is essential for reproducing creativity. The research regime's failure to resolve these contradictions introduces dysfunctions and pathologies that shortchange its ability to commodify creativity and to contribute to the reproduction of this most precious resource. Those dysfunctions also reflect the failure of managerial dogma to understand the new realities that accompany technocapitalism and the nature of the resources upon which it depends.

The external and internal pathologies of the systematized research regime pose a formidable challenge to the experimentalist corporation. They compound the contradictions between the external and internal domains of corporatism, setting the stage for frequent crises. As the research regime stumbles from crisis to crisis, it generates effects that are harmful, not only to those who provide creative power but also to society at large.

For all their technological clout and capabilities, experimentalist organizations and their research regimes seem out of touch with society in a century when technology and corporatism are likely to attract more public scrutiny than ever before. The call for social accountability and democratic scrutiny may therefore become more pressing as their social pathologies become more noticeable. These pathologies, more than any other factor, may pose major dilemmas as technocapitalism intrudes in most every aspect of life, work, and society.

Challenges

The most serious challenges posed by technocapitalism revolve around the need for accountability and public democracy. Given the power and reach of this phenomenon, greater accountability to society and the need for new forms of public democracy are important priorities. The new relations of power that accompany this new version of capitalism are likely to affect most every aspect of work and governance, our social relations, and life itself. Only through checks provided by greater social accountability and democracy can we hope to make technocapitalism responsive to human needs.

The sustenance of human emancipation, solidarity, and development rides on the democratization of technocapitalism and the new corporatism it is spawning. The new corporatism's authoritarian character and its insatiable quest for power and profit pose formidable obstacles to the struggle for greater accountability and democracy. The far-reaching pathologies it is introducing are likely to be with us for a long time. They may affect every corner of society and nature, leaving no institution, social relation, or life-form untouched. The twenty-first century may thus bear witness to some of the deeper transformations of human society, as technology and science are bound ever more closely to the power of this new version of capitalism.

These transformations, their pathologies, and the challenges they pose are intimately related to the fundamental split between commodification and reproduction, discussed in previous chapters. That split, which is a major characteristic of technocapitalism, is driving the decomposition of corporate organizations. Decomposition, in turn, makes corporate involvement in society more necessary than ever, as the manipulation of governance and all vehicles of power become more important for corporate survival. The new phenomena that make corporations more a product of society, and more dependent on it, also make it essential for corporate power to try to control society, its governance, and practically all avenues of power. As a result, corporatism's pathologies spill out into society more vividly and strongly than ever before.

Two important aspects of this dialectic, which are bound with decomposition and the split between commodification and reproduction, are corporatism's influence on public democracy and its drive for hegemony over society. These two aspects are explored in this chapter, to reflect how corporatism is reshaping the public domain. The discussion of these aspects is followed by a consideration of possible counteravenues of thought and action that can help check the social pathologies of corporatism. One of these counteravenues involves creativity, the most important resource of technocapitalism, to reclaim the human and social dimensions of technology. Other counteravenues involve a rediscovery of the social roots of technology and their implications for public democracy and for a humane reconstitution of society.

Downfall of Public Democracy

The erosion of public democracy is one of the most troubling effects of technocapitalism. It is becoming increasingly clear that the apparatus of public governance inherited from twentieth-century industrial capitalism is ineffective in protecting the public interest. This looming crisis poses a major challenge to public governance and to the need to hold corporatism accountable to society.

This challenge is all the more pressing given the relations of power between public democracy and the new corporatism. Public democracy is the mainstream form of governance commonly found in rich nations. Its apparatus is often referred to as representative democracy, with institutions that have nominally separate functions. Its capacity to safeguard the public interest has often been dubious, as powerful lobbies hold sway over policy making and regulation. Although its democratic substance was often in doubt, this system managed to implement the structures of governance for industrial society. It was both part and product of industrial market capitalism and created the institutions that allowed industrial capitalism to be established during the past two centuries.[1] Those structures are becoming increasingly ineffective, however, as the new corporatism erodes the legitimacy of public institutions.

The erosion of public democracy is largely due to the deeply asymmetrical relations of power between governance and the new corporatism. This situation is partly a result of the scale and scope of technocapitalist corporatism, which are global and mobile, unlike that of public democracy, which are national or local (and therefore confined to a specific territory). Through this asymmetry, the new corporatism can transcend limitations imposed by the boundaries of the national and the local. Accountability can thus be evaded through mobility and through strategies that pit governance structures in different areas against one another by engaging them in competition for investment.[2]

As a result, public governance is less capable of acting as a check on corporate power. Checks and balances become largely ineffective, turning into little more than words in official documents that seldom live up to their intent.[3] Political lobbying by powerful corporations to prevent competitors from marketing more effective products that can threaten their market power has become more common, as in the case of anthrax vaccines.[4] Research agendas and projects are also becoming more vulnerable to the interests of corporate power as government oversight and funding decline.

How far this situation has advanced can be seen in the frequent co-optation of researchers by corporate sponsors. Some of the more obvious examples of this development have occurred in health-related research, where pharmaceutical companies often finance research projects with the tacit understanding that results must be favorable to their products. Conflicts of interest thus arise frequently in medical research, as projects increasingly depend on corporate funding.[5] Flawed or ineffective new medications that can harm millions of people are being marketed, for the sake of higher profits and greater corporate power.[6] This situation now affects many research endeavors that require substantial funding. Researchers who do not bend to corporate power are more likely than ever to be left out of funding, if they do not face an early end to their careers.

At the same time, the very structures and mechanisms of democratic governance are being co-opted by the new corporatism. The agendas of public institutions and of governance itself become indistinguishable from those of corporate power.[7] Corporate power effectively sets the agendas of public institutions, sometimes subtly and at times forcefully. Public institutions become appendages of corporatism, adopting its mind-set, its priorities, and even its propaganda. The authoritarian nature of the new corporatism, seeking to control creativity, research, and the new technologies that will become symbolic of the twenty-first century, cannot spare the structures of public governance.

The common fallacy, often argued by mainstream (neoclassical) economists, that market competition is the best way to keep corporate power in check, is largely irrelevant to this issue.[8] The argument for market competition as a substitute for public governance misses the nature of the problem. Market competition might lower prices for consumers and producers, but it is not a substitute for public democracy.[9] The new reality that technocapitalism tries to impose is *a system*, an authoritarian system of corporate control over society. It matters little that market competition may end up vanquishing a company at the hands of another (or many others). The victors replace the vanquished and become the new powers in the competitive game, changing little or nothing of *the structure of the system* of authoritarian control. In fact, competition may end up strengthening the authoritarian power of corporatism over society by generating new strategies to co-opt public governance or by spawning more powerful corporations through the competitive game.

Another fallacy argues that the asymmetry of power favoring corporatism is necessary to sustain profits and technological innovation. This argument seems as justifiable as the ones that supported the use of child labor in factories more than a century ago. Child labor was needed, it was then argued, in order for industrial capitalism to sustain profits and acquire new technology.[10] Many arguments were put forth, from the ridiculous one that child labor built up a person's character, to the outrageous belief that child labor would reduce the numbers of the poor through shorter longevity. The antisocial and inhuman character of such arguments became obvious to many, and eventually led to the prohibition of child labor. Today, not very different arguments are put forth to justify the need for corporatist control over public governance as a way to generate higher profits and new technology.

Two phenomena stand out, in particular, as motivators of corporatism's quest for control of public governance. These phenomena have been discussed previously in this book, but they need to be kept in mind whenever the topic of corporate power over public governance is broached. One is the permanent state of urgency under which the experimentalist corporation operates. The state of urgency is tied to the control of research activities in the technocapitalist corporation, but this condition is not confined to the corporate setting. The new corporatism's need to manipulate all research endeavors is projected to the public arena. Public governance does, after all, set many of the conditions that regulate research. Clinical testing of biotech products, for example, is very much a function of public institutions charged with safeguarding our health. Moreover, hundreds of millions of dollars spent in research for a single prospective product are often at stake whenever such testing is undertaken or regulations are drafted.[11] It is not surprising, therefore, that control over regulators, and over public governance itself, has become a fundamental priority of the new corporatism.

The spread of this mind-set to sectors not symbolic of technocapitalism must also be taken into account. The state of urgency that pervades experimentalist organizations is becoming common in most every business activity. One must therefore look beyond the new activities symbolic of technocapitalism to see that many organizations engaged in services or production, and certainly low-tech ones, are now also engaged in research. Research functions of one kind or another—even rudimentary ones in some cases, but research nonetheless—have been adopted by organizations that are far removed from the model activities of the new corporatism. This phenomenon thus increases the pressure on corporatism, old or new, to control public governance for its own ends.

The second phenomenon behind corporatism's quest for power over public governance is the process of decomposition, which confronts most every corporate organization nowadays. Having to rely more on external networks, or externalizing what were previously in-house functions, tends to build up greater awareness of public governance. Such awareness often leads to strategies to manipulate public governance. The strategies can be quite diverse. Lobbying legislators, contributing to their political campaigns, bribing officials, implementing media campaigns through advertising, sponsoring one-sided journalism, and financing opinion surveys that favor corporatist agendas are but a few examples of the vast repertory of strategic tools available.[12]

Decomposition therefore elicits schemes to control the agendas of public institutions. Such efforts are often driven by uncertainties introduced by its own dynamic. Activities and transactions that used to occur within the corporate organization are thus forced out into the realm of societal mediation. Public governance is, after all, part of the realm of societal mediation, which, at its root, is driven by human actions and decisions. Actions and decisions therefore make governance subject to human will, and human will can be influenced to favor some interests over others. The calculus of the new corporatism is ever more keenly targeted to make governance favor its interests in a world where uncertainty increases the pressure on corporate power to have more control over the public domain.

Hegemony of Corporatism

Corporatism's attempt to control public governance is but one facet of a larger panorama. Control over society at large, and not just governance, is the larger concern involving technocapitalism and corporate power. No sphere of human activity, even those far removed from technology or science—whether in culture, the arts, the media, professional endeavors, or education—can be considered out of reach of the new corporatism.

Hegemony is domination, so deeply embedded that it appears quite normal (or "natural") to those who are dominated.[13] Those who are skillful at domination must therefore see to it that their hegemony is not perceived as such by those who must remain submitted. And, in the era of technocapitalism, the dominated could be entire societies, not just groups of individuals or disenfranchised minorities. The main tool for domination would be technology, introduced and applied for the benefit of corporatism, above all other possibilities.

Hegemony also involves colonization of new activities or those left untouched by prior stages of capitalism. Any aspect of human life, or nature itself, that has the potential to promote power and profit becomes a candidate for colonization. At the core of the new corporatism's quest for hegemony are the activities that are symbolic of technocapitalism. Genomics, nanotechnology, genetic engineering, biomedicine, molecular computing, and biopharmacology, to mention only a few, are targets of that quest. These activities will be hallmarks of twenty-first-century technological prowess. They will affect greatly how we view ourselves as humans, as social beings, and how we relate to life and nature.

Power and profit are part of the creation and development of those activities that are so typical of this new version of capitalism. They are corporate activities, first and foremost, even though their domain of knowledge is in engineering and science. Corporate power drives them, decides their priorities, and targets their dynamics. Thus, corporatism's conquest of technology and science and, more broadly, of "nature" is not a metaphysical undertaking but rather a matter of power over creativity and research.[14]

Choices over research agendas and new technologies are embedded in the new corporatism and cannot be considered independent of its power. These choices bring together the interests of corporatism *and* the functional rationality of a new technology to eventually attempt to exercise corporate power over social relations (and human resources). The propaganda so often spread by corporatism about technology having a functional rationality of its own, or at least one that is separate (or independent) from society, is a fiction. Such propaganda considers the social dimension, if it does so at all, in terms of the uses a technology is put to. Therefore, society is regarded only as the ultimate receiver rather than as an active participant in the creation of technology. In this regard, the propaganda is conspicuously similar to the long-standing precept that believes corporations to be separate from society.[15]

Research agendas and technologies are neither "neutral" nor "functional" in the new reality that technocapitalist corporatism tries to impose. And they are far from being separate or independent from society. Research agendas and technologies are choices made by corporatism, and they are intended to further its power. The values and interests of the new corporatism are in the very design of the new technologies and are therefore "installed" in them, in their rationality, and in their procedures.[16]

Based on technological conventions, the values and interests of corporatism may also be embedded in standardized procedures or "rules" that legitimize the exercise of corporate power. Standard setting provides many examples of how corporate priorities can be built into new technology.[17] Standards for new technology have often been set by corporate agents, by corporate organizations themselves, or by institutions that have been influenced by corporations. Most people in society are usually not technologically knowledgeable enough to understand (as experts) the technicalities of new technologies or the standards that are agreed upon behind the scene. Under technocapitalism, moreover, the highly complex (and often abstract) nature of new technology, the multidisciplinary talents needed to evaluate them, and the standards that will govern them are out of the reach of all but a very small group of experts. Once the standards are set, they become "reality." They must therefore be obeyed by everyone.

Under technocapitalism, therefore, technology and research are more than arrays of tools or procedures. Technology, in particular, becomes not a final "state" or "condition," and much less a "fate" or "destiny," but a potential scenario of struggle between corporatism and society. Given the power of corporatism over research and standard setting, the deck seems heavily stacked in its favor whenever the public interest is at odds with corporate power.

Technology and research under technocapitalism are thus largely a matter of *corporate choice*, despite their social character. The choices decided by corporatism ultimately affect society at large, even with the lack of democratic participation in the process. These choices, made by and for the interests of corporate power, also influence future choices. The farther removed society is from these decision processes, the less say it will have over the choices that are made. Preventing society from participating in these decisions, at least to the extent that such participation constrains corporate power (or is at odds with its interests) is a major concern of the new corporatism.

This is the nature of corporatist hegemony under technocapitalism: It neither recognizes nor respects boundaries in its quest for power. Respecting boundaries and limitations (if that occurs) tends to be subject to the calculus of power and profit rather than that of ethics or morality.[18] Breaking boundaries and limitations that would cost more than they are worth in power and profit are to be avoided, therefore. Those that are worth the power and profit of breaking them are not to be ignored.

Having considered the incipient hegemony of the new corporatism, it may seem paradoxical that this phenomenon should occur at a time when decomposition is making inroads into most every corporate organization. In a dialectical sense, decomposition would presumably make corporate power more "social" by externalizing its scope and scale. However, and also from a dialectical perspective, the process of decomposition actually makes corporate power all the more keen on control and hegemony. Having to deal with uncertainty outside its traditional boundaries (or, at any rate, with greater uncertainty than it has been used to), corporatism chooses to try to control the social environment—at large, and at scales and depths unfathomed by the corporate powers of previous times.

This phenomenon, paradoxical as it may seem, also accounts for the aggressive corporate efforts to manipulate external networks. Whether they involve public governance, researchers, customers, suppliers, financial patrons, or the media, networks have become too important to be left untouched.[19] Their vital role in reproducing creativity and thus eventually corporate performance (and market value) makes them a major source of interest for corporate power. Attempting to manipulate networks through diverse strategies, all with the intent of extracting favorable outcomes, is rapidly becoming a corporate "art."[20] Recipes on this subject can now be found in highly respected academic business journals, not to mention magazines and newspapers.[21] Books by well-known management "gurus" even provide recipes on how to go about developing "strategies" to bring such efforts to fruition.

One cannot be too surprised, therefore, if corporatism's attempts at social control often result in pathology—not only for corporate power itself but also for society at large. These pathologies will be part of the legacy of technocapitalism. The quest for hegemony coupled with poor social accountability can have far-reaching effects. It would not be shocking to see genetic engineering bound into the human realm to produce individuals with characteristics that are highly desirable to corporatism.[22] The "design" or "engineering" of humans with greater potential for creativity and innovation would be of great interest in this regard.[23] After all, most people want their offspring to be "successful" and "well adjusted." One can therefore expect corporatism to appeal to such sentiments that suit its need for power.

Empowering Creativity

As the most important resource of our time, creativity has a fundamental role to play in any effort to make technocapitalism accountable to the public interest. The exercise of research creativity, after all, involves corporatism in virtually all its dimensions. Hardly any aspect of technocapitalism and its corporate organization can be understood without taking into account the role of creativity. In this context, the empowerment of creativity takes on vital importance if there is any hope of making this new version of capitalism accountable to society.

Empowerment is defined here as enabling those who provide research creativity to develop independently of corporatism. *Those who provide creativity potentially hold the key to accountability, as the intangible resource they hold is vital to the survival of technocapitalism.* In a previous chapter, creative power is defined as the exercise of creativity by individuals or groups working under a systematized research regime. The empowerment of creativity must, however, rely on the possibility that creative power may be exercised independently of such regimes.

The systematized research regime is a corporatist artifact. Its fundamental objective is to structure the commodification of creativity such that power and profit can be extracted from this vital resource. The empowerment of creativity, to exercise this resource independently of those regimes, therefore implicitly involves a subversion of corporatism. Such empowerment is, by and large, contrarian to the interests of corporate power. Emancipating creativity from its organizational discipline would challenge corporatism's ability to structure research processes.

Without the systematized research regime, the new corporatism would find it very difficult to commodify creativity. As we saw in previous chapters, having to externalize the reproduction of creativity introduced a power split between commodification and reproduction. Commodification is handled internally, for which the structure of the systematized research regime is essential, while the reproduction of creativity occurs externally, out of direct (and often also indirect) control. Networks are the prime external medium through which the process of reproduction occurs. Thus, the new corporatism faces the daunting challenge of dealing with an external medium that it cannot control, while it tries to structure commodification internally by systematizing research.

In the struggle between corporatism's external and internal dimensions, networks can take up a major role in empowering creativity. The emancipative potential of social networks, external to the corporate setting and to corporate power, must be taken into account. Empowering creativity is about human emancipation and also about societal emancipation. It frees human creative potential from corporate domination so that it can serve society directly. Networks are a major tool in this struggle, and they have the potential to enlist public awareness, to educate, and to mobilize society as no other social medium can.

Empowering creativity through networks will likely subvert the corporate designs that structure technological research. Eventually, this struggle can transform social relations on a larger scale, perhaps including even the structures that govern everyday life and work. An important aspect of this process is network extent.[24] The larger and more inclusive a network becomes, the more influence it will likely have. This dynamic process of extent building can transform what at first might seem very limited nets into a major social movement.

An example of how this process expands can be seen in the proliferation of Open Source networks in recent times. Such networks, initially started for software research, have been adopted in various other activities. Open Source software design effectively subverted the research apparatus of the new corporatism, typified in this case by the global corporate power of Microsoft.[25] Microsoft's software innovations were proprietary and were based on a closed, systematized research regime. Open Source software innovations, in contrast, were free (or nonproprietary), open to anyone and everyone to use or modify, and were made in a voluntary (and nonhierarchical) research structure.

The expansion of network extent through open participation and access eventually ensured greater quality for Open Source software, whether as products to be used in specific applications or as ideas that could support new innovations. The emancipation of creativity through Open Source networks thus subverted the systematized research model. Open Source research was not undertaken for profit or to further corporate domination. Rather, it was a purely voluntary exercise of creativity, global in scope and practice, to potentially benefit all who cared to participate (or use its results) through the availability of software that was of higher quality than the alternatives provided by corporatism.

Creativity empowerment may also enlist the power of networks in other activities to subvert the structures imposed by corporatism. Individuals with very serious illnesses, for example, are typically subject to corporate priorities for obtaining care, where procedures are guided by cost-effectiveness criteria and profits. Pharmaceutical researchers and patients are thus relegated to passive roles. Corporate standards drive whatever treatment is provided.[26] Researchers are typically alienated from the patients whose lives they are supposed to improve or save. Patients know little or nothing about research that might help them, and they often contribute little in the way of immediate feedback to researchers.

Empowerment of creativity in this area would bring researchers and patients into close collaboration. Serious illnesses, after all, have a limited time horizon. Networks that include both researchers and patients might thus provide immediate feedback to researchers, who would be able to target their experimental activities. An Open Source strategy applied to such collaboration would subvert the proprietary models of pharmaceutical and biotech corporatism by making research results (involving medications or treatment) immediately and directly known to other researchers and to patients all over the world.

Such networks could expand rapidly, accumulating researchers' knowledge to benefit patients as well as researchers. The quality of the results would most likely be greater than the ones obtained through the corporatist model, where new knowledge is circumscribed and used as property instead of being shared openly. Treating such knowledge as proprietary typically means that researchers who share the knowledge are punished by corporate authorities. Firings and early career endings are a common outcome as employment contracts that require research results to be kept secret are enforced.

The outcome of corporatist appropriation of that research creativity is often seen in deadly side effects and ineffective treatments. Open researcher-patient collaborations through networks where new knowledge would be freely and immediately shared might do more than save lives and produce better results. It would also likely prevent some of the pathological practices of the new corporatism such as influencing medical practitioners to prescribe products or providing misleading information on new products to drive up share prices.

Rediscovering the Social

The empowerment of creativity must necessarily be part of a larger effort to democratize technocapitalism. This enterprise involves understanding the social character of the emerging era, curbing its pathologies, and improving its accountability to the public interest. It is a daunting proposition, given the power of corporatism, the intangible nature of creativity, the complexity of research, and the abstract character of the technologies embedded in this new era.

Industrial capitalism extracted advantages by sacrificing social values, social justice, human dignity, and the environment for its ends. It created great wealth with great inequity, and spawned technologies that allowed industrial corporatism to impose its priorities on work, our social relations, and nature.[27] Technocapitalism is poised to advance this agenda with deeper and farther-reaching impact, harnessing technology and science as no previous stage of capitalism could.

The new corporatism spawned by this new version of capitalism may not spare any aspect of life, society, or nature. As it demolishes old structures and colonizes new areas, the new corporatism leaves little space for dissent, and very limited tolerance for those who obstruct its quest for power and profit. Its authoritarian character is becoming evident in its conquest of sectors that not long ago were considered advocates of the public interest. Public governance at all levels—the media, the courts, legislation, health care, and even academia—are now more vulnerable to corporate power than ever before.[28]

Rediscovering the social dimension through this emerging era must start from the realization that technocapitalism and the new corporatism it has spawned are part of society. They are not separate from it. They are not the product of functional or natural "laws" that operate outside society.[29] Rather, their trajectory is both part and product of social struggles and of social forces. These forces and struggles shape the technologies that involve us as members of society. We, in turn, can shape them in terms of how they serve the common good, our social relations, and our well-being.

Technological creativity and research must be inserted into the fabric of society and its economic relations in a socially responsible and peaceful manner. Social well-being, human emancipation, social justice, and solidarity must take greater weight in the emerging era of technocapitalism if we are to contain its pathological tendencies and channel its technological prowess to benefit humanity. In this effort, it is important to realize that creativity and new knowledge are *social qualities*. No one really "owns" them—not corporations, individuals, or even institutions. Creativity and new knowledge depend on social mediation and culture and are therefore both part and product of society; they are "owned" by society at large.

One of the long-standing fictions of corporatism is the notion that technology is "neutral," meaning that the social context in which it is embedded does not matter. Technology is thus attributed to capital, to corporate governance, or to individual talent (genetically driven in whole or part). In this view, technology is simply "served" to society. Society is the receiver and passive consumer, with little or nothing to say on whatever happens before new technologies are "served." The market is the "tool" or vehicle through which new technologies are "served" on society. Society's only function is to provide feedback through the market's supply-and-demand mechanisms on a new technology's usefulness, quality, price, and other features.

That view ignores the role of society in shaping technological creativity, in articulating needs that channel research agendas, the relations of power in research and invention, and the social relations that frame the ethical expectations for any new technology. The history of technology is filled with evidence of how social needs and influences became drivers of research agendas. A social appreciation of life, for example, was a major influence on the invention of vaccines.[30] Many such inventions never turned a profit and therefore had only social value to offer in the form of saving lives or preventing illness. They were created, nonetheless, because of social influences that recognized the importance of human life and dignity. Had the corporatist notion of technology's social "neutrality" prevailed, they would have probably never been invented, as their potential for profit was often quite dim and could be determined beforehand.

Even when the potential for profit exists, social forces often shape invention and research agendas. The field of surveillance and its ties to nanotechnology, biorobotics, and software may provide some interesting examples in the years to come. New gadgets so minute that they can be placed most anywhere to spy on anyone may become commonplace. Social awareness of their harmful effects on privacy, political rights, and human dignity may curtail research agendas that seek to turn them into simple appliances, marketed alongside any household product.[31]

Examples of how social action affected or changed seemingly "neutral" technologies and research agendas can be found in most any field of research. Crash safety standards, for example, were incorporated in automotive design and research largely as a result of social pressures.[32] Those influences placed human life above "neutral" or functional considerations such as "efficiency" criteria based on vehicle weight or speed, production costs, and narrow benefit-cost analyses. Hundreds of thousands of lives were lost and countless people were disabled before those safety standards were incorporated in vehicle design and research. At the bottom of it all, social decisions about the importance of human life changed the technology and the research agendas that created it.

Another example was social action on environmental pollution, which helped change automotive engine research agendas. Social decisions about the importance of the environment, which is a public resource, radically channeled research creativity in new directions.[33] One of the results of this social struggle is the incipient (albeit gradual) abandonment of the internal combustion engine in favor of fuel cells and other technologies. For many years, however, those who advocated "neutral" criteria based on narrow pricing or benefit-cost considerations complained about how such "radical" change would damage the automotive industry and consumers' budgets.

Looking to the future and learning from history, there should be little doubt that social struggles will be entwined with research agendas in the activities that are symbolic of technocapitalism. It is possible, for example, that economic or military demands may at some point lead to the creation of humanoid beings, based on cloning, to raise productivity in some economic activities or wage war. Restrictions on immigration, neoimperial policies, or a decline in population might lead to that scenario in certain nations. As a result, social forces will have to be set in motion to articulate ethical agendas for research, not to mention life rights. Would euthanasia be applied to these humanoid beings when they are no longer economically (or militarily) useful? Would criminal laws enforced on humans apply to them, and would they be anyone's "property"? Society will have to play a central role in such research, if life and the dignity of all involved are to have meaning. Having the capacity to create humanoid beings does not mean that such technologies should be guided solely by "neutral" or functional criteria, any more than automotive crash safety, engine pollution, or surveillance can.

Technology and research, therefore, are not simply a means to an end, devoid of social meaning or context. Rather, the means are defined by society and social mediation, and vice versa. The social dimension and the functional character of technology are entwined with one another. One cannot exist without the other as long as humanity lives and functions through society.

We must therefore recognize that society is crucial to the meaning and nature of technology, and that technology is profoundly social and subject to social accountability. Their entwined existence, their struggles and contradictions end up defining a way of life. What way of life will technocapitalism represent? Unless we can insert it into the fabric of society in a socially responsible way, technocapitalism's contradictions and pathologies will likely endanger the meaning of life, nature, justice, human dignity, and our sustenance as social beings.

Notes

Introduction

1. Richard Levins, "Living the 11th Thesis," *Monthly Review* 59 (January 2008): 34. As head of the human ecology program at the Harvard School of Public Health, Levins researched the social dimension of science along a path that very few other scientists have been able to tread. See, for example, his and Richard Lewontin's *The Dialectical Biologist* (Cambridge, MA: Harvard University Press, 1985), and their *Biology under the Influence: Dialectical Essays on Ecology, Agriculture, and Health* (New York: Monthly Review Press, 2007).

2. It is therefore acknowledged that both functional and cultural considerations are at work in the creation of technology. Technology can be viewed as a systemic cumulation of culturally and functionally mediated knowledge that results in entities (such as organisms, tools, processes, methods, formulas, or ideas) that are of use to humanity. As we see in later chapters, such "use" or utility has a dichotomous nature: the social one (based on intrinsic social contributions) and the commercial one (based on market value). The term *technocapitalism* conflates that perspective (the essence of "technos") with the character of a new form of capitalism: an economic system based on the exploitation of *intangible* commodities executed through corporate organizations. Those corporate organizations have distinctive characteristics of their own, as we see later, and their collective ethos is assumed to represent a new kind of corporatism (experimentalist corporatism). The prime function of the new corporatism, to exploit intangible resources (most prominently technological

creativity), is at the core of its quest for power and profit. The character and pathologies of those forces and phenomena are addressed in the following chapters.

3. Although the culturalist (or substantivist) approach is associated with the work of Martin Heidegger, other authors such as Jacques Ellul contributed much evidence to support its philosophical apparatus. Heidegger's despair over the hopelessness of opposing technological forces and their authoritarian character in *The Question Concerning Technology* (New York: Harper and Row, 1977) was complemented by Ellul's documentation of their demeaning effects on occupations in *The Technological Society* (New York: Vintage, 1964). Criticism of the deterministic tendencies of culturalism was at the heart of the constructivist approach, which is closely associated with the work of Thomas Kuhn, *The Structure of Scientific Revolutions* (Chicago: University of Chicago Press, 1962) and Paul Feyerabend, *Realism, Rationalism and Scientific Method* (New York: Cambridge University Press, 1981). Their work argues that technological outcomes are not determined but instead are constructed through interaction between a particular technology (or scientific paradigm) and the social context (or social relations) in which it is embedded.

4. Earlier studies of industrial capitalism and the labor process showed that powerful economic interests had an important role to play in the design of industrial technology, a view most prominently expressed by Harry Braverman, *Labor and Monopoly Capital* (New York: Monthly Review Press, 1974), and those who continued his work. As with so many other currents, Marx's work on the labor process had a seminal influence on this line of inquiry; see, for example, Karl Marx, *Grundrisse* (New York: Penguin, 1973), 250–401.

5. A technocratic rationalization of technology that transfers decision making to corporatist "experts" is therefore opposed to the very meaning of democracy. One of the key questions for the democratization of technocapitalism is how the struggle between the power of experts (at the service of corporatism) and the public's interest will be shaped.

6. Such power is usually dispersed through numerous sectors, activities, and institutions in society, if Michel Foucault's studies of technocratic rationalization, *The Order of Things* (New York: Vintage, 1970), are taken into account.

7. The struggle must necessarily be democratic, but also radical. If, as Andrew Feenberg posits in *Critical Theory of Technology* (New York: Oxford University Press, 1991), the authoritarian character of technological development can only be effectively opposed by democratization and radical reform, then the creation of new means of public participation, and of new institutions, would be major elements of that struggle. This view is diametrically opposed to the notion (promoted in part by contemporary neoliberal thought) that technology, science, and society are governed by functional "laws" that are out of reach of human decision and social action. Debates on the relationship between science, social action, and radical political economy many years

ago addressed some of the fundamental questions on this matter. See, for example, John D. Bernal, *The Social Function of Science* (New York: Macmillan, 1939); John B. S. Haldane, *Dialectical Materialism and Modern Science* (New York: Labour Monthly, 1942). A consideration of the need for democratization and radical reform, in response to technocapitalism and its pathologies, must take these debates into account.

8. It must be acknowledged, nonetheless, that financial difficulties affecting conventional publishing are also an important factor in this phenomenon. Having to be more mindful of the "bottom line" than ever before, as the Web encroaches upon (and to a great extent takes over) publishing on the one hand, while shareholders (or stakeholders) demand maximal returns (or at least solvency) on the other, has made marketing an overwhelming priority for many publishers. This is reflected in the strategies of large corporate publishers, their increasing reliance on outsiders (from sectors unrelated to publishing) as chief executives, the overwhelming attention to "hit-driven" book publishing to generate revenue, and aggressive diversification into video games and other digital entertainment; see, for example, Jeffrey A. Trachtenberg and Mike Esterl, "Industry Outsider to Run Random House," *Wall Street Journal* (May 20, 2008): A9. Not surprisingly, the number of "coffee table" books that sell but have little in the way of critical scholarship has increased rapidly in academic publishers' lists. These issues have been the subject of attention at AAUP (Association of American University Presses) meetings, along with Web-generated threats to conventional publishing, such as Open Access. See, for example, "AAUP Statement on Open Access" (February 2007), available at www.aaup.org; Joseph J. Esposito, "The Devil You Don't Know: The Unexpected Future of Open Access Publishing," *First Monday* 9 (August 2004): 11; Marlie Wasserman, "How Much Does It Cost to Publish a Monograph and Why?" *Journal of Electronic Publishing* 4 (September 1998), available at www.press.umich.edu/jep.

9. The objective of reductionism—to attempt to understand complex entities by isolating their components—is often inadequate when considering social phenomena. Particularly, systemic effects, interrelations, and interactions are likely to be missed by reductionist approaches in the study of social phenomena. Such aspects are often at the core of a critical understanding of social relations, especially those involving domination, relations of power, and social pathology.

10. Robert Merton's expectations on scientific conduct in *The Sociology of Science* (Chicago: University of Chicago Press, 1973) seem out of place in a time when corporate influence over research (not to mention academia) sets agendas. Unlike previous times (and Merton's own historical frame of reference), most research in cutting-edge areas of science and technology today require vast resources, which often only corporations can provide.

Experimentalism

1. The collapsing of restraints in that phase of capitalism had a much slower dynamic, however. See, for example, Immanuel Wallerstein, *The Second Era of Great Expansion of the Capitalist World-Economy, 1730–1840s* (San Diego: Academic Press, 1989) and his *Historical Capitalism* (London: Verso, 1995); Eric Hobsbawm, *The Age of Capital, 1848–1875* (New York: New American Library, 1979). The collapse of social and institutional restraints was most vivid in the new factory towns of that era; see John Foster, *Class Struggle and the Industrial Revolution: Early Industrial Capitalism in Three English Towns* (London: Weidenfeld and Nicolson, 1974).

2. Networks can therefore be a vehicle for control and subjugation in the context of information technology and the globalization of corporate power; see Dan Schiller, *Digital Capitalism: Networking the Global Market System* (Cambridge, MA: MIT Press, 1999); Darin Barney, *The Network Society* (Cambridge, UK: Polity, 2004); Kevin Robins and Frank Webster, *Times of the Technoculture: From the Information Society to the Virtual Life* (New York: Routledge, 1999). Taken together, Schiller, Barney, and Robins and Webster make a very compelling case against the notion that networks are solely emancipative.

3. See Peter Wayner, *Free for All: How Linux and the Free Software Movement Undercut the High-Tech Titans* (New York: HarperBusiness, 2000); Richard Stallman, *Free Software, Free Society: Selected Essays of Richard M. Stallman* (Boston: Free Software Foundation, 2002).

4. See David Stauffer, *Business the Sun Way: Secrets of a New Economy Megabrand* (Oxford: Capstone, 2002).

5. See, for example, Jennifer Edstrom and Martin Eller, *Barbarians Led by Bill Gates: Microsoft from the Inside, How the World's Richest Corporation Wields Its Power* (New York: Holt, 1998).

6. Those companies have often been referred to as "gene-decoding factories" because of their intensive use of supercomputers for new gene discovery and their high rates of patent applications. See Ralph T. King, "Gene Quest Will Bring Glory to Some; Incyte Will Stick with Cash. Assembly-Line Sequencing Lets Firm Beat a Path to the U.S. Patent Office," *Wall Street Journal* (February 10, 2000): A1; Kathryn Brown, "The Human Genome Business Today," *Scientific American* 283 (July 2000):50–55.

7. See, for example, David Healy, *The Antidepressant Era* (Cambridge, MA: Harvard University Press, 1999). Among the more disturbing prospects for the commercialization of behavior-modifying drugs are those that would adjust economic behavior to suit corporate objectives, particularly mass consumption habits. Along this line, one major objective would be to increase feelings of "trust" such that it can be exploited to promote greater consumption (and thereby boost corporate profits). See, for example, Michael Kosfeld, Markus Heinrichs, Paul J. Zak, Urs Fischbacher and Ernst Fehr, "Oxytocin Increases Trust in Humans," *Nature* 435 (June 2, 2005): 673–676; Robert

Lee Holtz, "Researchers Find Trust to Be a Hormonal Affair," *Los Angeles Times* (June 2, 2005): A18; Antonio Damasio, "Brain Trust," *Nature* 435 (June 2, 2005): 571–572. A thriving market already exists for prescription drugs that enhance certain behaviors (many of them consonant with corporate needs), despite often serious side effects; see Karen Kaplan and Denise Gellene, "They're Bulking Up Mentally: Academics, Musicians, Even Poker Champs Take Pills to Sharpen Their Minds, Legally. Labs Race to Develop Even More," *Los Angeles Times* (December 20, 2007): A1.

8. A growing body of literature on the prospects for genetic manipulation is revealing the future that humanity faces. For a business-oriented (though critical) perspective, see Richard Donkin, "In Fear of Genetically Modified Recruitment," *Financial Times* (May 24, 2002): vi. The question of eugenics is a recurring one, as shown by Garland E. Allen, "Is a New Eugenics Afoot?" *Science* 294 (October 5, 2001): 59–61. Other authors view (in a broad way) the genetic engineering of human behavior as inevitable; see, for example, Peter McGuffin, Brien Riley, and Robert Plomin, "Toward Behavioral Genomics," *Science* 291(February 16, 2001): 1232; Gregory Stock, *Redesigning Humans: Our Inevitable Genetic Future* (Boston: Houghton Mifflin, 2002). Directed human evolution, whereby enhancements are added to human genes to affect certain professional aptitudes, seems a foregone conclusion, according to bioethicist Ronald M. Green's *Babies by Design: The Ethics of Genetic Choice* (New Haven: Yale University Press, 2007). In particular, Daniel A. Silverman's *The Neuro-Genetic Roots of Organizational Behavior* (Lanham, MD: University Press of America, 2000) provides views on how organizational skills might be genetically engineered, a topic that no doubt would interest many corporations and their shareholders.

9. An excellent philosophical discussion, from a Marxian perspective, on how life itself is being commodified can be found in Finn Bowring, *Science, Seeds, and Cyborgs: Biotechnology and the Appropriation of Life* (London: Verso, 2003).

10. See Wallerstein, *The Second Era*; Eric Hobsbawm, *Labouring Men: Studies in the History of Labour* (London: Weidenfeld and Nicolson, 1964), and Hobsbawm, *The Age of Capital, 1845–1875* (New York: New American Library, 1979).

11. Corporatism engineered those transfers of power by concocting performance standards that embedded its power and priorities over labor. See, for example, Harry Braverman, *Labor and Monopoly Capital: The Degradation of Work in the Twentieth Century* (New York: Monthly Review Press, 1974); Robert Kanigel, *The One Best Way: Frederick Winslow Taylor and the Enigma of Efficiency* (New York: Viking, 1997).

12. See David Gartman, *Auto Slavery: The Labor Process in the American Automobile Industry, 1897–1950* (New Brunswick, NJ: Rutgers University Press, 1986); David F. Noble, *Forces of Production: A Social History of Industrial Automation* (New York: Knopf, 1984); Rosalyn F. Baxandall,

Technology, the Labor Process, and the Working Class: Essays (New York: Monthly Review Press, 1976); and the articles in Andrew Zimbalist (ed.), *Case Studies on the Labor Process* (New York: Monthly Review Press, 1979).

13. Such pathologies are often taken for granted as "normal" features of the economy. A vast amount of literature has emerged over the years on their effects. See, for example, Steven C. High, *Industrial Sunset: The Making of North America's Rust Belt, 1969–1984* (Toronto: University of Toronto Press, 2003); Harley Shaiken, *Work Transformed: Automation and Labor in the Computer Age* (New York: Holt, Rinehart and Winston, 1984); and the articles in Rick Baldoz, Charles Koeber, and Philip Kraft (eds.), *The Critical Study of Work: Labor, Technology, and Global Production* (Philadelphia: Temple University Press, 2001).

14. See Daniel Bell, *The Coming of Post-Industrial Society: A Venture in Social Forecasting* (New York: Basic Books, 1973); and the articles in Bertram Silverman and Murray Yanowitch (eds.), *The Worker in "Post-Industrial" Capitalism: Liberal and Radical Responses* (New York: Free Press, 1974). Bell's characterization of "post-industrialism" is based on the dynamic growth of service activities in rich nations during the 1950s and 1960s.

15. See, for example, Eric Schlosser, *Fast Food Nation: The Dark Side of the All-American Meal* (Boston: Houghton Mifflin, 2001). A broader perspective on the societal implications of the spread of fast food can be found in George Ritzer, *The McDonaldization of Society* (Thousand Oaks, CA: Pine Forge Press, 2004).

16. Thus, some of the same tools (and mind-set) used to analyze industrial efficiency were applied to airline services. See, for example, Ronald E. Miller, *Domestic Airline Efficiency: An Application of Linear Programming* (Cambridge, MA: MIT Press, 1963).

17. Regulatory innovations involving transactions in the stock and bond markets often were part of that dynamic. See, for example, the articles in William N. Goetzmann and K. Geert Rouwenhorst (eds.), *The Origins of Value: The Financial Innovations That Created Modern Capital Markets* (Oxford: Oxford University Press, 2005).

18. This shift underlies most critical analyses of capital accumulation, starting with primitive forms up to contemporary analyses. See, for example, Joan Robinson, *The Accumulation of Capital* (London: Macmillan, 1956); Michael Perelman, *The Invention of Capitalism: Classical Political Economy and the Secret History of Primitive Accumulation* (Durham, NC: Duke University Press, 2000). For these and many other works, Marx's ideas on capital accumulation set the foundation upon which many subsequent critical views of accumulation flourished. See Karl Marx, "Original Accumulation of Capital," in *Grundrisse: Foundations of the Critique of Political Economy* (New York: Penguin, 1993), 459–549. In the late twentieth century, the Regulation School provided the most important critical, systematic view of capital accumulation. Its view of capital accumulation in the broader framework of "accumulation

regimes" provided a much needed adjustment of Marxian theory to the reality of late industrial capitalism (also referred to as "post-Fordism"). See Alain Lipietz, *Le Capital et son Space* (Paris: Maspero, 1977); Michel Aglietta, *A Theory of Capitalist Regulation: The U.S. Experience* (London: Verso, 2000).

19. Such flows have helped consolidate the power of capital in the global race to "corporatize" every corner of the earth. See, for example, Schiller, *Digital Capitalism*; Barney, *Network Society*.

20. Socially oriented overviews of these new fields are sparse. An excellent overview of biotech can be found in Bowring, *Science, Seeds, and Cyborgs*.

21. See U.S. Patent and Trademark Office, *Annual Report* (Washington, DC: U.S. Government Printing Office, various years); U.S. Bureau of the Census, *Historical Statistics of the United States* (Washington, DC: U.S. Government Printing Office, 1975).

22. Among the histories of individual inventors who were cast out of invention by corporate research, Evan I. Schwartz's *The Last Lone Inventor: A Tale of Genius, Deceit and the Birth of Television* (New York: HarperCollins, 2002) provides an excellent account of what happened with one of the most socially influential inventions of the twentieth century.

23. See, for example, Hugh D. Graham and Nancy Diamond, *The Rise of American Research Universities: Elites and Challengers in the Postwar Era* (Baltimore: Johns Hopkins University Press, 2004). The rise of public research universities was also part of a social vision where wide access to higher education was seen as a common good and an important contributor to economic development. See Roger L. Geiger, *Research and Relevant Knowledge: American Research Universities since World War II* (New York: Oxford University Press, 1993).

24. Microchip innovations and production led this advance, setting the stage for related sectors to emerge, such as personal computing and software design. See, for example, Ernest Braun and Stuart MacDonald, *Revolution in Miniature: The History and Impact of Semiconductor Electronics* (Cambridge: Cambridge University Press, 1982). In the early 1980s, Apple Computer became a prime example of how a high-tech corporation could master both cutting-edge research and production, coming out with a new product (the personal computer) that would revolutionize how people work and communicate; see Michael Moritz, *The Little Kingdom: The Private Story of Apple Computer* (New York: Morrow, 1984). Silicon Valley (the home of Apple Computer and of pioneer companies in microelectronics, such as Fairchild Semiconductor and, later, Intel) thus became the preeminent concentration of high-tech corporatism in the 1980s; see, for example, Dirk Hanson, *The New Alchemists: Silicon Valley and the Microelectronics Revolution* (Boston: Little, Brown, 1982).

25. U.S. Bureau of the Census, *Construction Reports: Value of New Construction Put in Place in the United States, 1964 to 1980* (Washington, DC: U.S. Government Printing Office, 1981); American Public Works Association,

History of Public Works in the United States, 1776–1976 (Washington, DC: U.S. Government Printing Office, 1976). For an analysis of cyclical patterns and dynamics of infrastructural construction over much of the twentieth century, see Luis Suarez-Villa and Syed A. Hasnath, "The Effect of Infrastructure on Invention: Innovative Capacity and the Dynamics of Public Construction Investment," *Technological Forecasting and Social Change* 44 (1993): 333–358.

26. A critical discussion of related aspects can be found in Andrew Feenberg, *Critical Theory of Technology* (Oxford: Oxford University Press, 1991), and his *Technology and the Politics of Knowledge* (Bloomington: Indiana University Press, 1995).

27. See, for example, Jennifer Edstrom and Martin Eller, *Barbarians Led by Bill Gates: Microsoft from the Inside; How the World's Richest Corporation Wields Power* (New York: Holt, 1998).

28. This debate has attracted attention over the years, and has involved a considerable number of scientists, engineers, and philosophers of science and technology. See, for example, Sergio Sismondo, *An Introduction to Science and Technology Studies* (Oxford: Blackwell, 2004), chap. 8.

Creativity as a Commodity

1. The organizational contexts involved, even when they are highly successful in their objective, have pathological effects of their own. Social critics of capitalism and its corporatist underpinnings long ago understood this important aspect. See, for example, Herbert Marcuse, *One-Dimensional Man* (Boston: Beacon, 1964).

2. Richard Levins and Richard Lewontin, *The Dialectical Biologist* (Cambridge, MA: Harvard University Press, 1985), 208.

3. This point is often supported implicitly in the literature on scientific-technological creativity. See, for example, Gerald J. Holton, *The Scientific Imagination: Case Studies* (Cambridge: Cambridge University Press, 1978); and Holton, *Thematic Origins of Scientific Thought: Kepler to Einstein* (Cambridge, MA: Harvard University Press, 1973). In particular, Albert Einstein legitimized greatly the notion that imagination may be more important than knowledge; see Paul Arthur Schilpp, *Albert Einstein: Philosopher-Scientist* (Evanston, IL: Library of Living Philosophers, 1949).

4. See Johan Söderberg, *Hacking Capitalism: The Free and Open Source Movement* (New York: Routledge, 2007). Samir Chopra and Scott D. Dexter, in their *Decoding Liberation: The Promise of Free and Open Source Software* (New York: Routledge, 2007), note the emancipative effect that a collaborative, network-grounded social context can have on individual and group creativity.

5. It has been thought that the transfer of ideas between disciplines has triggered much creativity in the recipient fields. However, the larger social

dimension of those transfers has been much neglected. Some of the more unexpected or unusual interdisciplinary transfers have involved art, which is an inherently (and multidimensional) social activity. See, for example, Pamela H. Smith, *The Body of the Artisan: Art and Experience in the Scientific Revolution* (Chicago: University of Chicago Press, 2004). Paolo Rossi, in his *Philosophy, Technology and the Arts in the Early Modern Era* (New York: Harper and Row, 1970), emphasizes how new philosophical currents underlie the relationship between art and technology, triggering new movements that affect both technological and artistic creativity. One interesting finding in this regard is that transcending intellectual and cultural barriers between science and the arts contributes to greater creativity; see, for example, David Edwards, *Artscience: Creativity in the Post-Google Generation* (Cambridge, MA: Harvard University Press, 2008).

6. Thomas S. Kuhn, *The Structure of Scientific Revolutions* (Chicago: University of Chicago Press, 1962).

7. See Jennifer Edstrom and Martin Eller, *Barbarians Led by Bill Gates: Microsoft from the Inside; How the World's Richest Corporation Wields Its Power* (New York: Holt, 1998).

8. The Open Source software research movement is, not surprisingly, often regarded as revolutionary. See Söderberg, *Hacking Capitalism*.

9. It must be recognized that regimentation and compartmentalization also often shortchange the providers of creativity by preempting their sharing in the resulting intellectual property rights or financial rewards. See, for example, Michael Perelman, *Steal This Idea: Intellectual Property and the Corporate Confiscation of Creativity* (New York: Palgrave, 2002); "Letters: The Problem with Patents," *Science* 308(April 15, 2005): 353. J. Rodman Steele's *Is This My Reward? An Employee's Struggle for Fairness in the Corporate Exploitation of His Inventions* (West Palm Beach, FL: Pencraft, 1986) provided an interesting personal account of how corporate policies can trump fairness in the appropriation of intellectual property.

10. The Marxian conception of value has, from a politico-economic perspective, been a subject of much debate over the years. It is indeed remarkable that it is as relevant to our contemporary context as it was a century and a half ago. See Karl Marx, *Capital: A Critique of Political Economy*, vol. I, *The Process of Capitalist Production,* ed. F. Engels (New York: International Publishers, 1967; orig. Hamburg: Verlag von Otto Meissner, 1867), chaps. 1 and 2.

11. High costs of experimentation are a hallmark of such diverse sectors as biotechnology, nanotechnology, bioinformatics, and practically all others associated with technocapitalism. In the case of many biotech activities, for example, long periods of testing (usually lasting several years) add to the high cost and uncertainty. High risk of failure is also a common feature as, for example, only about one out of eight thousand compounds usually manage to pass the long testing cycle and gain regulatory approval. Approval, however, does not guarantee at all that a product will be profitable. See, for example, Luis

Suarez-Villa and Wallace Walrod, "The Collaborative Economy of Biotechnology: Alliances, Outsourcing and R&D," *International Journal of Biotechnology* 5 (2003): 402–438.

12. The market value of a very new product for which a market does not (yet) exist would be practically none. A similar condition might apply to the case of an obsolescent product that has been replaced by a new and much more effective one, but that nonetheless continues to be used.

13. See, for example, Matthew Smallman-Raynor et al., *Poliomyelitis: A World Geography, Emergence to Eradication* (Oxford: Oxford University Press, 2006), Part II. Arthur Allen, in his *Vaccine: The Controversial Story of Medicine's Greatest Lifesaver* (New York: Norton, 2007), notes how the discovery and development of most vaccines were far removed from any notion of marketing or profit.

14. See Chopra and Dexter, *Decoding Liberation*. Eric S. Raymond's *The Cathedral and the Bazaar: Musings on Linux and Open Source by an Accidental Revolutionary* (Cambridge, MA: O'Reilly, 1999) provides insights on the importance of expanding network extent in the early years of that movement.

15. Parallel research networks in various fields of science have increased rapidly since the late 1990s. Beyond the immediate sharing of findings, savings on experimental hardware by most participants in such networks have been significant. See, for example, Stephanie Teasley and Steven Wolinsky, "Scientific Collaboration at a Distance," *Science* 292 (June 22, 2001): 2254–2255; Wesley Shrum, Joel Genuth and Ivan Chompalov, *Structures of Scientific Collaboration* (Cambridge, MA: MIT Press, 2007).

16. Some creativity was undoubtedly required for commodification, but the factory system of industrial capitalism and its labor processes required programming and serial tasking to such an extent that creativity was not a major objective or component of work. In addition, hierarchical, command-and-control management, a staple of the factory system even in its most recently evolved forms, greatly restricted creativity in work processes (in comparison with, for example, research endeavors in the technocapitalist context). Partly because of these characteristics, it became possible to automate labor processes in most factory operations. Discussions on the nature of work and labor under industrial capitalism are quite insightful in this regard. See Eric Hobsbawm, *Labouring Men: Studies in the History of Labour* (London: Weidenfeld and Nicolson, 1964); David F. Noble, *Forces of Production: A Social History of Industrial Automation* (New York: Knopf, 1984).

17. The term *reproduction* in Marxian political economy initially referred to capital. See Karl Marx, *Capital*, vol. I, chap. 23 and vol. II, chap. 20. The definition of reproduction used in this book corresponds with the notion of expanded reproduction (as opposed to simple reproduction). Expanded reproduction involves growth and the reinvestment of surplus value by corporate actors or the owners of capital. Creativity and its results are often thought to

contribute greatly to economic growth and productivity, and therefore seem more compatible with this definition of reproduction.

18. The spread of the market system to practically every corner of the world was one of the earlier and more noticeable effects; see Dan Schiller, *Digital Capitalism: Networking the Global Market System* (Cambridge, MA: MIT Press, 1999). Nick Dyer-Witheford's *Cyber-Marx: Cycles and Circuits of Struggle in High-Technology Capitalism* (Urbana: University of Illinois Press, 1999), in particular, considers the relevance of Marxian political economy to contemporary phenomena, showing that capitalism transcends the workplace to integrate diverse social activities and features into its frameworks of power.

19. Such alliances or communities of influence partly underpin the fame of individual scientists and of complex specialties whose ideas are not readily understandable to the public. Although much ignored in the literature, some accounts have appeared over the years about the role of social influence in major scientific awards. See, for example, Harriet Zuckerman, "The Scientific Elite: Nobel Laureates' Mutual Influence," in *Genius and Eminence*, ed. Robert S. Albert (New York: Pergamon, 1983); and Zuckerman, *Scientific Elite: Nobel Laureates in the United States* (New Brunswick, NJ: Transaction, 1996).

20. See Kevin Robins and Frank Webster, *Times of the Technoculture: From the Information Society to the Virtual Life* (New York: Routledge, 1999), chaps. 8 and 9. In the case of distance learning and online diploma programs, training (rather than education) seems to be a major objective and outcome; see David F. Noble, *Digital Diploma Mills: The Automation of Higher Education* (New York: Monthly Review Press, 2001).

21. The term craft-love is used here in the sense noted by Richard Sennett, *Respect in a World of Inequality* (New York: Norton, 2003). Craft-love can be considered a defense against mass production and the factory-based division of labor imposed by industrial capitalism; see Sennett's *The Craftsman* (New Haven, CT: Yale University Press, 2008). In the context of technocapitalism, craftsmanship (or "craft-love"), for example, may also be part of Open Source activities, such as software design.

22. Many such programs seem oriented toward mollifying what may be referred to as a deep state of social alienation (in the sense used by Marcuse), which occurs when individuals identify themselves closely with the (alienated) existence imposed on them. See "The New Forms of Control" in Marcuse, *One-Dimensional Man*, chap. 1.

23. Finding such anomalies is often the dream and hope of every creative researcher. All too often, however, overturning established ways becomes more a game of power than a search for (or recognition of) any scientific truth. See, for example, Georges Canguilhem, *Ideology and Rationality in the History of the Life Sciences* (Cambridge, MA: MIT Press, 1988); Levins and Lewontin, *Dialectical Biologist*. Bruno Latour's *Science in Action: How to*

Follow Scientists and Engineers through Society (Cambridge, MA: Harvard University Press, 1987), taking an ethnographic approach to the study of scientists' work and routines, made the point that controversies in science are often settled through social influences and games of power.

24. See, for example, Steve Lohr, *Go To: The Story of the Math Majors, Bridge Players, Engineers, Chess Wizards, Maverick Scientists and Iconoclasts, the Programmers Who Created the Software Revolution* (New York: Basic Books, 2001). Douglas Thomas, in his *Hacker Culture* (Minneapolis: University of Minnesota Press, 2002), notes how the social context created by computer programmers involved in hacking has become a cultural phenomenon in its own right, with language, social conventions, and mores that are distinctive and reflect the experimental aptitude of those involved.

25. However, it must be noted that artificial-intelligence (AI) regimens have often failed to produce expected results. In some ways, they also have contributed to demeaning the role of human initiative in the thought processes they tried to simulate. See Andrew Feenberg, *Critical Theory of Technology* (Oxford: Oxford University Press, 1991), chap. 5. The early history of AI also showed how futile some efforts at operationalizing humanlike thought processes would be; see Daniel Crevier, *AI: The Tumultuous History of the Search for Artificial Intelligence* (New York: Basic Books, 1993).

26. This is akin to Feenberg's definition of decontextualization, where the "objects of a technical practice are artificially separated from the systems and contexts in which they are originally found"; see Feenberg, *Critical Theory*, 184.

27. Alienation here is in the sense used by Levins and Lewontin, *Dialectical Biologist*. The term can also encompass the takeover of the results of creativity (legally or not) by corporate power; see, for example, Perelman, *Steal This Idea*; Pat Choate, *Hot Property: The Stealing of Ideas in an Age of Globalization* (New York: Knopf, 2005).

28. Corporate entities typically appropriate patents awarded to employees who use company resources to obtain them. However, in practice, most corporations have the power to appropriate any and all patent awards granted to any of their employees. The employees are at great disadvantage to contest a company's decision, since it is often very difficult to demonstrate conclusively that insights derived from company-related work did not influence a patent application. See, for example, "Letters: The Problem with Patents," *Science* 308 (April 15, 2005): 353; Steele, *Is This My Reward?*; Perelman, *Steal This Idea*; John Carreyrou, "Eli Lilly Faces Patent Challenge from a Long-Ago Collaboration," *Wall Street Journal* (May 10, 2006): A1.

29. The lag between the time when a new product is introduced and that of the appearance of a rival has declined significantly over the long term. See, for example, Rajshee Agarwal and Michael Gort, "First-Mover Advantage and the Speed of Competitive Entry, 1887–1986," *Journal of Law and Economics* 44 (2001): 161–177.

Networks as Mediators

1. Network range is therefore a composite feature that encompasses size and the heterogeneity (of interests) of participants; see Barry Wellman, *Networks in the Global Village: Life in Contemporary Communities* (Boulder, CO: Westview, 1999), 107. Network size is considered synonymous with scale in this discussion.

2. In the case of labor, for example, limiting external networks constrained its ability to organize or join unions and thereby enhanced corporate control over production and the labor process. See Harry Braverman, *Labor and Monopoly Capital: The Degradation of Work in the Twentieth Century* (New York: Monthly Review Press, 1974).

3. See, for example, Stephen Marglin, *The Dismal Science: How Thinking Like an Economist Undermines Community* (Cambridge, MA: Harvard University Press, 2008). Mainstream economics precepts have typically underpinned the neoliberal policies that have been applied around the world since the 1980s.

4. This is true particularly in the case of vertically integrated factories. See Eric Hobsbawm, *Labouring Men: Studies in the History of Labour* (London: Weidenfeld and Nicolson, 1964); Braverman, *Labor and Monopoly Capital*. As David Noble's *Forces of Production: A Social History of Industrial Automation* (New York: Knopf, 1984) points out, that kind of internal control made it possible for corporations to automate labor processes in factories, thus eliminating labor, limiting union activity, and increasing the power of corporate capital.

5. All results from participation in the Linux Open Source software network must be posted, and they are made freely available to anyone through the Web. This very important feature encourages openness, sharing, and collaboration. It also prevents appropriation by any participant. See Samir Chopra and Scott D. Dexter, *Decoding Liberation: The Promise of Free and Open Source Software* (New York: Routledge, 2007).

6. See, for example, Peter Wayner, *Free for All: How Linux and the Free Software Movement Undercut the High-Tech Titans* (New York: HarperBusiness, 2000); Steve Weber, *The Success of Open Source* (Cambridge, MA: Harvard University Press, 2004).

7. Pierre Gourdain, in his *La Révolution Wikipedia: Les Encyclopédies, Vont-elles Mourir?* (Paris: Mille et Une Nuits, 2007), emphasizes the perception that conventional encyclopedias will inevitably be replaced by Wikipedia (or by its model), despite the fact that its contents are sometimes not as well researched.

8. See "An Open-Source Shot in the Arm?" *Economist Technology Quarterly* (June 12, 2004): 17–19.

9. The Open Source movement is also generating "recipes" for doing business in diverse activities; see, for example, the Web site www.wikinomics.com.

The emergence of "Second Life," in particular, provided an Open Source–style approach to virtual business, allowing users to develop imaginary corporations and enterprises, along with a virtual currency, through the interactions supported by the Web site. See Wagner J. Au, *The Making of Second Life* (New York: HarperCollins, 2008); Peter Ludlow and Mark Wallace, *The Second Life Herald: The Virtual Tabloid That Witnessed the Dawn of Metaverse* (Cambridge, MA: MIT Press, 2007).

10. Parallel, network-based experimentation can promote cost-effectiveness in research, while enhancing creativity. See, for example, Wesley Shrum, Joel Genuth, and Ivan Chompalov, *Structures of Scientific Collaboration* (Cambridge, MA: MIT Press, 2007); Stephanie Teasley and Steven Wolinsky, "Scientific Collaboration at a Distance," *Science* 292 (June 22, 2001): 2254–2255.

11. See, for example, John Bohannon, "Grassroots Supercomputing," *Science* 308 (May 6, 2005): 810–813; Kenneth H. Buetow, "Cyberinfrastructure: Empowering a 'Third Way' in Biomedical Research," *Science* (May 6, 2005): 821–824.

12. Seeking and seizing larger market extent occurred at various levels. One of them involved offering free e-mail services. Creating a platform upon which many companies could build Windows-based applications was very important. See, for example, Jennifer Edstrom and Martin Eller, *Barbarians Led by Bill Gates: Microsoft from the Inside, How the World's Richest Corporation Wields Its Power* (New York: Holt, 1998). James Wallace, in his *Overdrive: Bill Gates and the Race to Control Cyberspace* (New York: Wiley, 1997), notes how domination of its market segment became a major corporate objective of Microsoft.

13. See Joshua Quittner and Michelle Slatalla, *Speeding the Net: The Inside Story of Netscape and How It Challenged Microsoft* (New York: Atlantic Monthly Press, 1998); Jim Clark and Owen Edwards, *Netscape Time: The Making of the Billion-Dollar Start-Up That Took On Microsoft* (New York: St. Martin's Press, 1999). Microsoft, however, eventually prevailed and drove Netscape into obscurity, using its near-monopoly power over the personal computer operating software market.

14. See David Stauffer, *Business the Sun Way: Secrets of a New Economy Megabrand* (Oxford: Capstone, 2002); Karen Southwick, *High Noon: The Inside Story of Scott McNealy and the Rise of Sun Microsystems* (New York: Wiley, 1999).

15. But it should be noted that distance-learning programs typically involve more training than education. David Noble's *Digital Diploma Mills: The Automation of Higher Education* (New York: Monthly Review Press, 2001) shows how and why such programs are attractive to the military and to many corporations.

16. This occurred mostly through users (many of whom were software specialists) who encountered problems and provided ideas or remedies through

the network of fellow users, including those in the organizations that set standards. See, for example, Tim Jordan, *Cyberpower: The Culture and Politics of Cyberspace and the Internet* (London: Routledge, 1999); Mark Stefik, *The Internet Edge: Social, Technical, and Legal Challenges for a Networked World* (Cambridge, MA: MIT Press, 1999).

17. However, this condition is at odds with the origins of the Internet as a tightly controlled, secretive network linking military research labs. See Janet Abbate, *Inventing the Internet* (Cambridge, MA: MIT Press, 2000). Katie Hafner and Matthew Lyon, in their *Where Wizards Stay Up Late: The Origins of the Internet* (New York: Simon and Schuster, 1996), note how the Internet's origins were intimately related to secret research, which prioritized the need to sustain interlab communications in the face of nuclear war.

18. See "Open-Source Shot," *Economist Technology Quarterly.*

19. See, for example, Richard Stallman, *Free Software, Free Society: Selected Essays of Richard M. Stallman* (Boston: Free Software Foundation, 2002). Although the Open Source software movement has often been described as "nonideological," it is difficult to see how a movement that purposefully operates outside the market system can be considered to have no ideology in an age when market processes control most everything. Operating outside the market system may be thought of as a tacit ideological statement, even though many in the Open Source software movement may not consider it to be so.

20. The Web is frequently associated with this characteristic. See, for example, David Weinberger, *Small Pieces Loosely Joined: A Unified Theory of the Web* (Cambridge, MA: Perseus, 2002). Bottom-up network building has occurred in many Web-based activities. One of these is the vast and highly diversified area of online games. See, for example, Julian Dibbell, *Play Money: Or, How I Quit My Day Job and Made Millions Trading Virtual Loot* (New York: Basic Books, 2006); Edward Castronova, *Synthetic Worlds: The Business and Culture of Online Games* (Chicago: University of Chicago Press, 2005); Au, *Making of Second Life.*

21. Beyond sustaining trust, consensual decision making, access, participation, and open debate help make technology and science more accountable to society. See Andrew Feenberg, *Critical Theory of Technology* (Oxford: Oxford University Press, 1991).

22. In the last years of the twentieth century, intercompany research unit–to–research unit (R2R) ties multiplied rapidly in Europe, North America, Japan, and South Korea; see John Hagedoorn, "Inter-firm R&D Partnerships: An Overview of Major Trends and Patterns Since 1960," *Research Policy* 31 (2002): 477–492.

23. The modern idea of modularity can be traced to decision theorist Herbert A. Simon and to architect Christopher Alexander. See Herbert A. Simon, "The Architecture of Complexity," *Proceedings of the American Philosophical Society* 106 (1962): 467–482; Christopher Alexander, *Notes on the*

Synthesis of Form (Cambridge, MA: Harvard University Press, 1964). Modularity is assumed to have important effects in Open Source software design; see, for example, Ilkka Tuomi, *Networks of Innovation: Change and Meaning in the Age of the Internet* (Oxford: Oxford University Press, 2002). Modularity's application in organizations is thought to have introduced greater flexibility; see, for example, Carliss Y. Baldwin and Kim B. Clark, *Design Rules, Volume 1: The Power of Modularity* (Cambridge, MA: MIT Press, 2000).

24. See Stauffer, *Business the Sun Way.*

25. See David Pilling and Francesco Guerrera, "Drug Giant Plans Radical Research Move," *Financial Times* (November 11, 2000): 16.

26. This phenomenon, the power-law effect, is frequently found in information communication networks; see Srinath Srinivasa, *The Power Law of Information: Life in a Connected World* (Thousand Oaks, CA: Response Books, 2006).

27. This condition can be extrapolated from individuals to organizations, and to an entire economic system. Historically, it was a common feature of imperial systems that were entwined with industrial capitalism, and of monopolistic industrial corporations. See Eric Hobsbawm, *The Age of Empire, 1875–1914* (London: Weidenfeld and Nicolson, 1987); Braverman, *Labor and Monopoly Capital.*

28. Skewed distributions are very much a symptom of inequity. In the case of the Web, such distributions reflect great inequities in connectivity. See, for example, Albert-László Barabási, *Linked: The New Science of Networks* (Cambridge, MA: Perseus, 2002), chaps. 6 and 7.

29. At least this was not intended in any explicit way. See Tim Berners-Lee and Mark Fischetti, *Weaving the Web: The Original Design and Ultimate Destiny of the World Wide Web by Its Inventor* (New York: Harper Collins, 2000).

30. Web-based Open Access publishing, despite its potential to empower authors and researchers, has not grown as rapidly as might be expected. Nonetheless, it is a worrisome development for noncorporate publishers (such as university presses), which often operate with losses. See, for example, "AAUP Statement on Open Access" (February 2007), available at www.aaup .org; and Joseph J. Esposito, "The Devil You Don't Know: The Unexpected Future of Open Access Publishing," *First Monday* 9 (August 2004): 11. In the area of academic journal publishing, the fact that articles cannot be published anywhere else once they appear in a journal (including on the Web) supports the oligarchic power of corporate publishers. Compounding this power is the fact that most journals treat the posting of any manuscript on the Web as "prior publication," and use this to automatically reject any such paper for publication. Nonetheless, electronic journals have begun to displace some of the best-established journals in some fields, thereby bypassing the power of corporate publishers. This trend is partly a response against the exorbitant subscription prices charged by corporate publishers, which took over and amassed large

collections of academic journals, thus securing captive audiences in many fields. Only the Web, it seems, holds promise for bypassing or opposing this kind of oligarchic power. See, for example, Bernard Wysocki Jr., "Peer Pressure: Scholarly Journals' Premier Status Diluted by Web," *Wall Street Journal* (May 23, 2005): A1. Schools and divisions at some universities have decided to pursue Open Access (Web-based) publishing on their own, thereby bypassing journals and corporate publishers; see, for example, *Los Angeles Times*, Editorials, "IvorytowerTube," (February 18, 2008): A20; Daniel Akst, "Information Liberation," *Wall Street Journal* (March 7, 2008): W13.

31. A major question in this regard is what distinctive expertise or value a corporate publisher adds, given the spread of digital publishing technologies and their facilitation of many aspects that were previously undertaken solely by publishing houses. John B. Thompson's *Books in the Digital Age: The Transformation of Academic and Higher Education Publishing in Britain and the United States* (Cambridge, UK: Polity, 2005) provides details on how digital technologies have impacted academic publishing and discusses prospects for the coming decades.

32. Corporate appropriation of others' ideas and intellectual property works at various levels, and includes not only other corporations' intellectual property but also the ideas of a company's own employees. The explosion of litigation in this domain since the early 1990s seems to have become a systemic pathology. See, for example, Michael Perelman, *Steal This Idea: Intellectual Property and the Corporate Confiscation of Creativity* (New York: Palgrave, 2002). Globalization has also propelled this pathology to new heights, as shown by Pat Choate's *Hot Property: The Stealing of Ideas in an Age of Globalization* (New York: Knopf, 2005). Another facet of this pathology is the de facto establishment of corporate espionage as a covert corporate strategy, as documented by Adam L. Penenberg and Marc Barry, *Spooked: Espionage in Corporate America* (Cambridge, MA: Perseus, 2000), and Hedieh Nasheri, *Economic Espionage and Industrial Spying* (Cambridge: Cambridge University Press, 2005).

33. Strategic maneuvers of this kind were thus often aimed at promoting stability in a company's external links and supply chains. See, for example, Robert F. Freeland, *The Struggle for Control of the Modern Corporation: Organizational Change at General Motors, 1924–1970* (Cambridge: Cambridge University Press, 2001).

34. Information technology has been a major force for "permanent change." Manuel Castells chronicled many features of the state of permanent change in his trilogy, *The Information Age: Economy, Society and Culture*, vols. I, II, III (Oxford, UK: Blackwell, 1996). Castells's work, however, brushed aside the critical, politico-economic dimension of information technology and its relationship with the global hegemony of market capitalism, pretending to adopt a mostly descriptive, nonideological approach that left out the most important aspects of the phenomena he tried to examine. Perhaps it should not

be surprising, therefore, that his work became interesting to many in the corporate high-tech field, among business journalists, and also even in business school technology management programs. In contrast to Castells's work, critical approaches to the study of information technology phenomena that grasp their ideological substance can be found in Dan Schiller, *Digital Capitalism: Networking the Global Market System* (Cambridge, MA: MIT Press, 1999); Nick Dyer-Witheford, *Cyber-Marx: Cycles and Circuits in High-Technology Capitalism* (Urbana: University of Illinois Press, 1999); Robert W. McChesney, Ellen Meiksins Wood, and John B. Foster, *Capitalism and the Information Age: The Political Economy of the Global Communication Revolution* (New York: Monthly Review Press, 1998). An earlier, insightful, and, in some respects, pioneering work on information technology capitalism grounded in the Japanese case during the 1980s was Tessa Morris-Suzuki's *Beyond Computopia: Information, Automation and Democracy in Japan* (London: Kegan Paul, 1988).

35. See, for example, Stephen J. Spignesi, *The 100 Greatest Disasters of All Time* (New York: Citadel, 2002); Mark Mayell, *Nuclear Accidents* (San Diego: Lucent, 2004).

36. Network extent in Open Source software research possibly may be considered the single most important feature that enhances participation. See Johan Söderberg, *Hacking Capitalism: The Free and Open Source Software Movement* (New York: Routledge, 2007); Samir Chopra and Scott D. Dexter, *Decoding Liberation: The Promise of Free and Open Source Software* (New York: Routledge, 2007).

37. The regularity of this pace, originally announced in April 1965 by semiconductor engineer (and Intel Corporation cofounder) Gordon Moore, became known as "Moore's Law." See, for example, Robert R. Schaller, "Moore's Law: Past, Present, and Future," *IEEE Spectrum* 34 (1997): 52–59.

38. See, for example, Robert F. Freeland, *The Struggle for Control of the Modern Corporation: Organizational Change at General Motors, 1924–1970* (Cambridge: Cambridge University Press, 2001). General Motors' strategy, in particular, emphasized the deepening of existing internal combustion engine technology through further development, such as the replacement of carburetors by fuel injection systems, in place of seeking radically new engines that would have provided both greater efficiency and less environmental damage. Part of the reluctance to change no doubt involved concern over the large investments previously made to develop the internal combustion engine.

39. This is an assumption that Mark Granovetter confirmed in his early studies of network-based social relations; see, for example, Granovetter "The Strength of Weak Ties," *American Journal of Sociology* 78 (1973): 360–380.

40. See, for example, Shrum, Genuth, and Chompalov, *Structures of Scientific Collaboration*.

Decomposing the Corporation

1. This was one of the most significant characteristics of corporate organizations during the nineteenth and twentieth centuries. Significant vertical disintegration nonetheless started to become noticeable during the second half of the twentieth century, particularly in sectors such as the automotive industry, which expanded globally and could tap low-cost resources in various nations. See, for example, Richard J. Barnet, *Global Reach: The Power of the Multinational Corporations* (New York: Simon and Schuster, 1974); Isabel Studer-Noguez, *Ford and the Global Strategies of Multinationals: The North American Auto Industry* (New York: Routledge, 2003). Vertical disintegration through outsourcing thus helped change the character of corporate organization. Much of this dynamic was a product of changes in management concepts that greatly influenced the thinking of corporate executives, and contributed to a reconfiguration of many corporate organizations in diverse sectors and activities. In various ways, this dynamic eventually contributed to the emergence of network-based organizations that are at the core of decomposition. See Luc Boltanski and Eve Chiapello, *The New Spirit of Capitalism*, trans. G. Elliott (London: Verso, 2005).

2. See, for example, Studer-Noguez, *Ford and the Global Strategies*; Robert F. Freeland, *The Struggle for Control of the Modern Corporation: Organizational Change at General Motors, 1924–1970* (Cambridge: Cambridge University Press, 2001).

3. See, for example, Studer-Noguez, *Ford and the Global Strategies*; David Gartman, *Auto Opium: A Social History of American Automotive Design* (New York: Routledge, 1994).

4. Such decomposition is increasingly global and involves locales that are geographically dispersed. See, for example, AnnaLee Saxenian, "Brain Circulation and Capitalist Dynamics: Chinese Chipmaking and the Silicon Valley-Hsinchu-Shanghai Triangle," in *The Economic Sociology of Capitalism*, ed. Victor Nee and Richard Swedberg (Princeton, NJ: Princeton University Press, 2005); Qiwen Lu, *China's Leap in the Information Age: Innovation and Organization in the Computer Industry* (Oxford: Oxford University Press, 2000).

5. This is based on the long-standing dogma that corporate organizations should look only after their own interests, or that they can best help society by looking solely after their own affairs. This narrow and self-serving precept has been proclaimed as a precondition for "freedom," but its actual outcome is greater corporate influence over society, and greater power for those who control capital. Milton Friedman and Rose D. Friedman's *Capitalism and Freedom* (Chicago: University of Chicago Press, 2002) has been a prime contemporary exponent of this precept. Greater corporate influence over society often results in the use of public resources and government to support corporate power and its interests; see, for example, Timothy P. Carney, *The Big Ripoff: How Business and Big Government Steal Your Money* (Hoboken, NJ: Wiley,

2006). Economic crises often reveal how corporatism wields its influence over government. In particular, the financial crisis that started in 2007 provided poignant examples of how megarich corporations use their influence to get government and the public to pay for their misdeeds, despite their usual advocacy of less government interference in business. See, for example, Damian Paletta, "Worried Bankers Seek to Shift Risk to Uncle Sam," *Wall Street Journal* (February 14, 2008): A2. The deepening of the financial crisis, moreover, led to the largest financial system bailout in history by the U.S. federal government, along with large bailout "loans" to other sectors. All of the bailouts were requested by interests that previously advocated governmental noninterference in their affairs.

6. Many of these tend to be biotech companies, which are more dynamic and versatile than the old pharmaceutical giants, mainly because of their external network relations. See, for example, Cynthia Robbins-Roth, *From Alchemy to IPO: The Business of Biotechnology* (Cambridge, MA: Perseus, 2000).

7. See, for example, Grady Means and David Schneider, *MetaCapitalism: The E-Business Revolution and the Design of 21st Century Companies and Markets* (New York: Wiley, 2000). B2B links are an example of how networks advance the market system, in the sense provided by Dan Schiller, *Digital Capitalism: Networking the Global Market System* (Cambridge, MA: MIT Press, 1999).

8. Pitting workers against each other through internal competitive schemes has been a fairly common tactic used by corporate power. See, for example, Harry Braverman, *Labor and Monopoly Capital: The Degradation of Work in the Twentieth Century* (New York: Monthly Review Press, 1974); Freeland, *Struggle for Control*; Lawrence E. Mitchell, *Corporate Irresponsibility: America's Newest Export* (New Haven, CT: Yale University Press, 2002).

9. See, for example, Johan Söderberg, *Hacking Capitalism: The Free and Open Software Movement* (New York: Routledge, 2007).

10. In contrast to Open Source, this prevents software code from being released to the public. Maintaining tight controls over such code typically means that research projects are compartmentalized to prevent any researcher from gaining complete knowledge of all the code that goes into a product. Researchers are also required to sign legally binding documents that prohibit the release of code or internal company projects to anyone outside the company. See, for example, Jennifer Edstrom and Martin Eller, *Barbarians Led by Bill Gates: Microsoft from the Inside, How the World's Richest Corporation Wields Its Power* (New York: Holt, 1998). In some cases, however, Microsoft has selectively released some components of its software code in order to allow others to build businesses, as part of a clever strategy aimed at sustaining its monopoly-like hold on personal computer software; see, for example, Robert A. Guth, Ben Worthen, and Charles Forelle, "Microsoft to Reveal Software Secrets on Internet," *Wall Street Journal* (February 22, 2008): A3.

11. See, for example, "An Open-Source Shot in the Arm?" *Economist Technology Quarterly* (June 12, 2004): 17–19.

12. See Means and Schneider, *MetaCapitalism*. Perhaps the most important attraction of B2B supplier networks to corporate power is their capacity to reduce costs.

13. See, for example, Daniel Stewart, "Social Status in an Open-Source Community," *American Sociological Review* 70 (2005): 823–842; Söderberg, *Hacking Capitalism*.

14. For many decades, this precept has been used to explain (or justify) outsourcing decisions, particularly in the context of industrial corporations. This (Nobel-winning) notion was espoused by Ronald Coase, "The Nature of the Firm," *Economica* 4 (1937): 386–405, and further developed in Coase, *The Firm, the Market and the Law* (Chicago: University of Chicago Press, 1990).

15. An exception was Walter W. Powell, "Neither Market nor Hierarchy: Network Forms of Organization," *Research in Organizational Behavior*, 12 (1990): 295–336. Breaking with the mold cast by mainstream economics, Powell set about to show how networks help structure organizations.

16. The "normative" excuse has allowed neoclassical (mainstream) economics to circumvent deeper questioning of its myths and has also enabled neoclassical economics to evade responsibility for the pathologies to which it has contributed (some of which are considered later in this chapter), particularly at the level of organizations. Neoclassical economic precepts have also been part of the ideological foundation of neoliberal policies, which have been applied around the world with nefarious effects. Deeper inequities, greater social injustice, and authoritarian governance have been some of their global effects. Radical political economists and social critics have grappled with these issues for some time, but they have been largely ignored by the mainstream discipline. Michael Perelman, in his *Railroading Economics: The Creation of the Free Market Mythology* (New York: Monthly Review Press, 2006), for example, exposes the mythology that has been constructed by neoclassical free marketeers to legitimize their ideology and its effects on society. Stephen Marglin, in his *The Dismal Science: How Thinking Like an Economist Undermines Community* (Cambridge, MA: Harvard University Press, 2008), has noted how the belief system of neoclassical economics often undermines the kinds of relations that sustain communities, such as collaboration, reciprocity, and a regard for the common good. A broad comparative perspective on the differences between neoclassical and Marxian politico- economic approaches is provided by Richard D. Wolff and Stephen A. Resnick, *Economics: Marxian versus Neoclassical* (Baltimore, MD: Johns Hopkins University Press, 1987), noting the neglect of social justice and inequality by the mainstream discipline.

17. It seems naïve, however, to expect that such sanctions will reduce malfeasance significantly, given corporatism's great influence over legislation and the institutions of governance, along with the very limited resources

employed to monitor wrongdoing. See, for example, Pat Choate, *Hot Property: The Stealing of Ideas in an Age of Globalization* (New York: Knopf, 2005). The case of Enron illustrates how a major corporation could evade scrutiny and engage in malfeasance over a long period of time. Only after its financial collapse was Enron's misconduct noticed. It seems doubtful that it might have been noticed at all if the company's financial troubles had not attracted attention. See Bethany McLean and Peter Elkind, *The Smartest Guys in the Room: The Amazing Rise and Scandalous Fall of Enron* (New York: Portfolio, 2004); Mimi Swartz and Sherron Watkins, *Power Failure: The Inside Story of the Collapse of Enron* (New York: Doubleday, 2003). Watkins's account, as a former top executive, is quite insightful about Enron's practices and how the company's troubles were grounded in decisions and actions at the very top of the company.

18. See Söderberg, *Hacking Capitalism*; Eric S. Raymond, *The Cathedral and the Bazaar: Musings on Linux and the Free Software Movement by an Accidental Revolutionary* (Cambridge, MA: O'Reilly, 1999).

19. See, for example, Philip Cooke and Kevin Morgan, *The Associational Economy: Firms, Regions, and Innovation* (Oxford: Oxford University Press, 1998); Ash Amin and Patrick Cohendet, *Architectures of Knowledge: Firms, Capabilities, and Communities* (Oxford: Oxford University Press, 2004).

20. This is a matter often ignored by those who regard the corporation as a separate entity from society. The social embeddedness of economic activities has long been a subject of interest to sociologists; see, for example, the articles in Mark Granovetter and Richard Swedberg (eds.), *The Sociology of Economic Life* (Boulder, CO: Westview, 2001).

21. See, for example, Cooke and Morgan, *Associational Economy*; Annalee Saxenian, *Regional Advantage: Culture and Competition in Silicon Valley and Route 128* (Cambridge, MA: Harvard University Press, 1994).

22. See, for example, Benjamin Gomes-Casseres, *The Alliance Revolution: The New Shape of Business Rivalry* (Cambridge, MA: Harvard University Press, 1996); John H. Dunning, *Alliance Capitalism and Global Business* (London: Routledge, 1997).

23. Cooperation in fast alliances is often halfhearted; see, for example, Wilma N. Suen, *Non-Cooperation: The Dark Side of Strategic Alliances* (New York: Palgrave Macmillan, 2005).

24. See, for example, Choate, *Hot Property*; Hedieh Nasheri, *Economic Espionage and Industrial Spying* (Cambridge: Cambridge University Press, 2005).

25. Modularity can be applied to diverse corporate functions, as long as they can be compartmentalized as entities or subsidiaries. See, for example, the articles in Raghu Garud, Arun Kumaraswamy, and Richard N. Langlois (eds.), *Managing in the Modular Age: Architectures, Networks, and Organizations* (Oxford: Blackwell, 2003).

26. Corporate executives, therefore, often rose to the top positions through

their experience with production. See, for example, Freeland, *Struggle for Control*; David R. Farber, *Sloan Rules: Alfred P. Sloan and the Triumph of General Motors* (Chicago: University of Chicago Press, 2002); Studer-Noguez, *Ford and the Global Strategies*.

27. This situation varied, however, from one industrial sector to another. In industries with complex industrial processes, research departments had a higher profile. But even in those cases, production had a higher priority than research. See, for example, Freeland, *Struggle for Control*; Farber, *Sloan Rules*; John D. Bernal, *Science and Industry in the Nineteenth Century* (London: Routledge and Paul, 1953); David F. Noble, *America by Design: Science, Technology, and the Rise of Corporate Capitalism* (New York: Knopf, 1977).

28. Evidence on this aspect is mostly fragmented and must be drawn from diverse sources. See, for example, Eric Hobsbawm, *Labouring Men: Studies in the History of Labour* (London: Weidenfeld and Nicolson, 1964); Braverman, *Labor and Monopoly Capital*; Dan Clawson, *Bureaucracy and the Labor Process* (New York: Monthly Review Press, 1980); David F. Noble, *Forces of Production: A Social History of Industrial Automation* (New York: Knopf, 1984). The earliest articulation of thoughts and evidence related to this point can be found in Marx's mid-nineteenth-century critique of early industrial capitalism; see Karl Marx, *Capital: A Critique of Political Economy*, vol. I, *The Process of Capitalist Production*, ed. F. Engels (New York: International Publishers, 1967; orig. Hamburg: Verlag von Otto Meissner, 1867).

29. The late Sumantra Ghoshal opened a window of consciousness on this aspect. His critique of contemporary management theories, education, and practice are insightful and need to be taken into account when considering contemporary corporate pathologies. See Sumantra Ghoshal, "Bad Management Theories Are Destroying Good Management Practices," *Academy of Management Learning and Education* 4 (2005): 75–91. Observations on Ghoshal's critical views by two contemporary management academics provide additional perspective on this issue. See Jeffrey Pfeffer, "Why Do Bad Management Theories Persist? A Comment on Ghoshal," *Academy of Management Learning and Education* 4 (2005): 96–100; Henry Mintzberg, "How Inspiring, How Sad. Comments on Sumantra Ghoshal's Paper," *Academy of Management Learning and Education* 4 (2005): 108. An earlier critique of American-generated approaches to management and their negative effects on organizations can be found in Lex Donaldson, *American Anti-Management Theories of Organization: A Critique of Paradigm Proliferation* (Cambridge: Cambridge University Press, 1995).

30. Their diffusion has relied greatly on the pronouncements of management "gurus," who usually turn them into simplistic "recipes" for any manager to practice. See, for example, James Hoopes, *False Prophets: The Gurus Who Created Modern Management and Why Their Ideas Are Bad for Business Today* (Cambridge, MA: Perseus, 2003). The importance of popularity "rankings" of management gurus to attract attention to their pet recipes should not

be underestimated. One major business newspaper has taken up the task of periodically ranking management gurus; see Erin White, "New Breed of Business Gurus Rises," *Wall Street Journal* (May 5, 2008): B1; and White, "Quest for Innovation, Motivation Inspires the Gurus," *Wall Street Journal* (May 5, 2008): B6.

31. The practice of these theories has spread well beyond corporate boardrooms. In the domains of education, public expression, and culture, their effects are likely to be both very damaging and long-lasting. See, for example, Jennifer Washburn, *University, Inc.: The Corporate Corruption of American Higher Education* (New York: Basic Books, 2005); Herbert Schiller, *Culture, Inc.: The Corporate Takeover of Public Expression* (New York: Oxford University Press, 1989); Stanley Deetz, *Democracy in an Age of Corporate Colonization: Developments in Communications and the Politics of Everyday Life* (Albany: State University of New York Press, 1992). These studies follow earlier works on the intrusion and influence of corporatism in most every aspect of society. See, for example, Maurice Zeitlin, *The Large Corporation and Contemporary Classes* (New Brunswick, NJ: Rutgers University Press, 1989), and the articles in Zeitlin, *American Society, Inc.: Studies of the Social Structure and Political Economy of the United States* (Chicago: Rand McNally, 1977). Leo Huberman's *America Incorporated: Recent Economic History of the United States* (New York: Viking, 1940) might be considered a pioneer in this line of critical thought.

32. See, for example, Fabrizio Ferraro, Jeffrey Pfeffer, and Robert I. Sutton, "Economics Language and Assumptions: How Theories Can Become Self-Fulfilling," *Academy of Management Review* 30 (2005): 8–24; Ghoshal, "Bad Management Theories," 77; Ken J. Gergen, "Social Psychology as History," *Journal of Personality and Social Psychology* 26 (1973): 309–320 (Gergen's article provided an early and insightful discussion of self-fulfilling theories in the social sciences; his work later influenced others to look into this matter). Self-fulfilling theories are also found in other fields related to corporate management. Theoretical models in modern finance theory, for example, are thought to have conditioned much decision making in financial markets; see, for example, Donald MacKenzie, *An Engine, Not a Camera: How Financial Models Shape Markets* (Cambridge, MA: MIT Press, 2006). The relationship between theory, practice, and nefarious social outcomes in mainstream (neoclassical) economics is incisively addressed in Marglin, *The Dismal Science*. Other authors have considered the self-fulfilling character of theoretical constructs in mainstream economics, from diverse viewpoints and in various specialties. See, for example, Michael A. Bernstein, *Perilous Progress: Economists and Public Purpose in Twentieth Century America* (Princeton, NJ: Princeton University Press, 2001); Robert H. Nelson, *Economics as Religion: From Samuelson to Chicago and Beyond* (University Park: Pennsylvania State University Press, 2001); and the articles in Donald MacKenzie, Fabian Muniesa and Lucia Siu (eds.), *Do Economists Make Markets? On the Performativity of Economics* (Princeton, NJ: Princeton University Press, 2007).

33. Fear of doing anything but "best practice" can be a powerful inducement to comply, regardless of the cost to one's mental and moral well-being. See, for example, Robert Jackall, *Moral Mazes: The World of Corporate Managers* (New York: Oxford University Press, 1988); Jill A. Fraser, *White-Collar Sweatshops: The Deterioration of Work and Its Rewards in Corporate America* (New York: Norton, 2001).

34. Human intent is usually a product of learning and behavioral adjustment. See, for example, Jon Elster, *Explaining Technical Change* (Cambridge: Cambridge University Press, 1983), and Elster, *Alchemies of the Mind* (Cambridge: Cambridge University Press, 1999). Among the most interesting critiques of the social sciences' claim to scientific status is Donald T. Campbell's "Can We Be Scientific in Applied Social Science?" in *Methodology and Epistemology for Social Science: Selected Papers*, ed. Donald T. Campbell (Chicago: University of Chicago Press, 1988).

35. Many contemporary corporate scandals can be traced to pressures, behavior, or beliefs instilled by these theories. The gamut of scandals and malfeasance encompasses practically every business sector. See, for example, Joel Bakan, *The Corporation: The Pathological Pursuit of Profit and Power* (New York: Free Press, 2004); McLean and Elkind, *Smartest Guys*; Swartz and Watkins, *Power Failure*; Mitchell, *Corporate Irresponsibility*; Daniel Litvin, *Empires of Profit: Commerce, Conquest and Corporate Responsibility* (New York: Texere, 2003); Adam L. Penenberg and Marc Barry, *Spooked: Espionage in Corporate America* (Cambridge, MA: Perseus, 2000). All of these works expose a range of corporate malfeasance that is typically tied to perceived pressures to maximize profits, all too often at any risk and regardless of the harm they may cause to employees, customers, and the public at large. Deception of customers is one of the most widespread kinds of corporate malfeasance, taking into account the evidence provided by numerous authors over the years; see, for example, Marcia Angell, *The Truth about the Drug Companies: How They Deceive Us and What to Do about It* (New York: Random House, 2004); Paul Blumberg, *The Predatory Society: Deception in the American Marketplace* (New York: Oxford University Press, 1990). The pharmaceutical sector, once an unlikely candidate for customer deception (given the potentially serious consequences for life and health), has nonetheless become prone to this sort of malfeasance as pharmaceutical companies try to enhance their profits by marketing their products directly to consumers (who usually have little understanding of the complex nature or side effects of the medications marketed to them). See, for example, Daniel Costello, "Healthcare: Two Former Amgen Salespeople Allege Improper Drug Marketing," *Los Angeles Times* (January 9, 2008): C1, and Costello, "Biotechnology: Amgen Needs Mojo Working," *Los Angeles Times* (March 12, 2008): C1; Rhonda L. Rundle, "Competitive Squeeze: Industry Giants Push Obesity Surgery," *Wall Street Journal* (March 31, 2008): A1; Daniel Costello, "Healthcare: Two Drugs Might Have No Benefit," *Los Angeles Times* (March 31, 2008): C1.

36. See Michael C. Jensen and William H. Meckling, "Theory of the Firm: Managerial Behavior, Agency Costs and Ownership Structure," *Journal of Financial Economics* 3 (1976): 305–360. This article is often considered to be the foundational piece of agency theory.

37. This is a historical precept of mainstream economics. It is espoused by most neoliberals and contemporary mainstream (neoclassical) economists. See, for example, Friedman and Friedman, *Capitalism and Freedom*, and critical comments in Ghoshal, "Bad Management Theories," 79. Among the authors who have questioned agency theory and its precept of maximizing shareholder value above all else is Paddy Ireland, "Company Law and the Myth of Shareholder Ownership," *Modern Law Review* 62 (1999): 32–57, and Ireland, "Capitalism without the Capitalist: The Joint Stock Company Share and the Emergence of the Modern Doctrine of Separate Corporate Personality," *Journal of Legal History* 17 (1996): 63.

38. See, for example, Ghoshal, "Bad Management Theories," 80–81. Empirical evidence on this matter can be found in Dan R. Dalton, Catherine M. Daily, Alan E. Ellstrand, and Jonathan L. Johnson, "Meta-analytic Reviews of Board Composition, Leadership Structure, and Financial Performance," *Strategic Management Journal* 19 (1998): 269–290.

39. See, for example, Catherine M. Daily, Dan R. Dalton, and Albert A. Cannella Jr., "Corporate Governance: Decades of Dialogue and Data," *Academy of Management Review* 28 (2003): 371–382.

40. See, for example, Ghoshal, "Bad Management Theories," 80–85; Donaldson, *American Anti-Management Theories*.

41. Perhaps the best-known work advocating corporate competitiveness, based on mainstream (neoclassical) economic precepts, is Michael E. Porter's *Competitive Advantage: Creating and Sustaining Superior Performance* (New York: Free Press, 1985). Among the followers who translated Porter's ideas on competition into practical "recipes" or strategies are George Stalk Jr., Robert Lachenauer, and John Butman, *Hardball: Are You Playing to Play or Playing to Win?* (Boston: Harvard Business School Press, 2004).

42. An example of the sort of corporate mind-set fostered by competition theory can be found in George Stalk Jr. and Rob Lachenauer, "Hardball: Five Killer Strategies for Trouncing the Competition," *Harvard Business Review* (April 2004): 62–71. The article's coauthors were vice presidents of a major global consulting outfit advising companies on competitive strategy. The popularization of aggressive strategic recipes is all too obvious in their high sales and related media articles. See, for example, "Business Books: Kicking Ass in an Unflat World," *The Economist* (November 3, 2007): 77–78.

43. Competition and the seemingly obsessive "need" to be competitive, is a likely driver of the rising wave of "white collar" crime. See, for example, Bakan, *The Corporation*; Stephen M. Rosoff, Henry N. Pontell, and Robert Tillman, *Profit without Honor: White-Collar Crime and the Looting of America* (Upper Saddle River, NJ: Prentice Hall, 1998); Ralph Estes, *Tyranny of*

the Bottom Line: Why Corporations Make Good People Do Bad Things (San Francisco: Berrett-Koehler, 1996).

44. Perhaps this is in the sense noted by Marcuse in his social critique of mid-twentieth-century capitalism. See Herbert Marcuse, *One-Dimensional Man* (Boston: Beacon, 1964).

45. The difference between "development" and "research" is not taken into account by statistical agencies, which typically lump the two categories together as one. This problem was, however, noticed and reported many years ago to no avail, despite the growing importance of research data. See, for example, John Jewkes, David Sawers, and Richard Stillerman, *The Sources of Invention* (New York: Norton, 1959), 105 and chap. VI.

46. "Teardowns" of competitors' products to reverse engineer proprietary innovations has become a fine art among many manufacturers. See, for example, Carl Hoffman, "The Teardown Artists," *Wired* (February 2006): 136–139.

47. See, for example, Means and Schneider, *MetaCapitalism*; Lawrence M. Fisher, "From Vertical to Virtual: How Nortel's Supplier Alliances Extend the Enterprise," available at www.strategy-business.com/casestudy/01113/(First Quarter 2001), February 2002.

48. This might be referred to as "management in the wild," analogous (perhaps) to Michel Callon's definition of "economics in the wild," which distinguishes between the stipulations of economic theory and the reality of its practice. See the articles in Michel Callon (ed.), *The Laws of Markets* (Oxford: Blackwell, 1998).

49. Much of the initial conceptual apparatus of transaction cost theory is attributed to Oliver E. Williamson, *The Economic Institutions of Capitalism: Firms, Markets and Relational Contracting* (New York: Free Press, 1985).

50. This is partly based on the belief that the importance of the modern corporation is a result of its "efficiency." In this view, corporate power is assumed to be best placed to enforce contracts. Some sociologists have challenged this notion; see, for example, William G. Roy, *Socializing Capital: The Rise of the Large Industrial Corporation in America* (Princeton, NJ: Princeton University Press, 1999).

51. See, for example, Sumantra Ghoshal and Peter Moran, "Bad for Practice: A Critique of the Transaction Cost Theory," *Academy of Management Review* 21 (1996): 13–47.

52. This kind of thinking also pervades mainstream economics. Rationalizing trust, ethics, and justice in purely functional terms seems to be part of the presumptuous claim to be a "science," which has encumbered mainstream (neoclassical) economics since the middle of the twentieth century. See, for example, Gary Becker, "The Economic Way of Looking at Behavior" (Nobel Prize lecture), *Journal of Political Economy* 101 (1993): 385–409.

Experimentalist Organizations

1. These functions are part of the conventional corporate organization and usually have greater weight than research. In the industrial capitalist corporation, however, production was by far the most important function. See, for example, Stuart Crainer, *The Management Century: A Critical Review of 20th Century Thought and Practice* (San Francisco: Jossey-Bass, 2000). Through production, labor processes are structured in the conventional corporation. Production and the labor process are, by and large, the most distinctive features of the industrial capitalist corporation. In the more evolved forms of industrial capitalism, however, the labor process came to be supplanted by automation, thereby modifying the relations of production. See, for example, Harry Braverman, *Labor and Monopoly Capital: The Degradation of Work in the Twentieth Century* (New York: Monthly Review Press, 1974); David F. Noble, *Forces of Production: A Social History of Industrial Automation* (New York: Knopf, 1984).

2. Tangible resources and production were the main preoccupation of the industrial capitalist enterprise. This aspect is obvious from the vast literature on industrial corporate management and history, particularly labor history. See, for example, Eric Hobsbawm, *Labouring Men: Studies in the History of Labour* (London: Weidenfeld and Nicolson, 1964); Noble, *Forces of Production*; and the articles in Rick Baldoz, Charles Koeber, and Philip Kraft (eds.), *The Critical Study of Work: Labor, Technology, and Global Production* (Philadelphia: Temple University Press, 2001).

3. Licensing genetic patents to large corporations has become a profitable business strategy for many research-intensive biotech companies. See, for example, Paul Rabinow and Talia Dan-Cohen, *A Machine to Make a Future: Biotech Chronicles* (Princeton, NJ: Princeton University Press, 2005); "Man on the Run," *The Economist* (February 17, 2001): 68.

4. Genentech is one of the best examples of a corporate organization dedicated to research. See Betsy Morris, "No. 1 Genentech: The Best Place to Work Now," *Fortune* (January 2006): 79–86; Maureen D. McKelvey, *Evolutionary Innovations: The Business of Biotechnology* (New York: Oxford University Press, 2000).

5. Research regimes in some of the better-known technology companies are often orchestrated by top executives, who tend to have considerable research experience. See, for example, Matthew Symonds, *Softwar: An Intimate Portrait of Larry Ellison and Oracle* (New York: Simon and Schuster, 2003); Larry MacDonald, *Nortel Networks: How Innovation and Vision Created a Network Giant* (New York: Wiley, 2000); Karen Southwick, *High Noon: The Inside Story of Scott McNealy and the Rise of Sun Microsystems* (New York: Wiley, 1999).

6. Although different in character from the conception of labor power in Marxian political economy (relevant to industrial capitalism), the notion of

creative power presented here shares a common critical ground with it. For a consideration of the role of labor power in industrial corporatism, see Hobsbawm, *Labouring Men*; Braverman, *Labor and Monopoly Capital*. As with so many other ideas, the conception of labor power can be traced to Marx's seminal critique of capitalism; see Karl Marx, "The Production Process of Capital," in *Grundrisse: Foundations of the Critique of Political Economy* (New York: Penguin, 1993), sec. 1, 293 (this work is based on notes initially drafted in 1857–1858).

7. Although such theft is common, the literature on this pathology is sparse. Self-censorship by publishers and, in some cases, by authors themselves (due to fear of lawsuits and various forms of corporate intimidation) is part of the reason. Among the relatively few sources available are, for example, Michael Perelman, *Steal This Idea: Intellectual Property and the Corporate Confiscation of Creativity* (New York: Palgrave, 2002); Pat Choate, *Hot Property: The Stealing of Ideas in an Age of Globalization* (New York: Knopf, 2005); J. Rodman Steele, *Is This My Reward? An Employee's Struggle for Fairness in the Corporate Exploitation of His Inventions* (West Palm Beach, FL: Pencraft, 1986); "Letters: The Problem with Patents," *Science* 308 (April 15, 2005): 353. This pathology seems to have much to do with the rising corporate pressure to accumulate intellectual property rights. Strategies and recipes to build up such rights have gained increasing importance in the management literature since the late 1990s. See, for example, Anthony L. Miele, *Patent Strategy: The Manager's Guide to Profiting from Patent Portfolios* (New York: Wiley, 2000); Kevin G. Rivette and David Kline, *Rembrandts in the Attic: Unlocking the Hidden Value of Patents* (Boston: Harvard Business School Press, 2000).

8. The separation of value from creativity is grounded in creativity's intangibility, as noted in the chapter "Creativity as a Commodity."

9. This condition can be considered a result of commodification and its alienation of the providers of creative power from the results of their creativity. The alienation of scientists from their work through commodification is very relevant to this point; see Richard Levins and Richard Lewontin, *The Dialectical Biologist* (Cambridge, MA: Harvard University Press, 1985).

10. Such transfers are fraught with great risk and uncertainty because of the contingent and localized character of much research practice, even in cases where the research is supposedly "standardized," as various studies of laboratory contexts have shown. See, for example, Michael Lynch, *Art and Artifact in Laboratory Science: A Study of Shop Work and Shop Talk in a Research Laboratory* (London: Routledge and Kegan Paul, 1985); Karin Knorr Cetina, *The Manufacture of Knowledge: An Essay on the Constructivist and Contextual Nature of Science* (Oxford: Pergamon, 1981). Part of the reason for the difficulty in transferring creative power from one organizational context to another lies in the fact that it is typically exercised through teamwork, and is specific to the individual talents involved. Also, in many cases, intellectual

property claims can preclude the transfer of specific skills and knowledge from one organization to another.

11. The spread of analytical templates since the mid-1990s is a symptom of the difficulties faced by systematized research regimes in most any aspect related to creativity. Nonetheless, the use of templates has attracted significant attention in the management and scientific literatures; see, for example, David Rosenberg, "The Brainstormer," *Wall Street Journal* (May 13, 2002): R14; Jacob Goldenberg, David Mazursky, and Sorin Solomon, "Creative Sparks," *Science* 285 (September 3, 1999): 1495–1496; Jacob Goldenberg and David Mazursky, *Creativity in Product Innovation* (Cambridge: Cambridge University Press, 2002).

12. Intrapreneuring relies greatly on making employees feel empowered to make significant decisions, mostly on products or marketing. See, for example, Gifford Pinchot and Ron Pellman, *Intrapreneuring in Action: A Handbook for Business Innovation* (San Francisco: Berrett-Koehler, 1999); Dean Takahashi, "Reinventing the Intrapreneur," *Red Herring* (September 2000): 189–196. In reality, however, intrapreneuring is often at odds with the hierarchical character of corporate governance.

13. In its essence, this approach seems oriented toward enhancing self-esteem as an antidote to the alienation that is part and parcel of commodification. Numerous guides on this subject have appeared in the management literature since the mid-1990s; see, for example, James L. Adams, *Conceptual Blockbusting: A Guide to Better Ideas* (Cambridge, MA: Perseus, 2001); John J. Kao, *Jamming: The Art and Discipline of Business Creativity* (New York: HarperBusiness, 1996).

14. In other words, this is storytelling. See, for example, Daniel H. Pink, "What's Your Story?" *Fast Company* (January 1999): 32–34; Brenda Laurel, *Computers as Theatre* (Reading, MA: Addison Wesley, 1993).

15. Role acting to elicit or demonstrate "proper" and "improper" attitudes is a feature of this scheme. Conflict prevention (or resolution), in order to make the organization and its personnel more compliant with managerial objectives, seems to be the overarching goal. See, for example, B. Joseph Pine and James Gilmore, *The Experience Economy: Work Is Theatre and Every Business a Stage* (Boston: Harvard Business School Press, 1999); Michael Schrage, *Serious Play* (Boston: Harvard Business School Press, 2000).

16. See Braverman, *Labor and Monopoly Capital*; Hobsbawm, *Labouring Men*.

17. Speed has attracted increasing attention as a management topic in recent times. It seems that the old proverb "time is everything" is being replaced by "speed is everything." This concern goes well beyond the historical emphasis on speeding up work and work processes. Its contemporary scope seems to be strongly strategic and therefore broader and more comprehensive. "Fast" strategies for attacking most any corporate problem have attracted more attention in the managerial literature. See, for example, the articles in Anne

Y. Ilinitch, Arie Y. Lewin, and Richard D'Aveni (eds.), *Managing in Times of Disorder: Hypercompetitive Organizational Responses* (Thousand Oaks, CA: Sage, 1998); Peter M. Senge and Art Kleiner, *The Dance of Change: The Challenges of Sustaining Momentum in Learning Organizations* (New York: Currency/Doubleday, 1999). Nigel Thrift's "Performing Cultures in the New Economy," *Annals of the Association of American Geographers* 90 (2000): 674–692, provides a critical perspective on the rising importance of speed in corporate culture.

18. For a discussion of the increasing importance of maximizing shareholder value and its negative consequences on contemporary corporate management, see Sumantra Ghoshal, "Bad Management Theories Are Destroying Good Management Practices," *Academy of Management Learning and Education* 4 (2005): 75–91. Short-term financial performance (of which shareholder value is a major ingredient) has become deeply embedded in contemporary management, to the point of pushing aside many other important concerns. See, for example, William Lazonick and Mary O'Sullivan, "Maximizing Shareholder Value: A New Ideology for Corporate Governance," *Economy and Society* 29 (2000): 13–35; Karel Williams, "From Shareholder Value to Present-Day Capitalism," *Economy and Society* 29 (2000): 1–12.

19. This often involves laboratories in different locales. Globalization has made it necessary; the Internet and the Web have made it feasible. See, for example, Kenneth H. Buetow, "Cyberinfrastructure: Empowering a 'Third Way' in Biomedical Research," *Science* (May 6, 2005): 821–824; Stephanie Teasley and Steven Wolinsky, "Scientific Collaboration at a Distance," *Science* 292 (June 22, 2001): 2254–2255.

20. Modularity involves compartmentalization and is quite compatible with the character of commodification. It also adds flexibility and is therefore supportive of corporatist control. See, for example, the articles in Raghu Garud, Arun Kumaraswamy, and Richard N. Langlois (eds.), *Managing in the Modular Age: Architectures, Networks, and Organizations* (Oxford: Blackwell, 2003).

21. User involvement in corporate R&D has sometimes been portrayed as a "democratization" of innovation. In effect, however, it enlists users to try to improve products (usually without compensation for their time and effort) for the benefit of corporate organizations. For a detailed consideration of the importance of user involvement for corporate R&D, see Eric von Hippel, *Democratizing Innovation* (Cambridge, MA: MIT Press, 2005); Patricia B. Seybold, *Outside Innovation: How Your Customers Will Co-Design Your Company's Future* (New York: HarperBusiness, 2006).

22. Histories of labor processes under industrial capitalism provide many insights on these aspects. See, for example, Braverman, *Labor and Monopoly Capital*; Hobsbawm, *Labouring Men*; Noble, *Forces of Production*; Harley Shaiken, *Work Transformed: Automation and Labor in the Computer Age* (New York: Holt, Rinehart and Winston, 1984).

23. Research collaboration is a major avenue for corporate appropriation of others' ideas and intellectual property, in what is now part of a long history of malfeasance. Research collaboration is also often a means for corporate espionage, as it provides easier access to other companies' personnel and internal activities. These issues have been broached in numerous works on corporate espionage; see, for example, Hedieh Nasheri, *Economic Espionage and Industrial Spying* (Cambridge: Cambridge University Press, 2005); James Croft, *Corporate Cloak and Dagger: Inside the World of Industrial Espionage* (London: HarperCollins, 1994). However, espionage is but one branch of a broader trend of corporate malfeasance, particularly regarding intellectual property or ideas. See, for example, Choate, *Hot Property*; Perelman, *Steal This Idea*. The increase of such malfeasance has motivated new approaches for detecting corporate fraud, which some authors refer to as a "new forensics." See, for example, Joe Anastasi, *The New Forensics: Investigating Corporate Fraud and the Theft of Intellectual Property* (Hoboken, NJ: Wiley, 2003).

24. An important aspect is the complexity and novelty of required knowledge, along with the cost of research hardware. It is practically impossible for most companies to gather internally all the resources needed to undertake research in the emerging fields of research associated with technocapitalism (such as nanotechnology, proteomics, quantum computing, biorobotics, and many others). These aspects are brought up in various works; see, for example, Julian Brown, *Minds, Machines, and the Multiverse: The Quest for Quantum Computing* (New York: Simon and Schuster, 2000); Peter Menzel and Faith D'Aluisio, *Robo Sapiens: Evolution of a New Species* (Cambridge, MA: MIT Press, 2000); and the articles in Daniel Figeys (ed.), *Industrial Proteomics: Applications for Biotechnology and Pharmaceuticals* (Hoboken, NJ: Wiley, 2005); Barbara Webb and Thomas R. Consi (eds.), *Biorobotics* (Cambridge, MA: MIT Press, 2001). Much of the economic interest (and investment) in all these emerging fields is driven by their potentially wide-ranging effects. See, for example, Douglas Mulhall, *Our Molecular Future: How Nanotechnology, Robotics, Genetics, and Artificial Intelligence Will Transform Our World* (Amherst, NY: Prometheus, 2002).

25. The human and social ramification of these new fields should not be underestimated. The impact of biotechnology on medicine will likely result in the emergence of biomedicine as a replacement for established medical practice. This may, in turn, lead to a redefinition of therapeutic practices, disease, the human body, and life itself. The emergence of biomedicine will also likely be accompanied by a new, biotech-derived biopharmaceutical industry that may help redefine how and why medications are taken. See, for example, Peter Keating and Alberto Cambrosio, *Biomedical Platforms: Realigning the Normal and the Pathological in Late Twentieth-Century Medicine* (Cambridge, MA: MIT Press, 2006). The emergence of a new field, personal genomics, and its integration with clinical care may also result; see Amy L. McGuire, Mildred K. Cho, Sean E. McGuire, and Timothy Caulfield, "The Future of Personal

Genomics," *Science* 317 (September 21, 2007): 1687. In all of these new fields, and the ones mentioned in note 24, intercompany research collaboration may become indispensable, since no single company may be able to accumulate internally all the resources needed to undertake research in any one field. This will also likely be the case in biopharmaceutical research and in the establishment of the biomedical platforms that will be needed to support the new fields and their corporate actors.

26. Although corporate malfeasance has a long history, its increasing frequency and the magnitude of the sums of money involved have no precedent, if one takes into account recent works that expose its pathologies. See, for example, Joel Bakan, *The Corporation: The Pathological Pursuit of Profit and Power* (New York: Free Press, 2004); Perelman, *Steal This Idea*; Choate, *Hot Property*.

27. See, for example, Nasheri, *Economic Espionage*; Croft, *Corporate Cloak and Dagger*; Adam L. Penenberg and Marc Barry, *Spooked: Espionage in Corporate America* (Cambridge, MA: Perseus, 2000). Outsourcing of corporate espionage to specialized contractors that provide "CIA-type services" to large companies is gaining importance. One of its benefits is that it allows corporate power deniability, and the opportunity to distance itself from any spying that might go wrong. See, for example, Jeremy Scahill, "Blackwater's Bright Future," *Los Angeles Times* (June 16, 2008): A15.

28. Reverse engineering is one of the older tactics; see, for example, Carl Hoffman, "The Teardown Artists," *Wired* (February 2006): 136–139. The repertory of predatory tactics is quite broad, however; see, for example, Choate, *Hot Property*; Nasheri, *Economic Espionage*; Croft, *Corporate Cloak and Dagger*; Justin Scheck and Lauren Pollock, "Former H-P Executive Pleads Guilty," *Wall Street Journal* (July 14, 2008): B8.

29. "Second-mover" corporate research strategies caught the attention of some economists long ago, when it was noticed that imitation was often more profitable than originality. Among the earlier publications on this aspect is William L. Baldwin and Gerald L. Childs, "The Fast Second and Rivalry in Research and Development," *Southern Economic Journal* 36 (1969): 18–24.

30. Strategic alliances can be prone to such opportunism. See, for example, Wilma N. Suen, *Non-Cooperation: The Dark Side of Strategic Alliances* (New York: Palgrave Macmillan, 2005).

31. Such strategies seem to be becoming a staple of the "recipes" provided by some management consultants. See, for example, George Stalk Jr. and Rob Lachenauer, "Hardball: Five Killer Strategies for Trouncing the Competition," *Harvard Business Review* (April 2004): 62–71; George Stalk Jr., Robert Lachenauer and John Butman, *Hardball: Are You Playing to Play or Playing to Win?* (Boston: Harvard Business School Press, 2004). The pathological effects of aggressive business practices and strategies have been documented, for example, by Bakan, *The Corporation* (a book that served as the basis of a 2.5-hour documentary, "The Corporation"); Croft, *Corporate Cloak and*

Dagger; Penenberg and Barry, *Spooked*; and Ralph Estes, *Tyranny of the Bottom Line: Why Corporations Make Good People Do Bad Things* (San Francisco: Berrett-Koehler, 1996).

32. Contemporary management education feeds this pathology by making competition and competitiveness a major component of corporate strategy, where collaboration, ethics, and morality are often ignored. Being "competitive" thus becomes a highly desirable condition, regardless of the cost. "Competitive" strategies and behaviors are therefore taught and implemented, thereby becoming self-fulfilling. See Sumantra Ghoshal, "Bad Management Theories Are Destroying Good Management Practices," *Academy of Management Learning and Education* 4 (2005): 75–91.

33. A common view popularized by the popular business media and some "how-to" management books is to consider business competition as war, where most any strategy is valid as long as it succeeds. See, for example, C. Kenneth Allard, *Business as War: Battling for Competitive Advantage* (Hoboken, NJ: Wiley, 2004); Stalk, Lachenauer, and Butman, *Hardball*.

34. This objective is often unsuccessful, except where procedures and criteria are rigid and highly codified. See, for example, the articles in Stefano Franchi and Güven Güzeldere (eds.), *Mechanical Bodies, Computational Minds: Artificial Intelligence from Automata to Cyborgs* (Cambridge, MA: MIT Press, 2005).

35. Inadequate compensation of researchers is common among research-intensive corporations, despite the frequently reported stock option plans and similar programs. See, for example, Perelman, *Steal This Idea*; Choate, *Hot Property*; Steele, *Is This My Reward?*; *Science*, "Problem with Patents."

36. Avoidance of complexity in management practice may account for the proliferation of "recipes" that provide simple guidelines, despite their often negative consequences. See, for example, Ghoshal, "Bad Management Theories"; Jeffrey Pfeffer, "Why Do Bad Management Theories Persist? A Comment on Ghoshal," *Academy of Management Learning and Education* 4 (2005): 96–100; Lex Donaldson, *American Anti-Management Theories of Organization: A Critique of Paradigm Proliferation* (Cambridge: Cambridge University Press, 1995). The popularity of these "recipes" may be attributed, in part, to the emergence of numerous management "gurus" who profess to have answers for most any kind of management problem. See James Hooper, *False Prophets: The Gurus Who Created Modern Management and Why Their Ideas Are Bad for Business Today* (Cambridge, MA: Perseus, 2003).

37. Agency theory seems to have acquired a mythical dimension in management education, despite its failures and pathological effects. See, for example, Lazonick and O'Sullivan, "Maximizing Shareholder Value"; Ghoshal, "Bad Management Theories"; Paddy Ireland, "Company Law and the Myth of Shareholder Ownership," *Modern Law Review* 62 (1999): 32–57. The last article shows that the power conceded to shareholders by agency theory (and contemporary management theory and practice, in general) has, in fact, little

or no legal standing. Shareholders are all too often assumed to be "owners" or "co-owners" when their only claim is to a portion of a corporation's profits.

Challenges

1. It must be noted, however, that their establishment was quite uneven across industrialized nations. See, for example, Immanuel Wallerstein, *Historical Capitalism* (London: Verso, 1995); Eric J. Hobsbawm, *The Age of Capital, 1848–1875* (New York: New American Library, 1979); Michel Beaud, *A History of Capitalism: 1500–2000* (New York: Monthly Review Press, 2001). In the case of labor, for example, labor unions and governmental institutions concerned with labor created safeguards that tried to protect workers' rights. Nonetheless, late twentieth-century industrial capitalism brought about a breakdown of safeguards, with serious consequences for many aspects of work and labor. See Harry Braverman, *Labor and Monopoly Capital: The Degradation of Work in the Twentieth Century* (New York: Monthly Review Press, 1974).

2. Such competition is increasingly global. The globalization of corporatism and its quest for hegemony can be considered part of a larger panorama of conquest that is political and cultural. Neoliberal policies (typically based on neoclassical economic precepts) have been the most important instrument of conquest. See, for example, James F. Petras and Henry Veltmeyer, *Empire with Imperialism: The Globalizing Dynamics of Neo-Liberal Capitalism* (New York: Palgrave Macmillan, 2005); Noam Chomsky, *Profit over People: Neoliberalism and Global Order* (New York: Seven Stories Press, 1999); and Chomsky, *Hegemony or Survival: America's Quest for Global Dominance* (New York: Holt, 2004).

3. Corporatist co-optation of political agendas has deteriorated governance in practically every area of public concern. See, for example, Ted Nace, *Gangs of America: The Rise of Corporate Power and the Disabling of Democracy* (San Francisco: Berrett-Koehler, 2005); David J. Sirota, *Hostile Takeover: How Big Money and Corruption Conquered Our Government* (New York: Crown, 2006); Carl Boggs, *The End of Politics: Corporate Power and the Decline of the Public Sphere* (New York: Guilford, 2000). Nace, Sirota, and Boggs provide examples and expose cases of the ways in which corporate power has been able to co-opt and manipulate government, usually by legal means and all too often out of view of the public and the press. Lawrence C. Soley's *Censorship, Inc.: The Corporate Threat to Free Speech in the United States* (New York: Monthly Review Press, 2002) exposes how the increasing control of the media by large corporations has resulted in tacit forms of censorship, usually self-imposed.

4. See, for example, Marcia Angell, *The Truth about the Drug Companies: How They Deceive Us and What to Do about It* (New York: Random House, 2004).

5. See David Willman, "New Anthrax Vaccine Sunk by Lobbying," *Los Angeles Times* (December 2, 2007): A1.

6. See, for example, Jerome Kassirer, *On the Take: How Medicine's Complicity with Big Business Can Endanger Your Health* (New York: Oxford University Press, 2004); and Kassirer, "Tainted Medicine: Financial Conflicts of Interest are Raising Some Upsetting Questions about the Trustworthiness of Research," *Los Angeles Times* (April 6, 2008): M6.

7. Among them, and most dangerously so, is the conflict between the public interest and biotech companies. See, for example, Steven P. McGiffen, *Biotechnology: Corporate Power versus the Public Interest* (London: Pluto, 2005); Sheldon Krimsky, *Science in the Public Interest: Has the Lure of Profits Corrupted Biomedical Research?* (Lanham, MD: Rowman & Littlefield, 2003).

8. This argument overlooks the fact that corporate competition is often a source of pathology, particularly in the area of intellectual property and new ideas. See Pat Choate, *Hot Property: The Stealing of Ideas in an Age of Globalization* (New York: Knopf, 2005); Michael Perelman, *Steal This Idea: Intellectual Property and the Corporate Confiscation of Creativity* (New York: Palgrave, 2002). Joel Bakan's *The Corporation: The Pathological Pursuit of Profit and Power* (New York: Free Press, 2004), in particular, provides cases and details on how corporate actions or strategies that seem perfectly logical to corporate executives and insiders turn out to be both illegal and socially pathological (from a legal scholar's perspective). Bakan's book became the basis for a 2.5-hour documentary, "The Corporation," which attracted considerable notice and was shown around the world and in many classrooms.

9. The view that market competition can serve as a substitute for public governance is often implicit in neoliberal arguments; see, for example, Milton Friedman, *Why Government Is the Problem* (Stanford, CA: Hoover Institution, 1993). Such views may be considered part of the mythology surrounding free markets (and their assumed effects), which is very much embedded in mainstream (neoclassical) economics; see, for example, Michael Perelman, *Railroading Economics: The Creation of the Free Market Mythology* (New York: Monthly Review Press, 2006). Curiously, although corporate interests typically oppose government intervention, they are not shy about using their power to try to get government (and the public) to bail them out in times of crisis; see, for example, Damian Paletta, "Worried Bankers Seek to Shift Risk to Uncle Sam," *Wall Street Journal* (February 14, 2008): A2.

10. Such arguments were espoused by industrialists, and were also based on the premise that children "needed" to work and were made "useful" through factory work. See, for example, Peter Kirby, *Child Labour in Britain, 1750–1870* (New York: Palgrave Macmillan, 2003); Lionel Rose, *The Erosion of Childhood: Child Oppression in Britain, 1860–1918* (London: Routledge, 1991).

11. See, for example, McGiffen, *Biotechnology*; Cynthia Robbins-Roth, *From Alchemy to IPO: The Business of Biotechnology* (Cambridge, MA: Perseus, 2000).

12. See, for example, Nace, *Gangs of America*; Sirota, *Hostile Takeover*. Among the most egregious examples is the behind-the-scenes influence that food industry corporations wield on legislators, public agencies, academic institutions, professional associations, and the courts (while curtailing the public's access to relevant data and knowledge) to promote consumption of highly profitable products that damage health. See, for example, Marion Nestle, *Food Politics: How the Food Industry Influences Nutrition and Health* (Berkeley: University of California Press, 2002). An increasingly common strategy is the funding and use of company-sponsored trials to dispute adverse findings issued by public agencies or independent scientific panels. This strategy has been used by corporations in various sectors, ranging from pharmaceuticals to metals, to autos and tobacco, for example. See David Michaels, "Doubt Is Their Product: Industry Groups Are Fighting Government Regulation by Fomenting Scientific Uncertainty," *Scientific American* (June 2005): 96–101; Gerald Markowitz and David Rosner, *Deceit and Denial: The Deadly Politics of Industrial Pollution* (Berkeley: University of California Press, 2002). Lobbying politicians and regulators is a common strategy whenever regulatory action can harm profits by approving a rival product; see Willman, "New Anthrax Vaccine." Attempting to influence professionals (often indirectly) who prescribe products, as in medical practice, is another strategy. It has been estimated, for example, that about 60 percent of the cost of continuing education that physicians must receive to revalidate their professional licenses in the United States is paid for by pharmaceutical and biotech companies. See, for example, Angell, *Truth about Drug Companies*; Kassirer, "Tainted Medicine"; and Kassirer, *On the Take*. Although it is rarely acknowledged, influencing well-known physicians who can contribute to medications' sales through public opinions and endorsements is a related strategy; see, for example, Jeanne Whalen, "Glaxo's Handling of Physician Criticized," *The Wall Street Journal* (November 17, 2007): A6. Obtaining patients' data from physicians to target promotions or advertisements for specific medications is another example; see Daniel Costello, "Healthcare: Two Former Amgen Salespeople Allege Improper Drug Marketing," *Los Angeles Times* (January 9, 2008): C1. In other cases, substantially more expensive (and very profitable) medications are marketed to replace cheaper ones, even when they are no more effective; see, for example, "Pharmaceuticals: Shock to the System," *The Economist* (February 2, 2008): 72–74; Daniel Costello, "Healthcare: Two Drugs Might Have No Benefit," *Los Angeles Times* (March 31, 2008): C1. Related to this strategy, very expensive (and substantially profitable) medications used to treat certain illnesses are sometimes targeted to treat other illnesses for which they are not effective (or not as effective as the medications they aim to replace). See, for

example, Daniel Costello, "Healthcare: Avastin OK'd for Breast Cancer," *Los Angeles Times* (February 23, 2008): C1.

13. This is in the sense provided by Herbert Marcuse, *One-Dimensional Man* (Boston: Beacon, 1964), chap. 1. Such "normalcy," in the identification of individuals with their domination, may also reflect a deeper state of social alienation.

14. This is therefore contrarian to views that assume a reification of technology as a separate entity from society; see Martin Heidegger, *The Question concerning Technology* (New York: Harper and Row, 1977). Technology becomes not, as Heidegger assumed, an independent force wielding overwhelming (and practically unopposable) power over society, but instead an instrument of corporatism, manipulated (and manipulable) to further profit and power.

15. This is based on the assumption that corporations serve society best by looking after their own interests. It is a central tenet of neoliberalism; see Friedman, *Why Government Is the Problem.*

16. It has long been noted that labor-management relations were impressed into the design of production technology. See, for example, Andrew Feenberg, "Subversive Rationalization: Technology, Power, and Democracy," in *Technology and the Politics of Knowledge*, ed. Andrew Feenberg and Alastair Hannay (Bloomington: Indiana University Press, 1995); Braverman, *Labor and Monopoly Capital*; David F. Noble, *Forces of Production: A Social History of Industrial Automation* (New York: Knopf, 1984); Douglas Kellner, *Critical Theory, Marxism, and Modernity* (Baltimore, MD: Johns Hopkins University Press, 1989).

17. In production technology, for example, the setting of performance standards reflected the relations of power between managers and workers; see Braverman, *Labor and Monopoly Capital*; Noble, *Forces of Production*; David Gartman, *Auto Slavery: The Labor Process in the American Automobile Industry, 1897–1950* (New Brunswick, NJ: Rutgers University Press, 1986). In recent times, the setting of standards (formally and informally) in new sectors such as software, for example, has also reflected corporate priorities, on appropriation and on the relations of power between management and researchers. See, for example, Jennifer Edstrom and Martin Eller, *Barbarians Led by Bill Gates: Microsoft from the Inside, How the World's Richest Corporation Wields Its Power* (New York: Holt, 1998). The recent battles between high-definition video disc formats (Blu-ray versus HD DVD) illustrate how important (and profitable) such standards can be whenever certain corporate interests impose them on the public (and on competitors); see, for example, "Consumer Electronics: And in the Blu Corner . . . ," *The Economist* (September 8, 2007): 68. Such impositions are typically driven by corporate interest for greater power and profit. Thus, "corporate champions" drive rival technological standards based on their own self-interest, narrowly defined. For example, the recent battle for a "4G" (fourth generation) technology standard for the

next generation of wireless networks has pitted two rival models vying for pre-dominance: WiMAX versus LTE. WiMAX is backed by Intel and Google for the simple, self-serving reason that it would astronomically increase demand for Intel's chips and for Google's advertising (promoted through its Web search services). Its rival model, LTE (long-term evolution), is backed by telecommu-nications hardware manufacturer Ericsson, for the also self-serving motive of greatly boosting demand and profits for its mobile network gear. See, for example, "Wireless Telecoms: Culture Clash," *The Economist* (July 19, 2008): 76–77. Corporate influence over technology standards has a long history. In the 1980s, for example, corporate interests backing Betamax battled those fa-voring VHS for a videocassette standard. The winners (backing the VHS stan-dard) derived considerable profits over time. Earlier in the twentieth century, corporate interests favoring phonograph discs won over those who supported cylinders. The winners reaped substantial profits over the years, and came to dominate much of the music-recording hardware industry. The outcomes of such battles are often difficult to determine and reflect the fact that technolo-gies are all too often the result of choices made by corporate entities.

18.   Contemporary management education is partly to blame on this mat-ter; see, for example, Sumantra Ghoshal, "Bad Management Theories Are De-stroying Good Management Practices," *Academy of Management Learning and Education* 4 (2005): 75–91.

19.   The increasing control of megarich (and often global) corporations over major media networks provides an example of this trend. See Robert W. McChesney, *Corporate Media and the Threat to Democracy* (New York: Sev-en Stories Press, 1997); and McChesney, *Rich Media, Poor Democracy: Com-munication Politics in Dubious Times* (Urbana: University of Illinois Press, 1999).

20.   The top target of network-based predatory strategies is often intel-lectual property; see, for example, Choate, *Hot Property*; Perelman, *Steal This Idea*.

21.   See, for example, George Stalk Jr. and Rob Lachenauer, "Hardball: Five Killer Strategies for Trouncing the Competition," *Harvard Business Re-view* (April 2004): 62–71; C. Kenneth Allard, *Business as War: Battling for Competitive Advantage* (Hoboken, NJ: Wiley, 2004).

22.   This prospect is the subject of debate among bioethicists, as shown by Ronald M. Green's *Babies by Design: The Ethics of Genetic Choice* (New Haven, CT: Yale University Press, 2007). Of greater relevance to corporatism, genetic characteristics that affect organizational behavior have been attract-ing attention for some time; see, for example, Daniel A. Silverman, *The Neuro-Genetic Roots of Organizational Behavior* (Lanham, MD: University Press of America, 2000); Richard Donkin, "In Fear of Genetically Modified Recruit-ment," *Financial Times* (May 24, 2002): vi. Taking these developments into account, Habermas's observations about human biological evolution becoming an outcome of conscious, short-term decisions implemented through genetic

engineering seem prescient; see Jürgen Habermas, *The Future of Human Nature* (Cambridge, UK: Polity, 2003).

23. The possible occurrence of this trend must be viewed from a broader perspective. It would likely be part of a larger social panorama involving the commodification of life itself. See Finn Bowring, *Science, Seeds, and Cyborgs: Biotechnology and the Appropriation of Life* (London: Verso, 2003).

24. It would seem that *network extent* (defined in the chapter "Networks as Mediators") must necessarily include substantial range (scale and heterogeneity), open accessibility, and diverse composition for networks to support the empowerment of creativity.

25. See, for example, Johan Söderberg, *Hacking Capitalism: The Free and Open Software Movement* (New York: Routledge, 2007).

26. Given the imposed corporate priorities, it should not be surprising that there are great inequities and a large portion of the American population is left without access to health care. See, for example, Susan Starr Sered and Rushika Fernandopulle, *Uninsured in America: Life and Death in the Land of Opportunity* (Berkeley: University of California Press, 2005); Colin Gordon, *Dead on Arrival: The Politics of Health Care in Twentieth-Century America* (Princeton, NJ: Princeton University Press, 2003). Risk evaluations in medical research often also follow corporate standards, based on potential market value and narrow cost-benefit criteria. This should be expected when research agendas are all too often set by (or through) corporate priorities. See Sydney A. Halpern, *Lesser Harms: The Morality of Risk in Medical Research* (Chicago: University of Chicago Press, 2004).

27. The effects of those priorities were adeptly summarized by Richard Levins and Richard Lewontin, *The Dialectical Biologist* (Cambridge, MA: Harvard University Press, 1985), 208: "Agriculture . . . is directly concerned with profit and only indirectly with feeding people. Similarly, the organization of health care is directly an economic enterprise and is only secondarily influenced by people's health needs. The irrationalities of a scientifically sophisticated world come not from failures of intelligence but from the persistence of capitalism."

28. See, for example, McChesney, *Corporate Media*; Boggs, *End of Politics*; Soley, *Censorship, Inc.*; Jennifer Washburn, *University, Inc.: The Corporate Corruption of American Higher Education* (New York: Basic Books, 2005). Much of this vulnerability was made possible by the extensive reconfiguration of capitalism that occurred during the late twentieth century, as corporatism abandoned hierarchical (Fordist) structures in favor of horizontal, flexible forms of organization that tended to enlist employee initiative for the benefit of corporate power (without adequately rewarding employees) and provided work "autonomy" at the expense of less work security. As a result, corporate power became more flexible and broader in its worldview, and also more influential publicly as it became more externally oriented. See Luc

Boltanski and Eve Chiapello, *The New Spirit of Capitalism*, trans. G. Elliott (London: Verso, 2005).

29. The view that socioeconomic phenomena exist beyond the reach of democratic deliberation (through functional or "natural" laws that operate outside society) has been characteristic of contemporary neoliberal thought. Antoinette Rouvroy's *Human Genes and Neoliberal Governance: A Foucaldian Critique* (London: Routledge-Cavendish, 2007) debunks this notion by taking into account the interrelations between biotechnology and our social, political, cultural, legal, and economic frameworks, where individual action and social choice play important roles. There is a long history of debate between views that espouse the functionalist (or natural) "laws" that are external to society and those that view society and science as results of human and social action. It is grounded in critical social analyses that involved prominent scientists in times past, as can be seen in the works of John D. Bernal, *The Social Function of Science* (New York: Macmillan, 1939); and John. B. S. Haldane, *Dialectical Materialism and Modern Science* (London: Labour Monthly, 1942).

30. See, for example, Arthur Allen, *Vaccine: The Controversial Story of Medicine's Greatest Lifesaver* (New York: Norton, 2007).

31. Rising awareness of this threat and the impact of new surveillance technologies are reflected in the increasing number of works that address related problems. See, for example, David Lyon, *Surveillance Society: Monitoring Everyday Life* (Buckingham, UK: Open University Press, 2002). John Gilliom's *Overseers of the Poor: Surveillance, Resistance, and the Limits of Privacy* (Chicago: University of Chicago Press, 2001), in particular, notes how surveillance can and has become an instrument of repression, even in a society that considers itself to be fully democratic.

32. These pressures were very diverse but (nonetheless) social at the core. See, for example, Joel W. Eastman, *Styling vs. Safety: The American Automobile Industry and the Development of Automotive Safety, 1900–1966* (Lanham, MD: University Press of America, 1984). The movement for greater automotive safety was pioneered by individuals who selflessly advocated views that contradicted the interests of corporate power and often attracted personal smear tactics. See Ralph Nader, *Washington under the Influence: A Ten Year Review of Auto Safety amidst Industrial Opposition* (Washington, DC: Federal Consumer Product Safety Service, 1976); and Nader, *Unsafe at Any Speed: The Designed-In Dangers of the American Automobile* (New York: Grossman, 1965). Nader's role as a social activist and his ability to move large numbers of people to affect or change corporatist technological practices have been greatly neglected in the literature on technological change. His work showed that it is possible to oppose corporate power effectively, despite its substantial resources and capacity to damage those who oppose its interests.

33. Such creativity has transcended concerns over automotive pollution to affect many other areas and their research agendas. See, for example, Scott Frickel, *Chemical Consequences: Environmental Mutagens, Scientist Activism, and the Rise of Genetic Toxicology* (New Brunswick, NJ: Rutgers University Press, 2004). The important global problem of climate change is also attracting much social attention, despite the efforts of many corporate interests to downplay the problem and its effects; see, for example, John Firor, *The Crowded Greenhouse: Population, Climate Change, and Creating a Sustainable World* (New York: Yale University Press, 2002).

Index

accountability: empowering creativity and, 161; social, 100–108; of technology and science, 153–157, 183n21

accumulation: of capital, 17–20, 174n18; processes of, 24; of technological infrastructure, 23–24; of technological knowledge, 20–22. *See also* technocapitalism

agency theory, 114–115, 148, 194n37, 199n18 202n37. *See also* pathologies

agents of change, 132–135. *See also* systematized research regimes

Alexander, Christopher, 183n23

alienation: commodification of creativity and, 33–34, 37; creative power in systematized research regime and, 127–32; definition of term, 52-53, 180n27; mechanistic systematization and, 146; social, 179n22; transferring results of creative processes and, 52–53. *See also* systematized research regimes

alliances, strategic, 103–105, 190n23. *See also* decomposition

Apple Computer, 175n24

appropriation. *See* intellectual property; pathologies; systematized research regimes

art and science, 176–77n5

artifices, 129–32. *See also* systematized research regimes

artificial intelligence, 52, 146, 180n25

automotive safety, 166, 209n32

autonomous initiative artifice, 130

autonomous operations, 138

Bakan, Joel, 193n35, 194n43, 201n26, 204n8

behavior: commercialization of drugs modifying, 16, 172n7; genetic alteration of, 207n22; influence of management theories on, 111–112

Bernal, John, 170n7, 191n27, 209n29

bioinformatics, 14, 50, 57, 177n11. *See also* biotechnology; genomics

biomedicine, 10, 16, 158, 200n25. *See also* biotechnology; biopharmacology

biomimetics. *See* biorobotics

Luis Suarez-Villa is a Professor in the School of Social Ecology at the University of California, Irvine, specializing in the political economy of technology, development, and corporate capitalism.